W9-AYE-276

ADVENTURES IN SCUBA DIVING

ADVENTURES IN SCUBA DIVING

Mosby
Lifeline

St. Louis Baltimore Boston Carlsbad Chicago Naples New York Philadelphia Portland
London Madrid Mexico City Singapore Sydney Tokyo Toronto Wiesbaden

ADVENTURES IN SCUBA DIVING

Steven Barsky

NAUI

National Association of Underwater Instructors

Publisher: David T. Culverwell
Editor-in-Chief: Richard A. Weimer
Editor: Eric Duchinsky
Senior Developmental Editor: Cecilia F. Reilly
Developmental Editor: Julie Bauer
Assistant Editor: Carla Goldberg
Project Manager: Chris Baumle
Senior Production Editor: Shannon Canty
Electronic Publishing: Terri Schwaegel, Chris Robinson, Peggy Hill
Manufacturing Supervisor: Theresa Fuchs
Design Manager: Nancy McDonald
Cover Design/Chapter Openers: Sheriff-Krebs Design

Copyright © 1995 by the National Association of
Underwater Instructors (NAUI)

All rights reserved. No part of this publication may be reproduced, stored in a retrieval system, or transmitted, in any form
or by any means, electronic, mechanical, photocopying,
recording, or otherwise, without prior written permission from
the publisher.

Permission to photocopy or reproduce solely for internal or
personal use is permitted for libraries or other users registered
with the Copyright Clearance Center, provided that the base fee
of $4.00 per chapter plus $.10 per page is paid directly to the
Copyright Clearance Center, 222 Rosewood Drive, Danvers, MA
01923.. This consent does not extend to other kinds of copying,
such as copying for general distribution, for advertising or
promotional purposes, for creating new collected works,
or for resale.

Printed in the United States of America

Composition by: Mosby Electronic Production

Mosby, Inc.
11830 Westline Industrial Drive
St. Louis, MO 63146

International Standard Book Number 0-8151-6277-4
99/9

WARNING

Scuba diving is a wonderful adventure sport. However, like any adventure sport, there is a small but real chance that you can be injured or killed any time you enter the water to dive. Even if you do everything right, even if your equipment functions perfectly, there are always some risks in scuba diving. When you decide to become a scuba diver, you must do it of your own free will and be willing to accept the risks of the sport.

Naui Wants You to "Be a Responsible Diver"

The Code of the Responsible Diver:

As a responsible diver, I understand and assume all the risks I may encounter while diving.

My responsible diving duties include:

1. *Being familiar with and verifying my equipment's proper operation before and during every dive*
2. *Evaluating the conditions before every dive and ensuring they fit my present capabilities*
3. *Diving within the limits of my ability, equipment, and training, as well as my buddy's*
4. *Accepting full responsibility for my own safety on every dive*

CREDITS

Cover Photography
Stephen Frink-Water House Stock Photography, The Bettmann Archive

Interior Photography
Stephen Frink-Water House Stock Photography; pgs. 42, 58, 192. Charles Seabourne-Tony Stone Images; pg 2. Freddy Storhel-Tony Stone Images; pg 76. Kevin and Cat Sweeney-Tony Stone Images; pg 94. R. Whitby-FPG International; pg. 102. SuperStock, Inc.; page 78.

All other photography by Bret Gilliam-courtesy of Ocean Tech, Steven Barsky, Jeff Bozanic, Al Bruton, Lynn Hendrickson, Amos Nachom, Pete Nawrocky, Lloyd Orr, Tammy Peluso, Doug Perrine, David Sipperly

Illustration
Ben Clemens-Millennium Design

CONTENTS

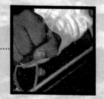

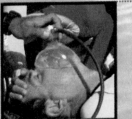

Scuba diving is the most unique adventure sport on earth. In the underwater world, you can watch the delicate beauty of tiny fish as they dart around a colorful tropical reef. You can experience the thrill of swimming eye to eye with a dolphin or a whale (Fig. 1-1). With very little training, you can shoot underwater video footage that will dazzle your family and friends. As a scuba diver, you can see history as you discover fabulous underwater treasures and lost sunken cities.

Scuba diving is an adventure sport you can pursue almost anywhere in the world. From the shipwrecks of the Great Lakes to the tropical reefs of Australia, from the kelp forests of California to the rocky coast of Maine, where there is water there is usually diving (Figs. 1-2 and 1-3). As long as you are in good health and have the proper equipment and training, you can enjoy diving.

Although it may seem that there is a great deal of information you must learn about diving, you do not need to be an expert to enjoy it. You can experience all the excitement of scuba diving by completing the training that you will receive in this NAUI Scuba Diver Certification course. There are more advanced dives and challenges that you may choose to experience later, but the basics of diving will allow you to participate in most underwater adventures.

To enjoy diving where you live, you will need to learn how to use the scuba equipment commonly used in your area. While the equipment may

Fig. 1-1. The underwater world will provide you with unique adventures.

Fig. 1-2. Exploring shipwrecks is an exciting part of diving.

Fig. 1-3. Diving in cold water can be just as enjoyable as diving in tropical water.

appear intimidating at first, it is very simple to use. As with driving a car, you don't need to understand the mechanics of how the equipment works to be able to use it. Keep in mind that if you dive in other areas or pursue certain specialized types of diving, you will need additional training and equipment.

LEARNING OBJECTIVES

Throughout this book, we will explain the objectives your instructor expects you to achieve by the end of this course. Each of these objectives must be met for you to receive Scuba Diver Certification. By the end of this chapter, you must be able to:

1. **Explain the difference between scuba diving and skin diving.**
2. **State the ultimate risk in scuba diving.**
3. **Explain what your obligations are during a Scuba Diver Certification course.**
4. **List three specialty scuba diving courses that you may take on successful completion of this Scuba Diver Certification course.**
5. **Explain what the word NAUI means.**
6. **Explain why running out of air is unlikely underwater.**

Additional objectives that you will need to meet for certification will be explained in subsequent chapters.

WHAT IS SCUBA DIVING?

When you enrolled in your Scuba Diver Certification course you probably already knew that the word **scuba** stands for **S**elf **C**ontained **U**nderwater **B**reathing **A**pparatus. Scuba diving is done with a compressed air "tank" (i.e., cylinder) that you wear on your back (Fig. 1-4). The air is supplied to your mouth through a regulator that reduces the high pressure inside the tank to that of the surrounding underwater pressure.

You will hear people refer to scuba diving as "recreational diving" and "sport diving." These terms are used interchangeably to refer to scuba diving for fun.

You also may hear people refer to "skin diving." Skin diving involves diving without any underwater breathing apparatus. In skin diving, you simply hold your breath and dive below the surface. Skin diving is also known as "free diving" or "breath-hold diving" (Fig. 1-5).

Fig. 1-4. Scuba diving is done with a compressed air "tank" that is worn on your back.

The primary objective of this course is to teach you to become a scuba diver. Your instructor will also teach you the fundamentals of skin diving. Mastering the skills of skin diving will make you a better scuba diver.

RISKS IN DIVING

Of course, in any adventure there are always risks. Scuba diving is a sport that has some risk, and you must understand this before you become a diver.

Most dives are very easy. On every dive, however, there is always the chance that you will need to exert yourself greatly. At times, diving can be very strenuous. This is particularly true if you make beach entries for diving through big surf, dive in strong currents, or dive in cold water (Fig. 1-6).

Your instructor will ask you to complete a medical history form before you can participate in the water-work sessions for this course. Depending on your age and overall physical condition, your instructor may require you to see a physician for a physical examination before diving. This is for your own well being.

The ultimate risk in diving is that you may be injured or killed while in or under the water. While this is extremely rare and most divers never suffer any type of mishap, you need to recognize that this risk exists. As a diver, you must be willing to accept this risk and take responsibility for your own actions. This book clearly explains each type of risk associated with diving. In addition, your instructor will explain the risks of diving in general and any risks that are unique to your local dive sites.

If you are a minor, your parents also need to understand the risks in diving. They will be asked to sign a Statement of Understanding and review your medical form.

Fig. 1-6. At times, diving can be quite strenuous, especially when the water is rough.

Fig. 1-5. Skin diving is also known as "breath-hold" or "free" diving. No breathing apparatus is used for this type of diving.

YOUR OBLIGATIONS

As a student enrolled in training for scuba diving, you have an obligation to attend, participate in, and satisfactorily complete every class session, both lectures and waterwork. Although diving is not complicated, the knowledge and skills you learn will build throughout the course. You must understand the most simple concepts in diving to be able to apply them to the diving you will do in open water. If you do not attend every training session, your knowledge and skills will be incomplete. If you do miss any sessions, it is your responsibility to arrange with your instructor to complete them satisfactorily.

Be sure to take notes during all classroom sessions. Your instructor will provide you with supplemental information that may not be in this textbook. In particular, you will learn about local diving techniques during the lecture and open water sessions.

You will learn the skills of diving in a "confined water" setting (Fig. 1-7). This may take place in either a swimming pool or a calm, clear body of water. Once you have learned these skills, your instructor will take you on a series of open water dives where you will practice these skills under actual diving conditions.

You will need to complete a final classroom, confined water, and open water evaluation of your diving knowledge and skills before your instructor will issue you a diving certification. Even if you pass all knowledge and skill exams, if your instructor does not believe you have the judgment needed to dive properly, it is his or her obligation to withhold your certification.

Fig. 1-7. You will learn the skills of diving in a confined water setting, such as a swimming pool.

WHAT IS SCUBA CERTIFICATION?

While there are no federal laws that govern recreational scuba diving, the professional instructors who work in diving have agreed on certain minimum standards of training for sport divers. You must meet these standards to receive a certification card that will enable you to receive scuba diving services. For example, once you become a diver you will need to produce your certification card to get your tank filled with air or to go on a diving trip.

Your NAUI Scuba Diver Certification course will teach you the fundamentals of how to dive. You will learn the principles of how to select and operate your equipment, the effects of diving on your body, and the basics of the local diving environment. On completing the course you will be qualified to dive under conditions that are similar to those where you learned to dive.

There are different levels of diving certification that signify special knowledge in diving. After you complete this NAUI Scuba Diver Certification course, you will be eligible to take "specialty courses" to learn about the different special interest areas in diving. For example, you might want to take a course on underwater photography or night diving (Fig. 1-8). There are also courses on underwater hunting and collecting, rescue diving, and many other topics.

Your instructor probably learned to dive in a course like the one you are taking now. In addition, he or she completed additional leadership courses in running organized dives and diver rescue techniques. To be certified as a diving instructor, he or she completed a demanding course that lasted at least 80 hours and then demonstrated the required knowledge and skills to a panel of experienced diving instructors.

Your NAUI Scuba Diver Certification card is just the beginning of your adventures in diving. In effect, it is your "license to learn" more about the

Fig. 1-8. Once you complete your initial training, you will want to participate in other NAUI programs, such as underwater photography specialty courses.

Fig. 1-9. Your initial Scuba Diver Certification is your "license to learn."

underwater world. There is no one who knows everything there is to know about diving, but in diving you'll find that the fun is in the learning (Fig. 1-9).

NAUI DIVING COURSES

Your Scuba Diver Certification course is being taught by an instructor certified through the National Association of Underwater Instructors, more commonly referred to as **NAUI**. Founded in 1960, NAUI is one of the oldest and most respected diver certifying agencies in the world. In the United States, NAUI is one of only two non-profit diver training associations. You can take pride in your NAUI certification, because NAUI courses are among the most demanding.

Your Scuba Diver Certification will teach you the fundamentals of diving, providing you with a great deal of information and many diving skills. There are many special interest areas in diving, however, and to become skilled in them you will want to take some or all of the NAUI specialty diving courses. For example, NAUI instructors teach specialty courses in such areas as wreck diving, deep diving, underwater photography and video, ice diving, cavern diving, underwater hunting, and numerous others (Fig. 1-10). These courses are exciting and fun, emphasizing the practical application of your new knowledge. Specialty courses give you the opportunity to learn these exciting activities more safely and quickly than if you tried to accumulate the same knowledge and experience on your own. The more experience you can gain under the supervision of a NAUI instructor, the more comfortable and confident you will be in the water.

Fig. 1-10. NAUI instructors teach many different types of diving courses.

To improve your overall skill and knowledge, eventually you will want to take the NAUI Advanced Diving course. To take this course, you need not be an advanced diver. The course will teach you advanced diving skills and knowledge.

Many people find that diving changes their lives and even their careers. By gaining diving experience and taking the progressive leadership courses in diving, you can eventually work your way toward certification as a diving instructor.

A Little Apprehension Is Normal

Most people who have not spent much time swimming in the ocean or other open bodies of water have a little apprehension about learning to dive. They have concerns about the strange equipment, the marine life, and the environment. This is normal and to be expected.

Diving is seldom, if ever, as it is portrayed in popular films or television shows. Once you become a diver, you will quickly begin to spot the flaws in most of the movies that feature diving. When you go underwater, you will find that most fish swim away from divers and that humans are the most fearsome creatures underwater.

While there are always some risks in diving, there are ways to minimize them. By knowing the risks you can deal with them and make the probability of their occurring extremely small, which is what diver training is all about.

One of the most popular misconceptions about diving is that divers frequently run out of air underwater. Certainly, the amount of time you spend underwater on any given dive is limited by the amount of air in your tank. All divers use a pressure gauge connected to their tank to monitor their air supply and help them determine when it is time to surface (Fig. 1-11). Just as a person driving a car will monitor the fuel gauge, you will monitor your pressure gauge underwater—except you must monitor it more frequently than you would a fuel gauge. As an extra precaution, most divers carry either additional regulators, which allow them to share air during an emergency, or a totally independent backup air supply. If you are a reasonably cautious diver, you should never run out of air underwater.

Most nondivers have the mistaken perception that even if you do not run out of air, diving equipment is unreliable. Few divers ever experience an equipment failure in diving gear that has been properly maintained. A poorly maintained regulator is more likely to freeflow and deliver more air than you need than to deliver no air at all. As a student diver, you will learn how to care properly for your equipment and inspect it before each dive. Occasionally, a piece of gear may become loose or go out of adjustment underwater, but you will learn how to deal with these minor nuisances as part of your course.

Another common concern is that when you are diving in the ocean, you will always be under the threat of a shark attack. Few divers ever have the opportunity to see a shark during normal scuba dives, however. In fact, it is so unusual to encounter a shark that many ordinary divers now go on special trips with the sole purpose of seeing and photographing sharks. Most experienced divers have come to realize that the opportunity to dive with these unique creatures is something rare and special.

In most cases where sharks do encounter divers, they show little or no interest in the people unless they have been "baited" with food. Divers who remain calm, swim slowly, and stay underwater usually receive little or no attention from a passing shark. They are like most creatures underwater and will leave you alone if you do not harass them.

When you see new things underwater, it often is easy to get excited while diving. One of the most important skills you will learn during your diving course is how to conserve your energy in the water and pace yourself to avoid fatigue. If you find yourself working hard and breathing shallowly yet rapidly, it is essential to slow down, stop what you are doing, and catch your breath. This will only take a second, and it helps prevent panic.

LET'S GET READY TO DIVE!

You will find that scuba diving is one of the most exciting and fun activities that you will ever enjoy (Fig. 1-12). By completing this Scuba Diver Certification course, you will be prepared to participate in diving adventures unlike anything you have experienced before. Read this book completely and follow your instructor's directions, and you will be ready to learn how to dive.

Fig. 1-11. You will always be able to know how much air you have during any dive by using a submersible tank-pressure gauge.

Fig. 1-12. Diving is fun and exciting!

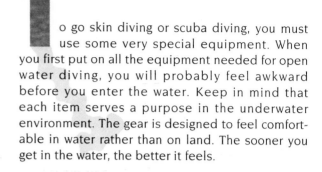

CHAPTER TWO

To go skin diving or scuba diving, you must use some very special equipment. When you first put on all the equipment needed for open water diving, you will probably feel awkward before you enter the water. Keep in mind that each item serves a purpose in the underwater environment. The gear is designed to feel comfortable in water rather than on land. The sooner you get in the water, the better it feels.

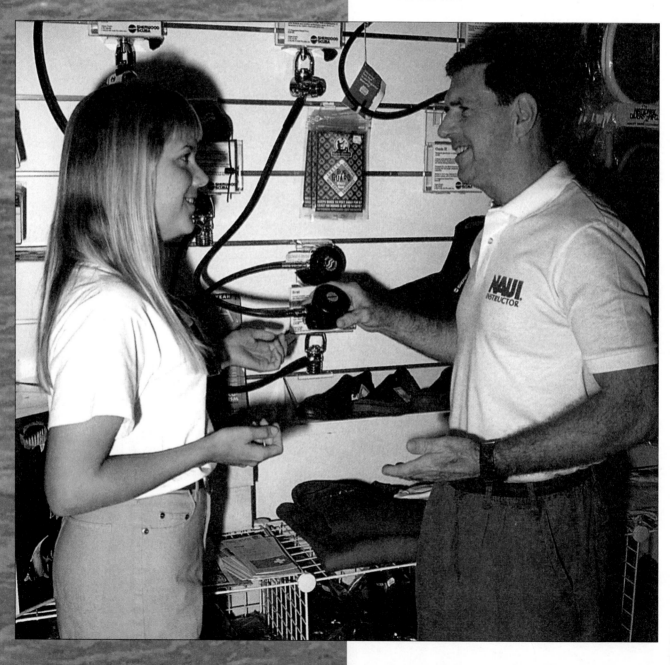

LEARNING OBJECTIVES

By the end of this chapter, you must be able to:

1. State four reasons why you should purchase your dive gear at a professional diving retailer.
2. List five items that are considered to be basic pieces of diving gear.
3. Explain how to select a diving mask.
4. Explain the two most important considerations in selecting a snorkel.
5. State the differences between an open-heel adjustable fin and a full-foot pocket fin.
6. Explain why a hood, boots, and gloves are important for diving in cold water.
7. Explain why some form of surface flotation is important for snorkeling.
8. Explain the maintenance procedures for a mask, fins, and snorkel.
9. List the two types of materials most commonly used to manufacture scuba tanks.
10. Explain the meaning of the terms p.s.i. and bar.
11. List three sizes of scuba cylinders.
12. List the two methods of attaching a scuba regulator to a valve, and explain the difference between them.
13. Describe the annual inspection that must be conducted on every scuba cylinder.
14. Explain the function of a scuba regulator.
15. State the proper maintenance procedures and precautions for scuba regulators.
16. List three types of alternate air sources, and explain their function.
17. State the function of a buoyancy control device.
18. List four features that are common to all buoyancy control devices.
19. State the most important feature of any weight belt.
20. List the three types of thermal protective suits worn by divers, and explain how they work.
21. Explain the importance of a submersible pressure gauge.
22. List three types of diving instrumentation.
23. List four types of information supplied by most dive computers.
24. Explain why backup instrumentation is important while diving.
25. Explain the primary concern regarding diving instrumentation and its effect on the environment.
26. List three uses for a diver's knife.
27. State two reasons for maintaining a diving log book.
28. List three minor accessories for diving.

WHERE SHOULD YOU BUY DIVE GEAR?

You can buy diving equipment from a variety of outlets, including mail-order catalogues, sporting goods stores, and stores that specialize in dive gear. All of these places are acceptable. Your best choice for purchasing equipment, however, is usually your local dive store or sporting goods store if it has a dedicated diving section.

There are several reasons why you should buy your gear from a specialized diving retailer, like a NAUI Pro Facility. These include:

- You can see and wear the equipment on dry land before you buy it.
- Some retailers will have an on-site pool and allow you to try the gear in the pool before you buy it.
- Your local retailer is able to help you adjust items such as buoyancy compensators (BCs) and to measure you properly for custom wet suits.
- Local retailers can provide you with the instruction needed when you purchase a specialized piece of gear such as a dive computer, video housing, or dry suit.
- Your local retailer is usually able to provide you with service on any gear that you buy there.
- Local retailers will frequently loan you equipment while yours is in the shop for repair.
- Your local retailer is the only source for scuba cylinder fills and last-minute accessory items.

If you develop a good relationship with your local diving retailer, the salespeople there will be able to help you select the right type of gear for local diving conditions and for your personal diving interests. Most new divers wait until they have finished their course to buy their scuba equipment. This is a good idea, because you will usually have the opportunity to try several different types of gear during the course. To take the course, however, most instructors will require you to have certain personal items of gear. These items generally include a mask, fins, snorkel, booties, and gloves (Fig. 2-1).

Fig. 2-1. Diving retailers generally have a wide selection of equipment so you can find the gear that best suits your needs.

THE BASICS

In its most basic form, you can go skin diving under optimal conditions with four basic pieces of gear: a mask, fins, snorkel, and some type of surface flotation. Because most pieces of dive gear are worn directly on your body, the comfort and fit of each item is extremely important.

Masks

If you have ever opened your eyes underwater without a mask, you know that it is impossible to see clearly without one. Our eyes are designed to see in air. A scuba mask places a layer of air between your eyes and the water, allowing you to see underwater objects without distortion.

A scuba mask differs from goggles in that it includes space for your nose. This is necessary to equalize the pressure inside the mask as you dive deeper in the water, where the pressure increases. The air pressure inside the mask is equalized with the water pressure outside when you exhale air from your nose into the mask.

The most important consideration in selecting a mask is how the mask fits on your face. To check the fit, hold the mask gently against your face without placing the strap over your head. Inhale briefly through your nose and hold your breath. If the mask sticks against your face and does not fall off, it is a good fit. If you must push the mask hard against your face or continually inhale to get it to stick, keep looking for a mask that fits. Be sure to try several different masks, even if the first one you try fits well. You may find another that fits better.

There are many different styles of masks from which to choose. Some of the features on masks are considered essential (Fig. 2-2), while others are considered optional. Essential features include:

Fig. 2-2. A diving mask must have certain essential features such as a split head strap, tempered glass, a solid frame, and a nose blocking device of some type.

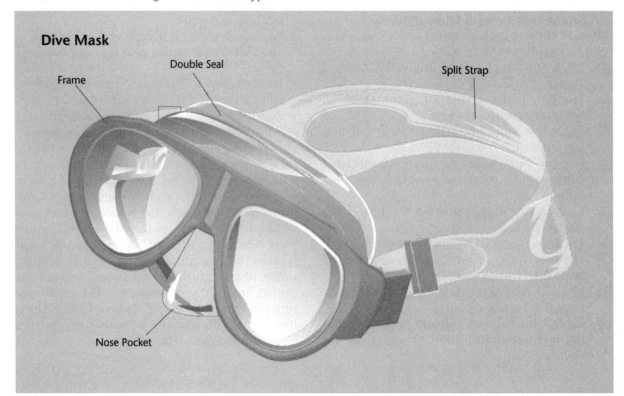

Dive Mask

Frame

Double Seal

Split Strap

Nose Pocket

1. Tempered glass to help avoid injury if the lens breaks.
2. A solid frame to hold the lens in position.
3. An adjustable, split headstrap that covers a wide portion of the head.
4. Some device for blocking off your nose to help equalize the pressure in your ears.

There are numerous optional features that you may desire when you select your mask. Some of the more popular optional features include:

1. A double-feather edge seal to help the mask fit on your face.
2. Side windows to provide a wider field of view.
3. A purge valve to help clear water from the mask (not required).
4. Prescription lenses.

A small number of people are allergic to certain types of rubber products that may be found in some dive masks. If you have this condition, be sure to select a mask made from silicone because this material is hypoallergenic.

New masks are covered with a thin film of lubricant, which was used to get the mask out of the mold when it was manufactured. To remove this lubricant, you can use dishwashing detergent or toothpaste. Wash the lens of the mask vigorously with either substance and plenty of fresh water (Fig. 2-3). This will help keep the lens from fogging, which happens when condensation forms on the inside of the lens.

Each time you don your mask for diving, you will need to prepare it further so that it will not "fog" because of the temperature difference inside the mask compared with that of the surrounding water. The most common way to prevent fogging is to spit into the mask and rub it on the lens. If you prefer, you can buy a commercially available anti-fog solution.

Fig. 2-3. New masks must be cleaned with dishwashing soap or toothpaste prior to first use.

Snorkels

Have you ever seen a dolphin and noticed how its blowhole is on the top of its head? With this arrangement, a dolphin does not need to lift its head out of the water to breathe, so it can swim more efficiently.

Without a snorkel, you would need to lift your head out of the water every time you want to breathe while swimming on the surface and looking at the bottom. This gets very tiring after just a few minutes. With a snorkel, you can swim along and watch the bottom continuously without lifting your head. This helps you conserve energy—and the air in your scuba tank—any time you must swim on the surface.

There are many different types of snorkels for diving, with a variety of features. Simple snorkels are "J" shaped, while others have flexible hoses and special valves. Other snorkels may have mouthpieces that rotate and contoured designs (Fig. 2-4).

Fig. 2-4. Snorkels should have a gentle, curved shape.

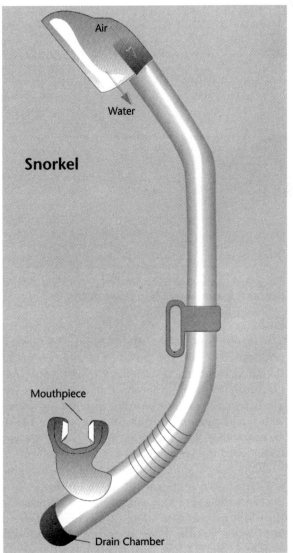

Air

Water

Snorkel

Mouthpiece

Drain Chamber

The two most important considerations in selecting a snorkel are its length and the diameter of its barrel. Snorkels should be neither too short nor too long. The ideal length is between 12 and 14 inches (30.5 and 35.5 cm). A snorkel that is too long will make it difficult to breathe, while one that is too short will constantly fill with water. Of course, the snorkel you choose must fit comfortably in your mouth.

The inside diameter of a snorkel should be approximately three quarters of an inch (1.9 cm). Snorkels that are too thin make breathing difficult, while those that are too thick are awkward to use. There must be no sharp bends or angles in the snorkel.

Learning to use a snorkel properly is one of the most important skills in scuba diving. Surprisingly, many scuba accidents occur at the surface when divers become fatigued and are unable to swim back to the boat or beach. In this course, you will learn to use your snorkel properly (Fig. 2-5).

Fig. 2-5. Learning to use a snorkel properly is one of the most important skills in scuba diving.

Fins

Without fins, scuba diving would be almost impossible. Once you put on the gear for scuba diving, it becomes very difficult to use your arms efficiently to swim underwater. In addition, if you are carrying a camera or other equipment underwater, it is even more difficult to use your hands for swimming. With fins on, you can go further and faster using the larger muscles of your legs.

While there are many different fin designs, there are two basic foot-pocket arrangements. One encloses the entire foot and is appropriately called "full-foot pocket fins." The other incorporates a heel strap, but the back of the foot is otherwise exposed. This is known as the "open-heel design."

Within the open-heeled arrangement, there is yet a further distinction between adjustable and non-adjustable fins. For cold water diving, most divers prefer "open-heel adjustable fins" because they are easier to use with booties.

Fins come in sizes that normally span a range of shoe sizes, such as small, medium, large, and extra large. Your fins should fit snugly without cramping your toes or pinching your feet (Fig. 2-6). Fins that are too loose are easily lost. If you plan to wear anything under your fins (e.g., socks, booties), you must try the fins on with whatever you plan to wear beneath them.

If your fin is equipped with adjustable straps, your instructor may have you tape the straps to avoid having them snag on kelp or other types of marine plants or debris. Minor modifications such as these will help make your diving more enjoyable.

You will frequently hear divers discussing the merits of different fins, arguing which they feel is "best." In fact, there is no one best fin for all divers. Because each person's body is different, each fin performs differently on different people. In general, you want to select a fin that is comfortable on your foot and does not cause cramping of your toes or foot muscles. In particular, you should be able to kick with the fin for long periods of time without causing your leg muscles to cramp. Large, stiff fins are not the best for all divers under all circumstances. In some cases, a shorter, more flexible fin will be more comfortable to wear and more efficient.

Fig. 2-6. Like any piece of diving gear, fins must fit properly to be effective.

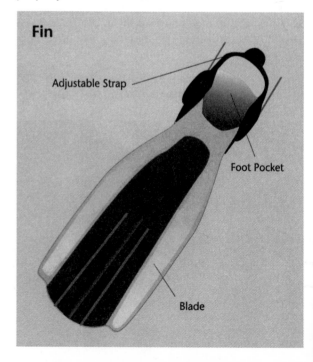

Fin

Adjustable Strap

Foot Pocket

Blade

Fins are manufactured from a variety of materials. They must withstand exposure to sun, salt, and sand, so you should purchase good-quality fins that will take this kind of hard use.

Most new fins today come with plastic inserts, similar in function to a shoe tree, that are designed to maintain the shape of the foot pockets when the fins are being stored. These inserts are not meant to be used for diving but should be used when storing your fins between dive trips.

If you dive in cold water, you will definitely want to wear some type of thermal protection on your feet, besides your fins, to keep them warm and protect them from cuts. Wet-suit booties made from foam neoprene are the most commonly used protection. Booties can be worn with either full-foot fins or open-heel fins.

Booties

Booties are like socks made out of wetsuit material, except that most have a hard sole designed for walking on rocks or other rough surfaces (Fig. 2-7). They will help keep your feet warm and protect them from cuts when climbing on rocks or walking on the rough deck of a boat. During the summer months, booties will help protect your feet from the hot surfaces found in most parking lots as you prepare to dive. Booties will also help to prevent most fins from causing blisters on your feet.

If you plan to buy booties, you should buy your fins at the same time, because most booties will require you to use fins that are one size larger. Trying to use booties with fins that fit your bare feet properly usually will not work. Like your fins, the booties should fit snugly but comfortably on your feet (Fig. 2-8).

Fig. 2-7. Booties are essential for cold water diving and will also provide protection for your feet while walking over rough surfaces as you go to and from the dive site.

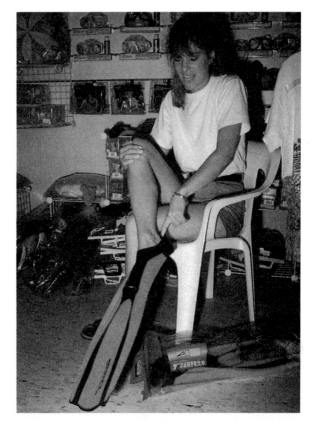

Fig. 2-8. If you plan to buy booties, be sure to purchase them at the same time as you purchase your fins to make sure they work together. Otherwise, if you buy your fins without booties, they probably won't work if you try to use booties with them later.

Some booties have zippers down the side, making them easier to put on. Zippers are acceptable provided they have a backing that prevents cold water from entering the boots.

Booties come in different thicknesses for different water temperatures. As you might expect, thicker boots are used in colder waters. Many booties have a nylon lining inside that makes them easier to put on.

Gloves

Gloves are considered to be an essential piece of diving gear in most situations (Fig. 2-9). Whether you dive in warm or cold water, gloves will protect your hands from nicks and cuts. In cold water, your hands will quickly grow numb if you do not wear gloves.

In the tropics, almost any type of glove will work for diving. Inexpensive cotton gloves are usually more than adequate. In colder waters, divers use neoprene gloves or mittens. There are also gloves that can be connected directly to certain types of diving suits to keep your hands completely dry. Your instructor will advise you about the type of gloves that are usually worn in your area.

Fig. 2-9. Gloves help to protect your hands from cuts and abrasion.

Whichever type of gloves you choose, they must fit properly so you can handle all of your equipment while you are wearing them. Most instructors will want you to wear your gloves during your training so you learn how to work with them on.

When you are wearing gloves, there is a great temptation to touch or handle many of the marine creatures you will find underwater, because the gloves give your hands some protection. This should be avoided, however, because in many cases, the mere act of touching certain animals or plants will hurt or kill them. For example, coral reefs are particularly sensitive to touch, and many corals are easily broken. Many fish are also covered with a protective slime that, when removed, makes them subject to infection or parasites.

Surface Flotation

Any time you are snorkeling or skin diving, you should always have some additional flotation with you in case you get tired. This includes both personal flotation and some type of surface support station as a backup.

All divers must wear some type of personal flotation when snorkeling. The most commonly used piece of flotation equipment is an inflatable vest that is worn on the chest and is usually referred to as a "snorkeling vest" (Fig. 2-10). The vest is designed to slip over the head and fasten around the waist with a strap. Most vests of this design have some type of oral inflation tube as well as a mechanism to inflate the vest automatically using a CO_2 cartridge (i.e., a small, disposable canister of compressed gas).

Fig. 2-10. Snorkeling vests can be inflated to provide positive buoyancy at the surface.

Your surface support station can be anything from an inflatable inner tube to an inflatable surf mat, or even a yacht. It does not matter which of these items you use as long as some type of object that can support you if you become tired is close at hand (Fig. 2-11).

Maintenance of Your Basic Gear

The maintenance of most diving gear is extremely simple. All that is usually required is a good rinse with fresh, clean water at the end of each diving day (Fig. 2-12). Do not leave your gear lying in the sun any longer than necessary, and store it in a cool, dry place between dives. The sun's rays are very damaging to dive gear.

If you live in an area with heavy smog, rubber products will usually last longer if they are stored in a sealed plastic bag, such as a large trash bag. Just be sure that any gear is completely dry before you seal it up to avoid mold or mildew formation.

Fig. 2-11. A surface support station, such as an inner tube, provides a place to rest on the surface.

Fig. 2-12. Your diving equipment should be rinsed with fresh water after every dive.

Remember that no matter how well you take care of your dive gear, parts of your gear will need to be replaced periodically. Fin straps and mask straps will wear out, as will the foot pockets on most fins. Inspect your gear regularly to make sure it is working as it should, and replace worn items before they break.

TEST THE DEPTH OF YOUR KNOWLEDGE

If you have read the preceding text carefully, you should be able to answer the following questions regarding basic diving equipment.

1 The **two** most important features for the selection of your mask, fins, and snorkel are:
   a. Comfort   b. Style
   c. Fit   d. Color

2 One feature that is not essential in a dive mask is:
   a. Purge valve   b. Tempered glass
   c. Nose block device d. Frame

3 List three factors that can reduce the ease of breathing of a snorkel:
   a.
   b.
   c.

WHAT DOES A SCUBA TANK DO?

When most people think of scuba diving, they immediately think of the scuba tank that divers wear on their backs. You will hear tanks referred to by a variety of terms, including "bottles," "jugs," and "cylinders." They all mean the same thing.

The scuba tank provides a method of storing a large quantity of air in a relatively small space. The air in the tank is highly compressed, so the tank walls must be strong to withstand the pressure. Most diving tanks operate at pressures that range from between 2250 p.s.i. (pounds per square inch), or 155 bar, to 4500 p.s.i., or 310 bar. The term **p.s.i.** is commonly used in diving, and it is used frequently throughout this book. The term **bar** refers to approximately one atmosphere of pressure, which equals 14.7 p.s.i. It is a term commonly used in Europe or in countries where the metric system is used. These are terms that you should know.

To maintain the high pressures found in scuba cylinders, tanks must be made from rugged material. Most cylinders available for sport diving are made from either steel or aluminum. Both materials have advantages and disadvantages.

Both steel and aluminum tanks can corrode if water is allowed to enter the tank. In an aluminum tank, this corrosion occurs as aluminum oxide, a chemical that retards further corrosion. When a steel tank corrodes, it rusts. Aluminum tanks are more easily damaged externally than steel tanks, and the threads where the valve screws into these tanks must be serviced periodically.

Some steel tanks are capable of operating at higher pressures than aluminum cylinders. Thus, they are able to pack a larger volume of air into a smaller cylinder.

Scuba tanks come in a variety of sizes, from as small as 15 cubic feet (424 L) to well over 100 cubic feet (2831 L). You can also get cylinders that are hooked together with a common valve or "manifold." For most sport diving situations, however, a single cylinder is the optimum combination of weight, size, and tank volume. For average sport-diving depths, an 80-cubic-foot (2266-L) cylinder is more than adequate. Smaller divers, who have less lung volume, may be able to use a cylinder as small as 50 (1415 L) to 65 cubic feet (1840 L) yet still be able to dive for a reasonable length of time.

Most divers buy an accessory "boot" to protect the bottom of their tank. The boot provides mechanical protection to the tank bottom. If the cylinder is a steel tank with a round bottom, the boot makes it easy to stand the tank up while you are attaching your regulator or back pack. The boot should be removed periodically so the bottom of the tank can be rinsed properly.

Do not leave your tank standing by itself when you are not right next to it. Tanks should be laid down so they do not fall over and damage the valve or injure another person.

All scuba tanks have a set of markings stamped on the shoulder of the cylinder. As a diver, you will need to understand some of these markings. (This way, when you buy a cylinder, you will know what you are buying.) The markings may differ slightly depending on whether the tank is a steel or aluminum cylinder and where the tank was manufactured. The three most important marks you should be able to identify are the service pressure of the tank, the last test date, and the serial number.

The service pressure of the tank is the pressure at which it is designed to operate. As mentioned previously, this varies depending on the type of tank, but the minimum could be as low as 1800 p.s.i. (124 bar) to as high as 4500 p.s.i. (310 bar). Whatever the pressure, it will be indicated clearly so the person who fills the tank will know the maximum allowable pressure. You need to know this number so you can be sure the tank is full (Fig. 2-13).

The last test date reflects the last time the tank was pressure tested to ensure that it still has adequate strength to hold pressure. This must be done once every 5 years in the United States, and the procedure is known as a "hydrostatic test" (Fig. 2-14). If a tank is past its test date, it cannot be filled. In Japan, this test must be done every 3 years and in Australia every year.

Fig. 2-13. The numbers stamped on the top line of this aluminum cylinder signify that it may be filled to a pressure of 207 bar, while the second line indicates an equivalent pressure of 3000 p.s.i.

The serial number of the tank is the unique identifying number assigned to a particular tank. If you buy a tank, you should write the number down and keep a record of it in a safe place in the event your tank is stolen (Fig. 2-15).

Every Tank Needs a Valve

Every scuba tank must have a valve to hold the air in the cylinder when it is not in use, to control the flow of air from the tank, and to provide an attachment point for the regulator. In its simplest form, a scuba tank valve operates much like a water faucet in your home. The valve is opened by turning a knob counterclockwise, and it is closed by turning the knob clockwise.

The most common valves you will find are designed like a post. The "yoke" attaches the regulator to the post. It slides over the valve, and a set screw on the regulator is used to tighten it against the valve. Regulators with yokes are not normally used at pressures above 3000 p.s.i. (207 bar).

The other type of valve design is known as a "DIN" valve. The DIN valve system originated in Europe. In this system, the valve has a large, threaded opening, and the regulator actually screws into the valve (Fig. 2-16). You will also hear divers refer to this system as a "captured O-ring system." DIN valve systems are less commonly seen in the United States than yoke systems. They are more reliable, however, and capable of operating at pressures higher than 3000 psi (207 bar). They are also more expensive.

The seal between the tank valve and the regulator is made by a rubber gasket known as an "O-ring." If the O-ring is damaged or missing, the regulator will not seal and air will escape. When you buy your own tank, be sure to get several extra O-rings, because they wear out frequently and must be replaced regularly.

Fig. 2-14. Diving cylinders must be hydrostatically tested on a regular basis.

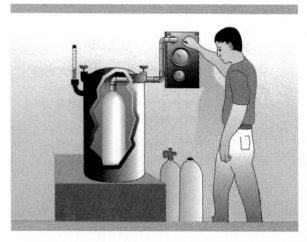

Some valves are equipped with mechanical reserve mechanisms designed to hold back a few hundred pounds of air pressure until the mechanism is activated. These valves are known as "J valves." These mechanisms are not entirely reliable, and it is easy to accidentally bypass the reserve. When this happens, there is no air left in the tank at the time when you usually need it the most. These valves are more expensive to buy than other valves, and they are more expensive to service. Although these valves were popular in the early days of diving, they are less popular today.

Valves without a reserve mechanism are commonly referred to as "K valves." These valves are designed only to turn the air on and off. The logical question you might ask regarding a "K" valve is: How do you know when you are running low on air? The answer is simple: All responsible divers use a submersible pressure gauge that attaches to their regulator and indicates how much pressure is in their tank at all times. The submersible pressure gauge performs a function much like the fuel gauge in a car. Today, most divers use tanks equipped with "K" valves and regulators with submersible pressure gauges (Fig. 2-17).

Every scuba valve is equipped with a pressure relief disk, which you may also hear referred to as a "burst disk." The purpose of the pressure relief disk is to allow the tank to vent pressure rather than rupturing if the pressure within the tank becomes too high. In most cases, the only time a pressure relief disk will vent a tank is if the tank becomes extremely hot.

Maintenance of Scuba Tanks

Although scuba tanks are rugged pieces of equipment, they must not be abused. Probably the single most important thing you can do to care for your scuba cylinder is never to use all of the air in the tank. Apart from the danger of using all your air while you are in the water, there is nothing to keep water out of the tank if there is no air pressure inside it. Once moisture enters your tank, oxidation begins. In addition, if there is water in your tank, this will introduce moisture and oxidation products into your regulator, which could cause your regulator to malfunction. During storage, your scuba tank should always have a minimum of approximately 100 p.s.i. (7 bar) inside, and preferably 300 p.s.i. (20 bar).

The outside of your tank should be rinsed thoroughly with fresh, clean water after every dive. It should be stored standing up in a protected location where it cannot be knocked over. To transport it by car, it should be on its side and securely blocked to prevent damage to the valve.

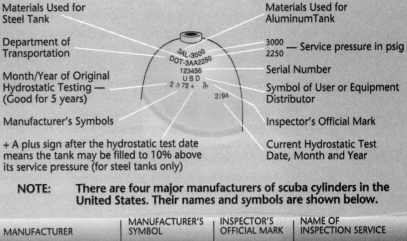

Materials Used for Steel Tank		Materials Used for Aluminum Tank
Department of Transportation	3000 — Service pressure in psig 2250	
Month/Year of Original Hydrostatic Testing — (Good for 5 years)	Serial Number	
	Symbol of User or Equipment Distributor	
Manufacturer's Symbols	Inspector's Official Mark	

+ A plus sign after the hydrostatic test date means the tank may be filled to 10% above its service pressure (for steel tanks only)

Current Hydrostatic Test Date, Month and Year

NOTE: There are four major manufacturers of scuba cylinders in the United States. Their names and symbols are shown below.

MANUFACTURER	MANUFACTURER'S SYMBOL	INSPECTOR'S OFFICIAL MARK	NAME OF INSPECTION SERVICE
Alcan Aluminum	Alcan	A	Industrial Analysis
Norris Industries	⬆	A	Industrial Analysis
Pressed Steel	PST	C	T.H. Cochrane Labratory
Walter Kidde	K or WK or WK & Co.	A H	Arrowhead Industrial Service or Hunt Inspection

Fig. 2-15. Be sure to record the serial number of your cylinder and other pertinent information.

Fig. 2-16. DIN valves are found throughout the world.

Fig. 2-17. "K" valves like this one are the most common type of valve found in the United States.

The inside of your tank must be inspected once a year at your local professional dive store or dive-equipment repair facility. This is known as a "visual cylinder inspection," or "VCI," and it must be done by a certified tank inspector (Fig. 2-18). Without a current visual cylinder inspection sticker and/or a current hydrostatic test date (if the tank is new), no dive store will fill your tank.

Provided the interior of the cylinder is in good condition, the inspector will apply a sticker to the tank to indicate that the tank has passed an annual inspection. If the tank is not in good condition, it may need to be cleaned to remove oxidation. While the tank is being inspected is a good time to have the valve serviced as well.

Backpacks

A backpack is designed to hold the scuba tank securely and comfortably on your back. The pack may be a separate item of equipment (Fig. 2-19) or may be part of a BC, which is a device used to adjust your buoyancy underwater.

The pack should be comfortable and have an easily adjustable harness with quick-release buckles at the waist and on at least one shoulder. The band that secures the pack to the tank may be rigid or soft and flexible. The flexible bands should be easily adjustable and should lock tightly onto the tank to prevent the tank from slipping from the pack.

Fig. 2-18. Your scuba tank must be inspected once a year by a qualified tank inspector.

Fig. 2-19. Traditional backpacks are designed to be used with separate buoyancy compensators.

Backpacks should be rinsed after each use. The straps should be secured around the pack so they do not drag and become frayed when your gear is being carried rather than worn.

WHAT IS A REGULATOR?

The scuba regulator is the mechanism you breathe through when you go underwater. The function of this device is to take the high-pressure air in the tank and reduce its level to match the surrounding pressure, also known as the "ambient pressure," so you can breathe. The air that is delivered to you through the mouthpiece is always at the exact same pressure as your body, no matter what depth you are at underwater. That is the magic of the scuba regulator (Fig. 2-20).

Fig. 2-20. Modern scuba regulators provide easy breathing. This regulator has a submersible pressure gauge attached to it.

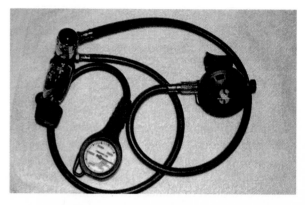

Scuba regulators break down the pressure in the tank in two steps. The first occurs in the "first stage," which is the part of the regulator that is attached to the tank valve (Fig. 2-21). In the first stage, the pressure in the tank is reduced to approximately 140 p.s.i. (9.6 bar) above the surrounding pressure. The air from the first stage is then delivered to the "second stage," which has the mouthpiece attached to it, through a short hose (Fig. 2-22). In the second stage, the air pressure is reduced to the surrounding or "ambient" pressure.

Fig. 2-21. The first stage of the regulator is the part that attaches to the scuba tank.

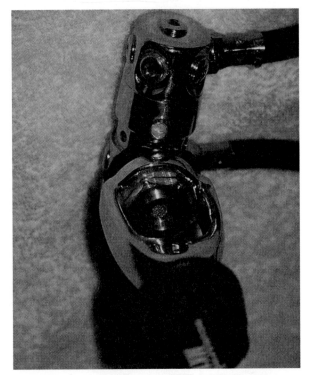

Fig. 2-22. The second stage of the regulator is the part that goes in your mouth.

All commercially available scuba regulators deliver air reliably under ordinary sport diving conditions. As you might expect, however, some regulators offer higher performance than others and deliver a greater volume of air at greater depths. This is important, because the harder you work underwater, the more air you need to breathe. If you plan to engage in deep diving, wreck diving, ice diving, or underwater hunting, you will almost certainly want a high-performance regulator.

You will add other hoses to the first stage of your regulator (besides the hose that connects the first stage to the second stage). At a minimum, you will have a second hose that connects the first stage to a submersible pressure gauge that monitors your air supply. Depending on the type of diving you do and where you dive, you may add the following hoses:

- Power inflator hose for a BC
- Dry suit inflator hose
- Alternate second stage or "octopus regulator"

The octopus regulator is an additional second stage that allows you to share air from your tank with another diver rather than trying to share a single mouthpiece. Using an octopus is just one of several methods for sharing air that you will learn about during your NAUI Scuba Diver Certification course.

Maintenance of Scuba Regulators

The inside of a scuba regulator is filled with a number of small parts that have been manufactured to very close tolerances. If saltwater, dust, or other foreign matter enters your regulator, it can seriously affect its performance, making breathing more difficult. In addition, many of the parts used in scuba regulators are made from rubber and must be replaced when they become worn. For these reasons, your regulator must be properly maintained and serviced annually by a professional technician trained in regulator service.

Professional regulator technicians have the correct tools and spare parts to maintain and repair regulators. They are trained by regulator manufacturers to properly identify and fix problems.

You can help maintain your regulator, and thus reduce your repair bills, by checking the device at the end of each diving day. One of the most important maintenance procedures is to be sure to install the "dust cap" that seals the first stage when the regulator is not in use. The dust cap must be dry before you install it, and the best way to dry the dust cap is to use a dry towel to remove all water droplets. Your instructor will show you the proper procedure for drying and installing the dust cap.

Some dust caps use an O-ring to create a seal to prevent foreign matter from entering the regulator.

You can tell if your dust cap requires an O-ring by looking at the large end of the cap. If an O-ring is present, it should always be present. If there is a large, empty groove in the dust cap, then the O-ring is missing and must be replaced.

With the dust cap in place, you should then rinse, or preferably soak, your regulator with clean freshwater. Gently rinse the regulator after it has been soaked, running water through the mouthpiece and exhaust ports (Fig. 2-23). Do not push the purge button, which is usually located in the center of the front of the regulator but also may be located on the side. Pushing the purge button will allow water to run back into the first stage and cause corrosion inside your regulator, further decreasing the regulator's performance.

During storage, the hoses on your regulator must not be coiled tightly or allowed to hang at an angle with weight on them, which causes the hose to kink. Hoses that have been stressed are prone to premature failure and must be replaced. Like your other gear, your regulator must be stored in a cool, dry place.

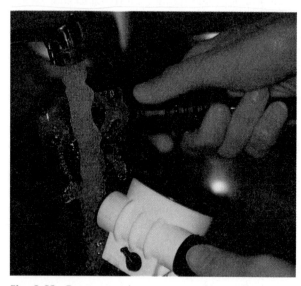

Fig. 2-23. Be sure to rinse your regulator after each day of diving.

Why Do You Need an Alternate Air Source?

In the rare event that you or your diving partner run out of air underwater, it is essential that each of you be equipped with some form of "alternate air source." Several different options are available to you that will satisfy this requirement.

True alternate air sources, or "contingency scuba," provide a totally independent regulator and air supply. Two main types of equipment that fall under this category:
• A small scuba cylinder (though containing at least 15 cubic feet [424 L] of air) equipped with a sepa-

rate regulator. This type of setup is known as a "pony bottle" (Fig. 2-24). It is most commonly used by wreck divers and is the preferred option for deep dives.
• A tiny scuba cylinder with a special, compact regulator that places the mouthpiece directly on the cylinder. This is a commercial product known as "Spare Air®" (Fig. 2-25).

These systems can serve as a backup for your buddy or yourself if you should become separated.

Fig. 2-24. Small scuba cylinders like this one are usually referred to as "pony bottles."

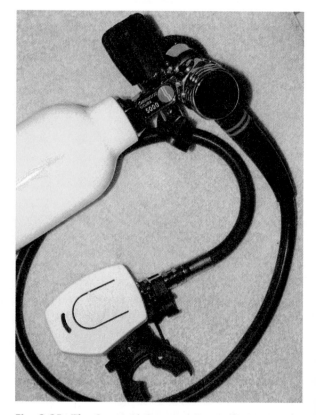

Fig. 2-25. The Spare Air® system is another type of alternate air source.

The disadvantage to contingency scuba systems is their additional expense, bulk, and weight. Because they are separate from your regulator, they represent another piece (or two) of equipment to carry with you when you dive.

"Octopus rigs" are the most common type of alternate air source used by divers (Fig. 2-26). Its hose must be at least 4 inches longer than a standard regulator.

The main advantages to using an octopus rig are its low price, the convenience of having it integrated into your existing regulator, its light weight, and its ease of use. The major disadvantage to using an octopus rig is that it does not represent an independent air supply. If your dive buddy is out of air, you probably will be. If you become separated from your buddy and run out of air, you also have no backup. While an octopus rig will function at all recreational diving depths, it does not represent the best choice for deep dives below 60 feet.

Yet another type of alternate air source (similar to the octopus rig concept) functions as a combination power inflator for a BC and regulator. This system is covered in more detail in the section on BCs (Fig. 2-27).

No matter what type of alternate air source you select, the location of the mouthpiece on your body is critical. An alternate air source does neither you nor your dive buddy any good if it cannot be located immediately during an emergency. The alternate air source must be visible, easy to identify, and available for instant use whenever it is needed.

The mouthpiece for your alternate air source must be located in the area known as the "golden triangle" (Fig. 2-28). This triangle is defined as the area located between your mouth and either side of your waist on the front of your body. Any other location for the mouthpiece is not acceptable.

Maintenance of alternate air sources is identical to that for your primary tank and regulator. These systems must be tested regularly, even though they will not be used on every dive.

Fig. 2-26. This regulator is equipped with an octopus rig.

TEST THE DEPTH OF YOUR KNOWLEDGE

Good divers are knowledgeable about their diving equipment. Let's see how much you know:

1 Briefly describe the difference between a "J" valve and a "K" valve.

2 What are the most important criteria when selecting a regulator?

3 What maintenance step must be performed before you rinse your regulator?

4 List one advantage of using an octopus regulator.

5 What is the primary advantage of contingency scuba over an octopus rig?

6 What two types of metal are most commonly used to make scuba cylinders?

Fig. 2-27. Alternate air source.

Fig. 2-28. "Golden triangle."

BUOYANCY CONTROL SYSTEMS

As a diver, there will be times when you want to float effortlessly on the surface of the water. This is known as "positive buoyancy." There also may be times when you want to rest firmly on the bottom, which is known as "negative buoyancy." Most of the time when you are underwater, however, you will want to achieve "neutral buoyancy," which enables you to hover underwater without effort. Being neutrally buoyant underwater is like being weightless in outer space!

You can achieve neutral buoyancy at any depth by carefully controlling what equipment you wear and how you use it. The primary device divers use to control their buoyancy is known as a "buoyancy compensator" (abbreviated as "BC") or "buoyancy control device" (abbreviated as "BCD"). By inflating or deflating this device, you can control your buoyancy precisely. Buoyancy control is one of the most important of all diving skills (Fig. 2-29).

In addition to buoyancy control, the BC plays a large role in determining your "trim" underwater. For diving purposes, trim is defined as the angle your body is in as you swim through the water. Trim is also affected by the type of diving suit you wear and the amount and placement of any weights on your body.

There are two main types of BCs that are presently in use. These are known as "back flotation systems" and "buoyancy jackets." Most BCs include some type of backpack as part of the system.

Fig. 2-29. By using a buoyancy control device you can control your buoyancy at any depth. This is a jacket style buoyancy compensator.

Back Flotation Systems

Back flotation systems provide good trim as you swim through the water. Because the bladder of the compensator is behind you, it leaves your chest and waist relatively uncluttered. For this reason, underwater photographers often have their models wear back-mounted systems (Fig. 2-30).

The disadvantage to some back-mounted systems is that they tend to push you forward into a face-down position on the surface if you do not actively kick to maintain a face-up position. If you are swimming on the surface and deliberately lie on your back, you will have no problem with the buoyancy of this type of system.

Buoyancy Jackets

Jacket-style BCs tend to be the most popular systems. These BCs are comfortable to wear, provide good trim underwater, and most enable you to maintain a face-up position when you are resting on the surface.

Integrated Weight Systems

Some jacket-style and back-mounted compensators include systems that allow you to integrate your weights into the BC rather than wearing a separate weight belt. The advantages to this type of system are that it eliminates the weight belt and holds the BC in position on your body. Because there is no weight belt, the weights cannot slide around on your body, and the weight is supported by your shoulders. If you

Fig. 2-30. Some divers prefer buoyancy compensators that are back mounted.

use this type of system, it must provide a mechanism for ditching the weights instantly during an emergency.

The disadvantage to an integrated weight system is that when the system is assembled, it can be quite heavy and awkward to handle. If you use this type of system, it is generally easier to remove the weights or wear the system if you must carry it for any distance on dry land.

Common features of BCs

All BCs are made of durable material designed for rugged use. They must be equipped with an overpressure relief valve to prevent damage from excessive internal pressure. All BCs have an inflation/deflation hose that should be at least three quarters of an inch (1.9 cm) in diameter. The mouthpiece used to inflate the BC orally must be comfortable and fit easily inside your mouth.

All BCs are equipped with a mouthpiece attached to the inflation/deflation hose that allows you to blow air into it. To inflate the BC, put the mouthpiece into your mouth, push a button (usually located on the end of the mechanism), and blow into the BC. The button must be released when you are not blowing air into the BC, or the air will flow out. To deflate the BC, push down on the oral-inflator button and hold the mouthpiece so it is over your head. This allows the air to flow out.

To get air out of the BC, it is easiest if the unit has a "dump valve" located on the shoulder. This valve is usually operated by a cable that connects to a knob on the chest of the BC. The valve also may be operated by a cable that runs inside the inflation/deflation hose. By pulling down on the hose, the cable is also pulled, and the valve is opened. This is a useful optional feature on many BCs.

One of the most important features you should have on your BC is a low-pressure power inflator. The low-pressure inflator uses air from your regulator to inflate your BC; you do not need to inflate the BC orally. A low-pressure hose similar to the one that supplies your regulator mouthpiece connects your regulator to the power-inflator mechanism. The power inflator also includes a mouthpiece and oral inflator valve that can be used should the power inflator fail. To put air into the BC using the power inflator, push a button on the unit, and air flows through the inflation/deflation hose and fills the BC (Fig. 2-31).

Power inflators that also include an alternate air source (i.e., regulator) for emergency use are quite popular. The great advantage to these systems is that they eliminate the need for the additional hose of an octopus unit. In addition, because you

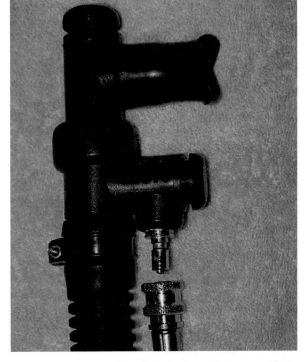

Fig. 2-31. Power inflators make buoyancy control easy.

frequently must use your power inflator as you dive, locating this unit during an emergency becomes second nature.

You occasionally may see older BCs with optional CO_2 cartridge inflator mechanisms. These mechanisms were designed to be used for emergency conditions only. Because of problems with corrosion, these mechanisms are highly unreliable and must not be depended on under any circumstances.

You must be capable of inflating your BC and controlling your buoyancy using either the oral or the power inflator. If the power inflator fails, you must be capable of putting air into the BC orally. This is covered in detail in the section on diving techniques.

Selecting a Buoyancy Compensator

The best way to select a BC is to try different models and see which is the most comfortable for you. A BC feels quite different when you try it on in the dive store compared with how it feels when you wear the rest of your dive equipment.

In particular, a BC must be as comfortable when it is inflated as when it is empty. The controls must be easy to locate and operate, and it should not ride up on your body when it is inflated.

Maintenance of Buoyancy Compensators

Modern buoyancy systems are costly, but with proper care they will last a long time. It is very important to rinse the unit both internally and externally after each use. Saltwater, dirty water, or chlorinated water inside the BC will cause damage. Every time you deflate the BC underwater, it usually gets some water inside it.

Through the oral inflator, fill the unit with several quarts of clean water, slosh the water around inside, and drain thoroughly. Then fully inflate the unit, both to allow it to dry and to be sure no leaks have developed (Fig. 2-32).

Be sure to rinse the power inflator mechanism thoroughly as well. Operate all of the buttons while you rinse the mechanism to dislodge any salts that may be present. Your power inflator must be serviced on an annual basis. If this is not done, it may malfunction.

Despite the best possible maintenance, BCs will wear out, although some of their parts can be replaced. Inspect your BC and test it before each dive.

Fig. 2-32. Drain the water from your buoyancy compensator before storing it away.

TEST THE DEPTH OF YOUR KNOWLEDGE

Let's review some of the important aspects of buoyancy systems:

1 What are the two main types of BCs?

2 List two essential features found on all BCs.

3 Why is it important to rinse the inside as well as the outside of your BC?

WHY MUST DIVERS WEAR WEIGHTS?

To offset the positive buoyancy of the diver's body, diving suit, and any other equipment the diver wears or carries, divers wear lead weights while diving (Fig. 2-33). These weights are available in many configurations, and as you gain diving experience, you will be able to determine which arrangement works best for you.

The various weight options include traditional weight belts, weight harnesses, and BCs with integrated weight systems. The weights themselves are usually either solid, molded lead or bags filled with lead shot.

Weight Belts

The most commonly used system is the 2-inch-wide nylon belt with a metal or plastic buckle. The weights themselves are normally molded into various shapes that can be slid onto the belt. Solid weights range in size from 1 to 10 pounds, and the weights may be bare or coated with a plastic covering (Fig. 2-34).

Fig. 2-33. Weight belts are worn to offset the positive buoyancy of your body, diving suit, and other equipment.

Fig. 2-34. Lead weights can be coated or uncoated, or provided in shot filled bags.

Many divers who use solid, molded weights prefer those that are curved to fit the hip. As you might suspect, these are called "hip weights." Other divers prefer to use a series of small, cylindrical weights that, when worn together, give the appearance that you are wearing a gun belt. These are known as "bullet weights." To hold solid weights in position on nylon weight belts, weight "keepers" are used to prevent the weights from moving.

Another type of available weight belt is equipped with a series of pockets that will accept either molded weights or pouches filled with lead shot. Many divers prefer to use shot, because it is more comfortable than a solid piece of lead against their hips. Shot pouches also are less likely to cause injury or damage than molded weights if they are dropped. There are also shot belts that have one continuous compartment circling the waist.

A popular feature of many weight belts is their ability to compensate for the compression of the diving suit as you go deeper. Without this compensating feature, ordinary weight belts usually become loose at depth. This allows the belt to rotate around your waist, and it may place the buckle on your side or back rather than in the front of your waist (where it is supposed to be).

A weight harness uses a belt and shoulder-harness system to support the weights on your shoulders rather than around your waist. This helps reduce the strain on your lower back and prevent the belt from sliding around on your body.

The length of any weight belt you use must be adjustable so there is not an excess amount of strap to get in your way. Your instructor can show you several methods of adjustment depending on the type of belt you select. It is preferable to adjust the belt to take up the excess strap rather than to cut the end of the belt. Usually, the tail of the belt should not exceed 6 inches in length.

TEST THE DEPTH OF YOUR KNOWLEDGE

You must remember the following essential points regarding weighting systems:

1 What is the most important feature of a weight belt?

2 Describe the purpose of a compensating weight belt.

3 What are two reasons some divers prefer shot pouches over molded lead weights?

No matter what type of weight system you select, it must provide a means for ditching the weights immediately using only one hand. This type of system is referred to as a "quick release." Weight belts typically use a quick-release buckle, while integrated weight systems use some type of ripcord or removable-pin arrangement. Any of these arrangements is acceptable.

THERMAL PROTECTION FOR DIVERS

Your normal body-core temperature is approximately 98.6° F (37° C). Any time the water temperature is colder than this, your body will lose heat to the water. In all but the warmest waters, divers need some form of thermal protection.

When you grow cold underwater, you lose your ability to perform at your best. Heat loss underwater affects your ability to think, and it causes you to fatigue rapidly. Cold water has been shown to be a contributing factor in many diving accidents. It is essential that you wear the right thermal protection for the conditions that exist where you dive.

The amount of insulation you need to wear depends on many factors, but the most important are the water temperature, your activity level during a dive, and your body size. In colder water, every diver needs to wear more insulation then he or she would in warm water. The harder you work underwater, the more heat your body generates as well, and the warmer you are. Larger divers also tend to need less insulation than smaller divers under the same conditions.

Different ranges of temperatures feel comfortable to different divers. You may need to wear far more insulation in the water than your dive instructor or dive partner. It is essential to wear what feels right for you rather than what someone else tells you to wear.

In the warmest tropical waters, you may be able to dive with nothing more than a Lycra® body suit, more commonly referred to as a "dive skin." As the water grows colder or if you make multiple dives the same day, you will probably want to wear a wet suit. In water below 55° F (12.7° C), dry suits are the most effective form of thermal insulation for sport divers.

Diving suits also provide protection from cuts, scrapes, and stings that can occur while a diver is in the water. Even if the water is not "cold," you should still wear some type of protection covering your body to avoid injuries and sunburn.

Dive skins

Dive skins are thin, one-piece suits that are designed to protect your skin from minor abrasions that can occur while diving in tropical waters. Most provide only the most minimal thermal protection, while some have capabilities that equal those of a wet suit intended for tropical waters (Fig. 2-35).

Fig. 2-35. Lycra® dive skins provide protection from minor skin abrasions.

The term "dive skins" can cover a wide range of products made from different materials. To determine what you are buying, it is important to ask what materials were used to make the suit. "Skins" that provide thermal protection will have layers of other insulating materials besides Lycra®. If most of your diving will be in tropical waters, this type of suit may be an acceptable choice.

By themselves, Lycra® dive skins provide almost no protection from the wind, especially when they are wet. This can be a problem on the surface after a dive with many suits, where heat is lost as the water outside your suit evaporates and carries heat away from your body.

Wet suits

Wet suits are made from foam neoprene, which is a synthetic rubber that provides good insulation in many diving situations. Insulation comes from the neoprene material, which is filled with thousands of tiny gas bubbles.

Wet suits are available in a variety of thicknesses, from 3 to 9 mm, and in many different styles. The thicker the suit, the greater the insulation, although thick suits can be bulky and awkward to wear. Wet suits are the most widely used thermal protection for divers because of their simplicity and relatively low initial cost (Fig. 2-36).

To work properly, a wet suit must fit your body quite snugly. Once you enter the water, a thin layer of water enters the suit and is trapped between your skin and the inner surface of the suit. This water is warmed to your body temperature.

Provided you do not dive deep or make multiple dives in cold water, a wet suit will provide you with reasonable insulation. As a wet suit ages, however, it loses much of its insulating capability, because some of the "cells" (i.e., gas bubbles) within the suit break down on each dive.

"Shorty" wet suits and thinner full-body suits are popular in warmer waters. The most popular suit thickness for warm waters is 3 mm. In colder waters, most divers prefer a suit thickness of 6 mm or greater. For cold-water diving, most divers prefer a bib overall set of pants (known as a "farmer john"), a jacket with a hood attached, booties, and gloves.

You can adjust the warmth of your wet suit to a certain extent by "layering." For example, during the winter months, you may want to add a vest underneath your farmer john to enhance insulation. During the warmer months, you can remove it to avoid overheating.

Wet suits come in a variety of colors, although the colors are not in the neoprene itself but in the nylon that coats the suit. Most divers select suits containing nylon both inside and outside. These suits provide better durability and are easier to don, but you sacrifice some elasticity.

Fig. 2-36. Wetsuits are available in a variety of thicknesses and styles. This diver is wearing a relatively thin suit for warm water diving.

Because a wet suit must fit you perfectly to function properly, many divers prefer to get a suit that is custom-made to their measurements. This is essential if you are especially tall, thin, muscular, or otherwise differ from the standard sizes.

When you order a custom suit, you will be able to choose from a wide range of options. For example, you can specify the number of zippers to be installed. Aside from the main zipper used in the jacket, many divers also like the convenience of having zippers at the wrists and ankles. While this makes the suit easier to put on, it also allows more water to enter the suit. If you dive in cold water, you will be warmest with the fewest possible number of zippers.

Other options you may want in your suit include knee pads, pockets, knife sheaths, and different types of fasteners for the "beaver tail" that holds the jacket in place. "Step-in" jackets are also popular. All of these items will help make your diving more enjoyable and convenient.

Check to see what type of suit your instructor and other divers in your local area use. Their recommendations will guide and help you select the type of suit most appropriate to where you will dive.

Dry Suits

For colder waters, dry suits are preferred. Dry suits are considerably more expensive than wetsuits, but for many diving situations, their increased comfort is well worth the additional cost. There are many different types of dry suits, and like any piece of diving equipment, each has certain advantages and disadvantages (Fig. 2-37).

Basically, a dry suit is designed to do one thing: keep you dry. It does this by using a combination of wrist seals, a neck seal, and a waterproof zipper. To stay warm, you wear additional insulation under the dry suit in the form of dry-suit underwear. The underwear traps a layer of air between you and the water. By layering your underwear, you also can adjust your insulation for any water temperature.

The amount and type of underwear you use beneath your dry suit is determined by the water temperature, your body size, your activity level during the dive, and other factors. The concept of layering applies for dry suits as well.

Dry suits can be made from foam neoprene, crushed neoprene, vulcanized rubber, or a variety of heavy-duty nylons with waterproof materials laminated to them. Certain types of suits are recommended for specific diving applications, such as wreck diving, underwater photography, or underwater hunting.

Fig. 2-37. Dry suits are quite popular for cold water diving.

Most of the options available for wetsuits, such as pockets, knife sheaths, and knee pads, are also available for dry suits. There are also special options available for dry suits, such as dry hoods, dry gloves, and other accessories. Almost all dry suits come with attached hard-sole boots.

Dry suits are somewhat easier to put on than wetsuits, although it does take training to learn how to do it properly. Most, but not all, dry suits are a bit bulkier than wet suits. Depending on the fit of your suit and the type of underwear you use, you may need a bit more weight with a dry suit than with a wet suit. In some cases, however, you may be able to use less.

Buoyancy control while diving with a dry suit is achieved with an inflator valve, which allows you to add air to the suit, and an exhaust valve, which allows you to vent air out. The inflator valve is similar to the power inflator used on a BC. A small amount of air is added to the suit as you dive deeper and then is vented as you return to the surface.

The most common location for the inflator valve is the middle of your chest. This is also the best location to avoid interference with your BC.

The exhaust valve should be a low-profile valve that automatically vents as you ascend. The most common location for the exhaust valve is on the outside of the left bicep. Different valve models vent at different rates. A faster exhaust is better, however, because it allows you to dump the air from your suit more quickly.

When you dive with a dry suit, you use the suit for buoyancy control and your BC for backup and surface flotation. Never add air to both your dry suit and your BC while you are underwater. It can be extremely difficult to control both devices at the same time. A BC must always be worn with a dry suit.

In some parts of the world, diving students learn to dive with a dry suit beginning with their very first class. This usually occurs in places where the water is extremely cold, such as Alaska or Canada. If this is the case where you are learning, your instructor will present supplemental material so you will understand thoroughly how to use your dry suit. If your class does not include training in dry suits but you decide to purchase one afterward, you will need to take a short specialty course to learn how to use the dry suit properly.

Thermal Protection for Your Head

You lose the greatest amount of heat from your head, hands, and feet. While we have already discussed protection of your feet and hands, thermal protection for your head is critical while you are diving. In cold water, you can lose up to 50% of your body heat through your head. For this reason, it is important to have thermal protection for your head that is appropriate for the waters where you dive (Fig. 2-38).

For most cold-water diving, you can use a simple hood made from wet-suit material. To help keep your neck warm, you may want a hood with a cold-water "bib" that tucks under the collar of your wet or dry suit. The warmest arrangement is an attached hood.

Fig. 2-38. A hood is essential for cold water diving.

If you are diving in water below 55° F (12.7° C) and using a dry suit, you may want to use a dry hood attached directly to the suit. A dry hood does exactly what its name implies; it keeps your head completely dry.

While most hoods are fairly uncomfortable out of the water, they become almost unnoticeable once you are underweater. If you find your hood is uncomfortable topside, you can usually remove it.

Maintenance of Diving Suits

Like your other diving gear, a diving suit must be rinsed thoroughly with fresh, clean water after each day of diving. Dive skins and wet suits should be rinsed both inside and out. Dry suits may not need to be rinsed inside provided they are completely dry inside all the way down to the inside of the boots.

Wet-suit zippers should be lubricated occasionally with a bit of silicone grease or spray. Dry-suit zippers may be lubricated only with paraffin wax or bee's wax. Check the owner's manual of your dry suit for any special care instructions.

Dry-suit valves and zippers must be inspected annually by a qualified repair technician. Dry-suit valves will malfunction if they are not regularly serviced.

Wet suits should be stored on wide hangers designed specifically for this purpose (Fig. 2-39). Most dry suits must be stored rolled up in a bag, away from heat and ozone-producing machinery such as hot-water heaters and electric motors.

Wet suits can be repaired using ordinary wet-suit cement. Dry suits require specific techniques depending on the specific type of suit. Again, consult your owner's manual or dive store for instructions on the materials you must use.

Fig. 2-39. Wetsuits should be dried and stored on wide hangers.

TEST THE DEPTH OF YOUR KNOWLEDGE

Let's review some important aspects of thermal protection:

1 Which type of diving suit is only suitable for warm, tropical diving?

2 Which type of diving suit is only made from foam neoprene?

3 Which type of diving suit is used with special undergarments beneath the suit?

4 Even if you did not learn to use a dry suit during your Scuba Diver Certification course, you do not need any additional training to dive with one. Is this statement true or false?

DIVING INSTRUMENTS

Just as a pilot relies on instrumentation to fly a plane, divers need instrumentation to monitor their depth, bottom time, direction, and remaining air supply. To monitor this information, divers use a variety of different gauges, or they may use a single electronic dive computer that integrates all of the needed information.

Submersible Pressure Gauge

The submersible pressure gauge (SPG) is an essential instrument for scuba diving (Fig. 2-40). It monitors your air supply and is equivalent to a fuel gauge in a car. You need to learn to interpret the gauge readings and refer to the gauge frequently while diving. By frequently monitoring your SPG, you will know when your air supply begins to get low and thus avoid running out of air.

All mechanical SPGs perform the same function: they measure the air pressure in your tank. Most give a reading in pounds per square inch (p.s.i.) or bar. When your tank is half full, the pressure in the cylinder will be half as much as when you started your dive, and so forth. By knowing the working pressure of the tank, you can determine the approximate amount of air in the tank through the gauge reading.

The SPG is a fairly sensitive instrument, so it should not be subjected to shocks or other abuse. Small leaks from the hose or connectors are no cause for alarm while diving, but the problem should be corrected at your local dive store as soon as possible. A gauge with water inside requires servicing, as it can become a hazard if repair is continually postponed.

Today, many dive computers integrate the function of the SPG into one complete package that monitors your air supply, depth, and bottom time. Dive computers that work this way are usually referred to as "air integrated computers" (Fig. 2-41).

Most electronic SPGs also monitor your breathing rate and, based on the amount of air left in your tank, will predict how long that remaining air will last. The disadvantage to this type of equipment is that if the electronics fail, you have no way of knowing how much air you have left.

Rinse your SPG after each use, and avoid harsh treatment to it and all diving instruments. Have minor problems corrected promptly by a professional, and then you will get many years of reliable service from your SPG.

Fig. 2-40. The submersible pressure gauge, whether analog or digital, is an important piece of scuba equipment.

Fig. 2-41. Most electronic submersible pressure gauges are integrated with dive computers.

Depth Gauges

As you will soon learn, there are limits to how deep you can dive and how long you can remain at any given depth. Thus, you must always have some means of measuring your depth to avoid exceeding established limits.

There are three main types of depth gauges: capillary, Bourdon tube, and electronic. Each type has certain advantages.

The capillary gauge is a simple, inexpensive instrument that uses an air column in a piece of clear tubing to register your depth. The air in the tube is compressed underwater, and the reading is indicated by the water/air interface inside the tube. The capillary gauge is very accurate for shallow depths of up to approximately 40 feet, but it is not recommended for use at greater depths.

Bourdon tube gauges use pressure to bend a curved metal tube. An open Bourdon tube (seldom seen today) allows water inside the metal tube; a closed gauge has the tube filled with oil (Fig. 2-42). The pressure is transmitted through a flexible part of the housing to the oil in the tube. Open Bourdon tube gauges require careful maintenance to keep the tube clear and open. The accuracy of these gauges is reasonable and fairly constant with depth, but initial and occasional accuracy checks are strongly recommended.

Fig. 2-42. This oil filled depth gauge is part of a console with a submersible pressure gauge. The depth gauge is the unit on top.

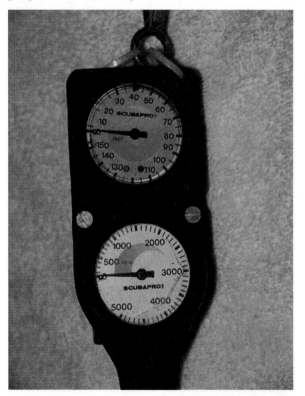

Electronic depth gauges are a part of all dive computers, and they are highly accurate and reliable. The electronic gauge registers your depth and displays it digitally. The computer compares the depth with your bottom time, which is also displayed, and your remaining allowable bottom time is then calculated and displayed as well. Today, most divers use dive computers as their primary means of monitoring their depth and bottom time. (Dive computers will be explained in more detail later.)

A desirable feature in a depth gauge is a way to record the deepest depth reached during a dive. The value of this will become apparent later. Capillary gauges have no means of recording your maximum dive depth, which means that you must record it on a slate during your dive. Bourdon tube gauges usually have a maximum depth recorder in the form of an indicator that is pushed by the depth needle. Electronic dive computers record your maximum depth during the dive and display it again once you surface.

Depth gauges need to be treated as the delicate instruments they are. They should be checked for accuracy when first obtained and at least annually thereafter. Reduced atmospheric pressure and high altitudes can harm some gauges, so they should be transported in a pressure-proof container when subjected to heights above 1000 feet (304.8 m).

Timing Devices

You are limited not only as to how deep you may safely dive, but also as to how long you can safely remain at a given depth. To keep track of your time underwater, you may use a diving watch, an underwater timer, or a dive computer.

Watches used for diving must be dive watches, not just water-resistant ones. Divers need a way to measure elapsed time, and this should be a feature of the watch. Analog watches can accomplish this with a rotating bezel around the dial, while a stopwatch mode is common for digital watches (Fig. 2-44).

Underwater dive timers are designed to measure elapsed time, but dive timers have another valuable feature that may make them more desirable than a dive watch. A pressure-activated switch automatically starts and stops the time as you begin your descent and return to the surface. Dive timers automatically record the elapsed time without assistance from the diver. When using a watch, you must remember to set the recording mechanism at the beginning of the dive and check it at the end, an often overlooked procedure.

Fig. 2-43. Watches used for diving must be designed to withstand the pressures found at diving depths.

Dive computers are the most convenient method for keeping track of your bottom time, because they integrate all of the data you need to dive. Many are designed to turn on automatically once you enter the water, just like an underwater timer.

Treat timing devices as you would any expensive instrument. They should be cleaned and lubricated as specified by the manufacturer. Wearing them in the shower or a jacuzzi is not advised. because the change in temperature from a cold lake or ocean to a hot shower or jacuzzi can cause condensation in your dive watch and ruin the mechanism. It is also possible to ruin the seals in the watch if the temperature is too warm, causing the watch to flood.

Compasses

When you are swimming underwater and visibility is poor, a compass becomes an important reference instrument. Some divers use a compass on every dive, even in clear, tropical water. It can also be useful at the surface when fog suddenly appears and you cannot see the beach or boat.

The way a compass works is very simple. A mechanical compass contains a magnetized needle that aligns itself with the Earth's magnetic field. The needle points to magnetic north provided there are no magnetic influences nearby that cause the needle to "deviate." This constant reference allows divers to know their position relative to the north-seeking needle and then set and follow a course accordingly.

A compass used for diving must be a diving compass. This means it will be liquid filled, have a reference line (called a "lubber line"), and have some means to specify a selected heading or direction. You will become more familiar with the compass and its use in the Skills chapter of this book.

A compass should receive common-sense care and not be left in the sun for prolonged periods. Heat can cause the liquid inside the compass to expand and leak.

Consoles

If you purchase individual diving instruments rather than an air integrated dive computer, it is more convenient to mount these instruments together on a "dive console." The console is a plastic enclosure molded with slots to accept a SPG and depth gauge (see Fig. 2-42). Most people find it is less cumbersome to mount their instruments in a console rather than to wear them on their wrists.

Dive Computers

We have already seen how many of the independent instruments that divers use can be combined into a single instrument: the dive computer. New dive computers are available every year with more sophisticated functions than those previously available.

At a minimum, most dive computers display your maximum depth, current depth, actual bottom time, remaining allowable bottom time, and water temperature. Between dives, most dive computers display the information from one or more previous dives, including your maximum depth and bottom time. They will also calculate the time you have been on the surface since your last dive as well as the allowable depths and times for your next dive.

One of the more advanced features available in the latest computers is the ability to upload information from your dive computer to a personal computer. This feature allows you to print out detailed information from one or more days of diving.

More detailed information on how to use dive computers is given in Chapter 5. Your instructor can give you current information on the latest models of available dive computers.

Backup Instrumentation

Even the best diving instruments will occasionally fail or malfunction. This normally does not create an emergency, but it can end your diving for the day unless some type of backup is avialable. If you use a dive computer to keep track of your bottom time, you should back it up with either a second computer or with a watch and depth gauge. If you have an air integrated computer and it fails, you will not be able to dive unless you have also brought along a mechanical SPG.

Maintenance of Instruments

Aside from rinsing your instruments thoroughly at the end of each diving day, your dive computer, depth gauge, timing devices, and SPG also need to be inspected and serviced annually by a qualified technician. While these devices are highly reliable, they can go out of calibration. In addition, O-ring seals wear out and must be replaced, or leakage can occur. If saltwater enters these instruments and is allowed to stay inside, they are quickly ruined.

Environmental Concerns

Some BCs as well as some dive computers now come with clips that allow you to attach your instruments to your BC so they do not dangle freely (Fig. 2-44). Without such clips, your instruments will naturally hang at your side, up to a foot or more below your waist as you swim horizontally through the water. If you happen to be swimming close to the bottom, your instruments are then free to hit any marine life that happens to stick up from the bottom. When corals and other delicate organisms are broken, they will not grow back.

Remember to clip your instruments to your BC on every dive to avoid environmental damage. Any clips you use must be fastened so it is possible for you to remove BC immediately. If your BC or instruments did not come with clips, you can buy accessory clips at most dive stores.

Fig. 2-44. Diving instruments should be clipped off to your buoyancy compensator so that they do not drag along the bottom.

TEST THE DEPTH OF YOUR KNOWLEDGE

Understanding your diving instrumentation will increase your enjoyment of diving. See if you can answer the following questions based on the information presented here:

1 Which type of depth gauge is accurate only at shallow depths?

2 What type of diving instrument is used to measure the amount of air pressure remaining in your tank while you are underwater?

3 Which type of diving instrument will calculate your remaining allowable bottom time while you are underwater?

4 Complete the following statement. To be acceptable for diving, a watch must be waterproof and _____.

DIVING ACCESSORIES

Numerous accessory items are available for diving that are used for specialized activities. There are also common items that almost all divers use. These items will make your diving more enjoyable and convenient.

Dive Knife

A diver's knife is a working tool used for many purposes, but its most important function is to cut fishing line or nets should you become entangled underwater (Fig. 2-45). Knives are not used as weapons or to fight with sharks, as you might think if you have watched a lot of television.

There are many different designs of diving knives, and you should select the most appropriate one for the type of diving you do. For example, a spearfisherman would probably want a very different type of knife than a wreck diver would. The spearfisherman might want a knife with a thin, sharp blade, while the wreck diver might want a knife heavy enough for prying or pounding.

All dive knives should be kept sharp and have their blades coated with a light film of oil when not in use. Many stainless-steel dive knives will still develop surface rust if they are not properly maintained because of the type of steel used to make the blade.

Dive knives must be sheathed when not in use. Sheaths for dive knives are made from plastic and

Fig. 2-45. Dive knives are useful tools.

mounted on either the inside of your calf, on your weight belt, or on the back of your instrument console. Some models can also be mounted on your BC shoulder strap. How and where the knife is mounted depends on the design of the sheath and your individual preference. Most divers, however, wear them on the inside of either calf, on their weight belt, or in a special sheath built into the thigh of their dive suit.

Gear Bag

Every diver should have a gear bag to transport his or her gear to and from the dive site. Without a gear bag, it is very difficult to handle your equipment and easy to drop delicate gear. If you do not have a gear bag on a charter dive boat, your gear may be lost or accidentally picked up by other divers.

Almost any heavy-duty nylon or canvas bag may be used as a gear bag. You can use a surplus canvas duffel bag, but nylon is usually preferred. This is because nylon will not get mold or mildew as easily as canvas. Your bag should be marked with your name, address, and phone number so it can be identified if you accidentally leave it aboard a dive boat.

Special gear bags are available from diving-equipment manufacturers. These bags are the easiest to use for diving, because they usually have special compartments for regulators, fins, and instruments. Many of these special bags also have dry compartments that may be used to store your clothing, log book, or other items that should not get wet.

Waterproof Tape/Waterproof Paint Markers

If you are taking a dive class with other people and everyone has bought their gear at the same dive store, it is safe to assume that at least a few of you will have identical masks, fins, and snorkels. Unless your gear is marked, it will be easy to confuse your equipment with someone else's.

Most dive stores sell a variety of waterproof paint or tape that can be used in various ways to mark your equipment. Every piece of personal dive gear you own must be marked to avoid its loss. Marking your gear becomes even more important if you dive aboard charter boats, where there sometimes may be 40 or more divers.

Dive Flags and Floats

When you are diving, it is almost impossible for a boat or jet ski moving through the water at high speed to see your bubbles, or for their operators to know you are in the area. To avoid a potentially disastrous accident, divers use a special "divers down flag" to let others know they are underwater.

The sport diver's flag is a red flag with a white diagonal stripe running from the upper left to the lower right corner of the flag. This flag must be flown from your surface support station any time you have free-swimming scuba divers in the area. In many states, the law requires this. Even where it is not, however, it would be foolish to go into the water without hoisting this flag.

In many states, when the red-and-white diving flag is flying, boats are supposed to stay at least 100 feet (30.5 m) away. If such laws apply in your state, you are obligated to stay within the perimeter defined by your divers flag. You also have an obligation to fly the flag only when you are actually diving (Fig. 2-46).

Charter boats must fly the blue-and-white "alpha" diving flag that indicates their maneuverability is restricted. Your instructor will inform you regarding local regulations for dive flags.

Log Book

Although a log book is technically not a piece of "equipment," it is an item intimately associated with your diving. Your log book should be carried with you for recording dive information as soon as possible after you leave the water. Each dive that you make should be recorded in your log book.

Fig. 2-46. Always fly a divers down flag when conducting diving operations from a boat.

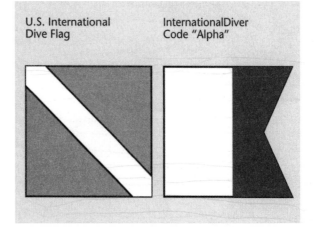

U.S. International Dive Flag

InternationalDiver Code "Alpha"

You are required to use a log book during all diver-training courses you take. In addition, many diving operators require you to provide proof of your diving experience before they will make diving services available to you. Your log book is your proof.

If you decide to take diving-leadership courses with the aim of working in diving, a log book is essential. As you progress in your diving skills, your log book allows your trainers to verify your diving experience (Fig. 2-47).

Fig. 2-47. Your log book will provide a useful record of your dives.

TEST THE DEPTH OF YOUR KNOWLEDGE

Can you recall the following points regarding accessory equipment?

1 What is the most likely use for a dive knife underwater?

2 What two obligations do you have when flying the dive flag?

3 List two reasons for recording your dives in a log book.

4 List two additional accessories you feel will be useful in your diving.

First-Aid Kit

It is always a good idea to have a first-aid kit handy on any dive trip. By adding a few items to meet the particular needs of diving, you can be prepared to deal quickly with minor injuries. Recommended contents are listed in Appendix VI.

Minor Accessories

The following are some items that can be extremely useful when diving:

Underwater slate: This is handy for recording data and communications (Fig. 2-48).

Goody bag: This is useful to hold game, specimens, artifacts, and other "goodies."

Underwater light: This obviously is necessary for diving at night, but it is also handy for daytime use to bring out vivid colors and peer into holes and crevices.

Marker buoy: This is excellent for marking the location of dropped items or a specific area.

Spare parts: This is a kit of items that can save a dive and includes such things as mask and fin straps, snorkel keepers, O-rings, and so on.

Checklist: This is a great way to remember all of the things you need for diving and includes personal articles as well as your dive gear. A sample is provided in the Appendix.

Fig. 2-48. An underwater slate is a good way for two divers to communicate.

CONCLUSIONS

Diving is an equipment-intensive activity, and by now, you should be convinced of that. Remember that all this equipment helps you adapt to the underwater environment and function there as safely and comfortably as possible. The more you work with the gear, the easier it becomes to use. Using and handling equipment will soon be second nature, and you will be able to devote much more of your attention to your surroundings and activities.

CHAPTER THREE

PHYSICS

You are probably familiar with many of the differences in the physical properties of air and water. This chapter examines these differences in greater detail. The better you understand these differences, the easier it will be for you to function as a diver.

LEARNING OBJECTIVES

By the end of this chapter, you must be able to:

1. State the composition of air.
2. List and explain the physical differences between air and water.
3. Explain two reasons why body heat is rapidly lost underwater.
4. Explain two ways that light is affected underwater.
5. Explain how sound transmission is affected underwater.
6. State the normal air pressure at sea level.
7. Explain how pressure increases underwater with depth, and show how to calculate the pressure at 33 feet (10 m), 66 feet (20 m), and 99 feet (30 m).
8. Explain the relationship between air pressure, volume, and density in a closed system.
9. Explain the difference between positive, negative, and neutral buoyancy.
10. List two ways that divers must deal with humidity while diving.
11. State the rule of thumb for pressure increase with temperature.
12. Explain how air consumption changes with depth while diving.
13. List two additional factors that affect air consumption while diving.

WHAT IS AIR?

Air is a mixture of different gasses. The gasses in air are colorless, odorless, and tasteless. Most of the time we do not even think about air, because breathing normally is an automatic activity and we cannot see or "feel" the air around us.

The most important component of air is oxygen, because without oxygen, we cannot survive. Oxygen makes up approximately 20.9% of the air that we breathe; the remainder of the mixture we call "air" is primarily made up of another gas called nitrogen. You can breathe pure oxygen for limited periods of time while you are topside, but pure oxygen can be extremely dangerous underwater. Some divers also breathe special mixtures of gasses for certain dives that may have more or less oxygen than normal. The use of special gas mixtures other than normal air requires additional training and is beyond the scope of this book (Fig. 3-1).

Nitrogen makes up approximately 78% of the air that we breathe, and it is considered to be an

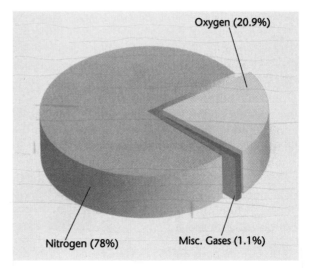

Fig. 3-1. Air is a mixture of gases.

"inert" gas. In other words, it does not react inside our bodies when we breathe it in under normal conditions. Nitrogen does have some interesting effects on divers, however, that you must understand.

Air also contains a small percentage of other gases. Carbon dioxide is one, although it is a very small part of the air that we breathe. The effect of carbon dioxide on the body is that it stimulates the urge to breathe.

Air Can Be Compressed; Water Cannot

Air can be easily compressed; when pressure is applied to a given volume of air, it can be forced to occupy a much smaller space. For example, an "empty" tire can be filled with air until it becomes hard. When it is full, the tire has an air pressure inside it that is greater than the surrounding pressure. When an 80-cubic-foot (2266 L) scuba tank is filled with compressed air, it has an air pressure inside it more than 200 times the normal air pressure at sea level.

Another example of the compressibility of our atmosphere is that the air surrounding the Earth is compressed at the surface by the weight of the air above it. In other words, the air at sea level is denser than air high in the mountains.

In contrast with air, water is considered to be incompressible. For all diving depths, water at those depths can be considered to have a density equal to that at the surface. When pressure is applied to water, the pressure is simply transmitted throughout the water.

Air Is Normally Less Dense than Water

If you pick up a bucket with nothing in it but air and another bucket filled with water, the water is much heavier than the air. This is because the water is more "dense." By this, we mean that the

Oxygen 20.9% Nitrogen 78%

molecules making up the water are closer together than the molecules making up the air. With the right equipment, however, we could actually compress air to the point where it is as dense as water and appears to be a visible liquid.

For our purposes, we can define "density" as the quantity of an element per unit of volume. By understanding this, you can see how a scuba tank filled with air weighs more than an empty one. The compressed air in the tank weighs approximately 0.08 pounds per cubic foot (1.25 g/L); thus, an 80-cubic-foot (2266-L) tank is over 6 pounds (2.7 kg) heavier when full (Fig. 3-2). Mathematically, this can be represented as:

$$80 \text{ ft}^3 \text{ (2266 L) of air} \times 0.08 \text{ lbs/ft}^3 \text{ (1.25 g/L)} = 6.4 \text{ lbs of air (2.7 kg)}$$

When you become familiar with the principles of buoyancy, you will see that this difference in weight will affect your diving.

The weight of 1 cubic foot of freshwater is approximately 62.4 pounds (1.0 kg/L), while 1 cubic foot of seawater, which contains dissolved salts, weighs approximately 64.0 pounds (1.025 kg/L). Because 1 cubic foot of air only weighs 0.08 lbs/ft³ (1.25 g/L), it is easy to see that 1 cubic foot of seawater weighs more than 800 times the same volume of air. We also can say that seawater is over 800 times more dense than air (Fig. 3-3).

This higher density of water provides much greater resistance to movement than in air. Have you ever tried to run in water when you have been submerged up to your neck? If so, you know how difficult this is to do compared with running on land. This resistance to movement is known as "drag," and it is something that you must deal with as a diver (Fig. 3-4).

Your drag through the water also is affected by the amount of surface area of your body and equipment. If your equipment is sleek and compact, it will be easier for you to swim than if your gear has

Fig. 3-2. Air has weight, as can be seen by the difference in weight between an empty scuba tank and a full one.

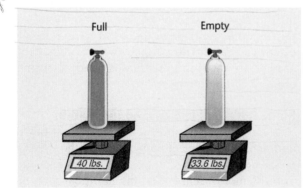

rough surfaces, dangling hoses, and loose straps. The more you can streamline yourself and your gear, the easier it will be for you to move through the water. A diver in a horizontal swimming position has much less resistance to forward progress than one in a semi-upright position (Fig. 3-5).

As Air Becomes Denser, It Does Not Flow as Easily

You probably have watched water flow through a hose at some time in your life. Compressed air flows through a hose in a similar way. When you dive, you breathe air that has been compressed, which is much denser than the air you breathe topside. The deeper you dive, the more resistance there is to the flow of this compressed air through the regulator. This resistance makes it more difficult for you to breathe the deeper you dive. When you combine the resistance of breathing compressed air with the restrictions of the equipment that you wear to dive, this imposes limitations on how hard you can exert yourself while underwater.

WHY DOES YOUR BODY LOSE HEAT UNDERWATER?

When air is 80° F (26.7° C), you would probably agree that the air is "warm." When the water temperature is 80° F (26.7° C), however, you will begin to grow chilled if you remain motionless for even a relatively short time.

Fig. 3-3. The variation in air density with changing altitude compared to constant water density with changing depth.

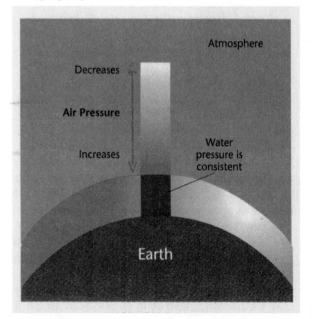

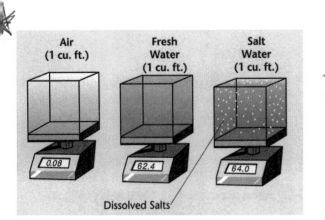

Fig. 3-4. Densities (i.e., weight per unit volume) of air and water.

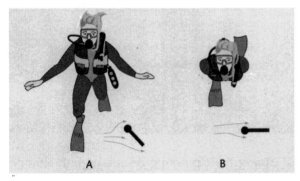

Fig. 3-5. Streamlining reduces drag and the amount of exertion that is required. For example, diver A must exert more effort than diver B.

Usually, you will be diving in water that probably is colder than 80° F (27° C). Because of this, you must understand why water causes such a rapid heat loss and how to protect yourself from it. First, because water is much denser than air, it can absorb a great deal of heat with very little change in temperature.

Another reason why water robs heat from your body is its density. Because the molecules of water are much closer together than those in air, heat can be conducted by direct contact between molecules at a rate nearly 20 times greater than in air.

With the great heat capacity of water and its high rate of conductivity, it is easy to understand how you can lose large quantities of body heat and become chilled while diving. The effects from loss of body heat and its prevention are covered later.

HOW LIGHT AND SOUND ARE TRANSMITTED THROUGH WATER

Things look and sound different underwater than when topside. Because of the density of water, sound travels through it rapidly. In fact, sound waves move so quickly through water that it usually is difficult to determine where their source is located.

While sound travels approximately four times faster in water than in air, light travels much slower. As light rays pass from the air into the water, they are slowed, and bending occurs. This bending is known as "refraction," and it causes changes in the way that you see objects underwater.

There is much more color in the underwater world than there appears to be if you depend solely on the sunlight from the surface to see. This is because most of the warmer colors (i.e., reds, oranges, and yellows) are "absorbed" by the water. These are the first colors to "disappear" as you descend through the water; at greater depths, the only colors that you can see without a flashlight are blues and grays. The first time you turn on a dive light at depth, however, you will be amazed by the colors that you will see. Most underwater photographs are made with artificial light (e.g., electronic flash) to bring out the magnificent, true colors of the underwater world (Figs. 3-6 and 3-7).

Fig. 3-6. Note the muted colors in this photograph taken with natural light underwater.

Fig. 3-7. With artificial light, colors become more apparent underwater.

TEST THE DEPTH OF YOUR KNOWLEDGE

Ⓦhile you are diving, the water will significantly affect your movement, warmth, senses, and breathing. To become a diver, you must learn how to handle these differences. This is what your equipment and the skills that you will learn during this course will help you to do.

Test your knowledge and understanding regarding these changes with the following questions:

1 Complete this statement: Air is approximately _20.9_ % oxygen, and the balance consists primarily of _Nitrogen_.

2 Air is more dense in the mountains (at altitude) than it is at sea level. True of false? _false_

3 The density of water is much greater at a depth of 100 feet (30 m) than it is at 10 feet (3 m). True or false? _True False_

4 Complete this statement: The difference in weight between a full and an empty 80-cubic-foot (2266-L) scuba tank is approximately _6.4 lbs_ pounds (_2.7_ kg).

5 Briefly describe how a diver can reduce the effects of drag while underwater. _Streamlining_

6 Describe why breathing resistance increases with depth. _Pressure_

7 List two reasons for the high rate of losing body heat while in the water. _Conductivity & heat absorption_

WHAT IS PRESSURE, AND WHY IS IT IMPORTANT TO DIVERS?

Ⓦhen you descend in water, the force from the combined weight of the air and the water above will affect you. Measured in pounds per square inch, this force is called "pressure." In this chapter, you begin to learn how pressure increases underwater and how it affects your body.

The weight of the atmosphere, that is, the air surrounding the Earth, is approximately 14.7 pounds per square inch (1.01 bar). This means that a 1-square-inch (1 cm × 1 cm) column of air extending from the Earth's surface to the outer edge of the atmosphere has a weight of approximately 14.7 pounds (1.01 bar). This constant force is referred to as "1 atmosphere (atm) of pressure" (Fig. 3-8).

Atmospheric pressure acts on our bodies at all times, but its effects usually go unnoticed. There are two reasons why this is true. First, our bodies are composed mainly of fluids, which are incompressible. Second, the air spaces in our bodies, such as our lungs and sinuses, are open to the surrounding atmospheric pressure. As long as the pressure inside these spaces equals the surrounding pressure, we do not feel any atmospheric effects, and we say that our bodies are "equalized" for the surrounding pressure. This is an important concept to understand, and you will shortly see how it relates to diving.

Atmospheric pressure decreases with altitude. Later, you will learn how decreasing atmospheric pressure affects people who dive in high mountain lakes. For now, however, we deal with atmospheric pressure and pressure changes at depth.

Remember that saltwater weighs 64 pounds per cubic foot (1.025 kg/L). If you were to take a 1-sqaure-inch column of water and keep adding to it vertically, you would find that at a height of 33 feet (10 m), the 1-square-inch column of water weighs

Fig. 3-8. Atmospheric pressure is approximately 14.7 pounds per square inch (1.01 bar), resulting from the weight of the air above the Earth's surface.

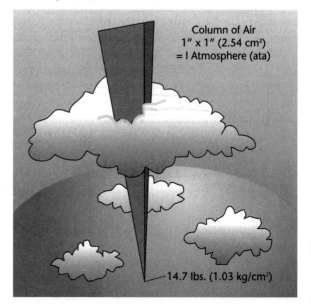

Column of Air
1" x 1" (2.54 cm²)
= 1 Atmosphere (ata)

14.7 lbs. (1.03 kg/cm²)

14.7 pounds (1.033 kg/cm²). This exactly equals the pressure exerted by the atmosphere at sea level. Thus, 33 feet of seawater is equivalent to 1 atm of pressure. Because freshwater is less dense than saltwater, 1 atm of pressure in freshwater requires 34 feet of water (10.3 m) (Fig. 3-9).

Because water is essentially incompressible and it transmits pressure freely, pressure in water increases at a constant rate, and its effect is cumulative. Simply stated, if 33 feet (10 m) of water equals 1 atm of pressure, then 66 feet (20 m) equals 2 atm, 99 feet (30 m) equals 3 atm, and so on.

While diving, you experience the pressure of both the water and the atmosphere above it. Both pressures must be considered. At sea level, you are under 1 atm of air pressure. At a depth of 33 feet (10 m) in the ocean, or at 34 feet (10.3 m) in freshwater, you are under 2 atm of pressure: 1 atm from the air, and 1 atm from the water. At 66 (20 m) feet in saltwater, you are under 3 atm of pressure. You must always consider atmospheric pressure when working with changing pressures.

Atmospheric pressure is nearly constant at sea level; therefore, most pressure gauges are adjusted so that they read zero at sea level. When a depth gauge indicates 33 feet (10 m) it is saying that the pressure is 1 atm greater than it was at the surface. The pressure measured on a gauge is termed "gauge pressure," but it is not the total pressure that is present. This is because gauge pressure does not include the atmospheric pressure. When atmospheric pressure is added to the gauge pressure, the sum is termed "absolute pressure," and this is the pressure to be used when determining your depth (Fig. 3-10).

Fig. 3-9. One cubic foot of saltwater weighs 64 pounds, and it exerts a pressure of 0.445 p.s.i. (0.03 bar). Multiplied by 33, this pressure shows how 33 feet of seawater (10 m) equals 1 atm of pressure.

For example, if you descend from the surface to a depth of 33 feet (10 m), you are doubling the pressure on your body. If you ascend to the surface from 66 feet (20 m), you are reducing the pressure to one third of what it was at 66 feet (20 m). Remember that absolute pressure is always 1 atm greater than the pressure of the water alone and that the atmospheric pressure must always be included in any calculations.

You may be wondering how to determine the pressure at depths not equal to increments of 1 atm. Although you do not need to know this as a beginning diver, it is interesting to note that pressure increases at a rate of 0.445 p.s.i. per foot (0.03 bar) of saltwater and at 0.432 p.s.i. (0.029 bar) per foot of freshwater. By multiplying this constant by the depth in feet and then adding 14.7 p.s.i. (1.01 bar), which is the average value for atmospheric pressure, you can determine the pressure at any depth in either freshwater or saltwater.

For example, the pressure at a depth of 100 feet (30 m) in the ocean is 44.5 p.s.i. (3.07 bar) of gauge pressure plus 14.7 p.s.i. (1.01 bar) of atmospheric pressure, yielding an absolute pressure of 59.2 p.s.i. (4.08 bar). As divers, we are concerned with both pressure and the volume changes caused by it.

Fig. 3-10. Water pressure alone is called "gauge pressure," but the weight of the atmosphere must also be considered. When combined, the atmospheric and the water pressure are called the "absolute pressure."

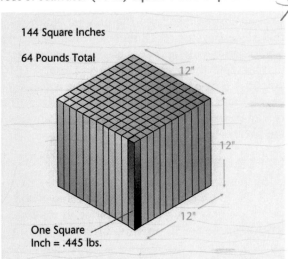

144 Square Inches

64 Pounds Total

12"

12"

12"

One Square
Inch = .445 lbs.

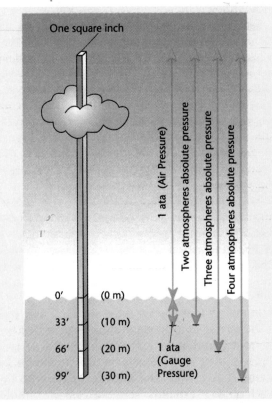

One square inch

1 ata (Air Pressure)

Two atmospheres absolute pressure

Three atmospheres absolute pressure

Four atmospheres absolute pressure

0'   (0 m)

33'   (10 m)

66'   (20 m)   1 ata
                      (Gauge
99'   (30 m)   Pressure)

TEST THE DEPTH OF YOUR KNOWLEDGE

Y ou have a good grasp of the concepts of atmospheric and water pressure if you can answer correctly the following questions:

1   One atm of pressure is equaled by ___34___ feet (____ m) of freshwater or by ___33___ feet (____ m) of seawater.

2   The pressure is ___5___ times greater at a depth of 136 feet (41 m) in freshwater than it is at the surface.

3   What is the absolute pressure in atmospheres at a depth of 66 feet (20 m) in the ocean? ___3 atm___

Pressure and Volume Relationships

As you descend below the surface, the increased pressure that your body experiences has both direct and indirect effects on you. For most of your time underwater, however, you will never be aware of or feel these effects.

To understand the direct effects of pressure, consider the effects of pressure on an open system. For our purposes, refer to the illustration of an inverted bucket (Fig. 3-11) held upside down and taken to a depth of 99 feet (30 m) in the ocean. As the bucket is forced below the surface, the pressure increases, causing the air inside the bucket to be compressed.

As the pressure inside the bucket increases, the volume of the air inside decreases. When the total pressure has doubled, at a depth of 33 feet (10 m), the amount of air in the bucket will be only one half of its original volume. No air has been lost from the bucket, however; it has merely been compressed. When the bucket is taken back up to the surface, the air inside will expand to its original volume, even though no air was added to it. The air simply expanded back to its original volume as the pressure on the air was reduced.

Now compare a different situation, one where a constant volume of air is maintained in the bucket during its descent. As the bucket is pulled down to depth, air is added to it through a hose. The volume of air inside the bucket is held constant by adding enough air to match the original volume.

Now assume that the bucket is taken to a depth of 33 feet (10 m), filled with air, and then raised to the surface. When the pressure decreases from 2 atm at 33 feet (10 m) to the surface, which is just 1 atm, the volume of air in the bucket doubles. Of course, the bucket cannot hold this much air as it expands, so the excess air bubbles

out of it. If the bucket were taken to 99 feet (30 m) and filled with air, a volume of air equal to three buckets would escape as the bucket was raised back to the surface.

This inverse relationship between pressure and volume is known as "Boyle's Law," which is named for the scientist who first recognized it. Knowing the law is not as important as understanding the concepts behind the relationship between pressure and volume.

The effects of pressure on a closed system, such as the air space inside your ears or your lungs, can be much more dramatic if you do not understand how to cope with them. Dealing with these effects is easy, however, as long as you understand the principles involved (see Fig. 3-11).

Imagine a sealed plastic bag (i.e., a closed system) that is filled with air and pushed below the surface of the ocean. As we pull the bag down to depth, the bag becomes smaller and smaller as it is compressed. When the bag is returned to the surface, the air inside the bag expands and returns the bag to its original volume.

Now imagine that the bag is opened at depth, filled with air to its original volume, resealed, and then raised to the surface. In this case, a different situation will result during the ascent than occurred with the open bucket. The air that was added at depth also will expand inside the bag, but it cannot escape as the bag is sealed.

If the sealed bag were opened, filled with air at a depth of 33 feet (10 m) at 2 atm, resealed, and then brought to the surface, the volume of air inside the bag would increase to twice its original volume. This would occur as the water pressure on the outside of the bag decreased.

Because the bag does not stretch and could not handle this additional volume, it would burst. If you filled the bag at a depth of 66 feet (20 m) or 3 atm and then brought it to the surface, the volume of air inside would triple. The only way to prevent this closed system (i.e., the bag) from rupturing would be to vent the excess air during its ascent.

The same thing would happen to your lungs if you took a deep breath from a scuba regulator at depth, held it, and then swam to the surface. This is why you must never hold your breath when you are breathing compressed air underwater.

More on Pressure and Density

By increasing pressure, we also affect the density of air. In an open system, air is compressed as depth increases. A given amount of air occupies a smaller space as the pressure increases. Thus, the density of air is twice as great at 2 atm, three times as great at 3 atm, and so on (Fig. 3-12).

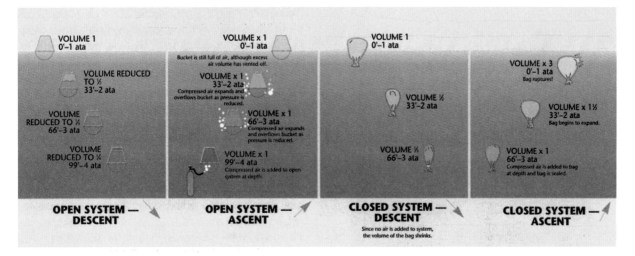

Fig. 3-11. Effects of pressure on open and closed systems. In an open system, compressed air is free to escape during ascent. In a closed system, compressed air expands and can cause the container to rupture if the pressure is not relieved.

If air is added to an air space to maintain its original volume, the air space will contain twice as much air at 33 feet (10 m) as at the surface, three times as much air at 66 feet (20 m), and so on. The overall effect is that the deeper you dive, the denser the air inside a given air space becomes, whether that space is your lungs, sinuses, or middle ear. This explains why you use air faster when you dive deeper, and why breathing resistance increases with depth—you are moving more air through your lungs with each breath you take.

You can function almost normally beneath the pressure of water. To achieve this comfortably, we must do as we do on land: keep the pressure in the air spaces inside our bodies equal to the pressure outside. One of your most important goals during this course is to learn how to do this.

Fig. 3-12. The density of air increases as the pressure increases.

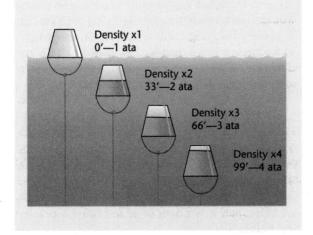

Density x1
0'—1 ata

Density x2
33'—2 ata

Density x3
66'—3 ata

Density x4
99'—4 ata

TEST THE DEPTH OF YOUR KNOWLEDGE

Ⓒomplete the following chart for a given quantity of air in a balloon:

Pressure	Volume	Density
Doubles	Halves	Doubles
	One third	
Halves		
	One Quarter	Quadruples

MAKING BUOYANCY WORK FOR YOU

Ⓦhen different objects are placed in water, some of them float, others sink, and a few remain suspended between the surface and the bottom. These objects all have varying amounts of buoyancy. By understanding buoyancy, you can control it to your advantage for diving.

Any object that is placed in water is buoyed up by a force equal to the weight of the water that is displaced by that object. If an object displaces an amount of water weighing more than itself, it floats, and a diver who is floating on the surface without any effort is said to have "positive buoyancy" (Fig. 3-13).

Exhaling reduces the air volume in the lungs and the consequent displacement of water, and it results in a loss of buoyancy. Buoyancy control with lung volume is important for divers to understand.

You can observe displacement by filling a glass to its brim with water. If you push a ping-pong ball

Fig. 3-13. With their lungs filled with air, the average person can float motionless.

into the glass, water will run over the side. The volume of water that overflows the glass is the volume that has been displaced.

If the object weighs more than the amount of water that it displaces, that object sinks. In other words, objects that are more dense than water sink, while objects that are less dense float. A diver who is resting on the bottom and not able to float without inflating his buoyancy compensator (BC) is said to have "negative buoyancy" (Fig. 3-14).

Objects with the same density as water will "hover" anywhere they are placed in the water column. Divers can hover underwater by adjusting their buoyancy for their depth. This ability to hover without effort is one of the signs of a good diver, and it is known as "neutral buoyancy" (Fig. 3-15).

By examining actual diving situations, the principles of buoyancy will be more easily understood. Most people find that when their lungs are full of air, they have slight positive buoyancy when they rest motionless in deep water. In this type of situation, if they let their body hang vertically in the water, they will float with the top of their head (or even more of their body) out of the water.

Different people have different amounts of "personal buoyancy," and they will float at different levels. Some people will float higher, some will float lower, and some will actually sink, even if their lungs are completely full of air.

Those people who float when their lungs are full of air usually find that their buoyancy changes significantly if they exhale some or all of the air from their lungs. As you breathe out, your chest deflates and consequently displaces less water. This results in less buoyancy.

Wet suits are much less dense than water because of the thousands of nitrogen gas bubbles

that are trapped in the material. If you wear a full 6-mm-thick wet suit and jump into the water wearing no other dive gear, it will be impossible for you to sink at the surface.

You cannot dive with a wet suit and a standard 80-cubic-foot (2266-L) aluminum dive tank without wearing additional weights. The lead weights that divers wear to adjust their buoyancy are many times more dense than seawater. By selecting the right amount of weight, you can adjust your buoyancy so that you will be neutrally buoyant at depth.

If you can imagine making a dive in a wet suit, you can begin to understand how your buoyancy might change over the course of a normal dive. As you begin to descend, pressure increases and compresses the nitrogen gas bubbles in your wet suit. Once the suit is compressed, it displaces less water and loses some of its buoyancy (Fig. 3-16). To compensate for this decrease, you add air to your BC, restoring the lost volume to regain the lost buoyancy. From this example, you can understand how the BC received its name.

As you begin to ascend at the end of your dive, the volume of your wet suit and BC begin to expand as the pressure on them is reduced. This increases your buoyancy, and it can cause your ascent to become quite rapid if it is not controlled. An uncontrolled ascent can be extremely dangerous, so to avoid this situation, vent air from your BC.

Besides the two factors already identified as affecting buoyancy (i.e., weight and volume), a third factor must be considered as well. Specifically, the density of the water in which you dive also affects your buoyancy.

Saltwater is more dense than freshwater. Therefore, more weight will be displaced by an object in saltwater than by that same object in freshwater. This simply means that you will have greater buoyancy in saltwater than in freshwater.

If you are weighted to dive and are neutrally buoyant in saltwater, but you dive in freshwater with the same weights, you will find that you are negatively buoyant. Conversely, if you are weighted for diving in freshwater but dive in the ocean with the same gear, you must add weights to adjust for your greater buoyancy in saltwater.

As a diver, you usually want to avoid negative buoyancy (i.e., sinking). Neutral buoyancy beneath the surface is your constant goal, and it is important to help protect marine life. Negatively buoyant divers who sit, kneel, or stand on coral reefs or other marine life may damage or kill these creatures. This is considered to be unacceptable behavior, and it is a sign of an unskilled, uncaring, and unthinking diver.

Whenever you are on the surface, you will usually want to be positively buoyant so that you need not exert yourself to stay afloat (Fig. 3-17). This is easily accomplished by using your BC.

Be sure to recheck your buoyancy if you use different equipment or if you lose or gain a large amount of weight (e.g., > 10 lbs or 4.5 kg). Also, you must always remember to recheck your buoyancy whenever you go from freshwater to saltwater, or vice versa.

TEST THE DEPTH OF YOUR KNOWLEDGE

1 What are the three factors affecting buoyancy?

2 List three ways that you can change your buoyancy.

3 Complete the following statement: During descent, a diver's buoyancy tends to _____.

4 Does an ocean diver need to add or remove weight to dive in freshwater?

Fig. 3-14. This diver is exhibiting negative buoyancy. While it is acceptable to kneel on sand, it is not acceptable to kneel on coral or other underwater organisms.

Fig. 3-15. On most dives, you will want to be neutrally buoyant while underwater.

Fig. 3-16. As you dive, pressure will compress your wet suit and make you less buoyant.

Fig. 3-17. Whenever you are on the surface, you will generally want to be positively buoyant.

THERMAL EFFECTS OF DIVING

As already mentioned, when the water temperature is colder than our body temperature, we must usually wear some type of insulation while diving. Divers lose heat underwater in several ways. First, water conducts heat away from your body very rapidly, much more rapidly than air conducts heat. Also, you lose heat by breathing underwater, because each time that you take a breath from your regulator, you breathe in cool, compressed air that must be warmed to your body temperature. Each time you exhale underwater, you lose the heat energy that was used to warm the air you just inhaled (Fig. 3-18). In addition, you will lose heat if you urinate underwater.

Humidity

The amount of water vapor in the air is referred to as "humidity." The higher the temperature of the air, the more water vapor that it can hold. If air that contains water vapor is cooled, the water vapor in that air condenses.

Fig. 3-18. Each time you exhale underwater, you lose body heat.

When you enter the water and descend, the air inside your mask and scuba tank cools. This causes water vapor in the air to condense, which can fog your faceplate and cause other problems. In extremely cold water, condensation can even cause scuba regulators to freeze and "freeflow" (i.e., to emit air continuously) unless special precautions are taken.

When water condenses on the faceplate of a mask, it tends to contract into beads unless the surface tension is reduced. Defogging solutions or saliva are used on the inner surface of masks to reduce the surface tension of water. Any moisture that does condense then spreads out in a thin film instead of forming drops that can obscure vision (Fig. 3-19).

Normally, the air in scuba tanks is very dry; almost all of the water has been removed from it following compression. This is necessary to keep moisture out of your scuba tank and prevent extensive corrosion. Therefore, not only must you supply heat to each breath of air that you take while scuba diving, you must also humidify it. This can cause dehydration in a diver, so it is a good idea to drink plenty of fluids before, between, and after dives. This helps to replace the lost fluids. Dehydration decreases your ability to exercise at full capacity, and it makes you more prone to decompression sickness, which is discussed in the following chapter.

Anything that you drink before diving must be nonalcoholic, and it should not contain caffeine. Caffeine is a "diuretic," which means that it will cause you to urinate and lose additional fluids while underwater. Drink decaffeinated coffee, herbal tea, caffeine-free soft drinks, juices, and water.

Fig. 3-19. When water condenses on the lens of your mask, it causes that lens to fog.

How Heat Affects Your Scuba Cylinder

When a container filled with a gas is heated, the gas molecules inside that container become more active, and one of two things will occur. Either the container will expand, or the pressure inside will increase. In a rigid container such as a scuba tank, the pressure will rise.

Scuba tanks should be cooled as they are filled, which allows more air to be stored in the cylinder at a given pressure than if the tank is hot. If the tank is subjected to heating or cooling once it is filled, the pressure inside it can vary by several hundred pounds. Internal pressure will increase or decrease by approximately 5 p.s.i. (0.03 bar) for each change of 1° F (or by 0.6 atm or 0.3 bar for each change of 1° C) even though no air has been added or lost (Fig. 3-20).

This phenomenon occurs simply because of the change in molecular activity caused by the change in temperature. Car trunks, which can reach temperatures of over 120° F (49° C), are not a particularly good place to store air-filled scuba tanks for pro-

Fig. 3-20. When the temperature of a scuba tank increases, the molecular activity inside also increases. This causes the pressure inside of the tank to rise.

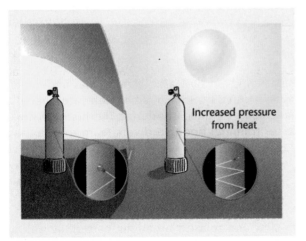

Increased pressure from heat

TEST THE DEPTH OF YOUR KNOWLEDGE

1 What are the two primary ways that divers lose heat underwater?

2 What causes the water vapor in air to condense into a liquid?

3 How can you prevent a mask from fogging up underwater?

4 Why should you drink lots of fluids when diving?

5 Briefly explain the relationship between pressure and temperature for a rigid container.

longed periods. There is no danger from the pressure increase because of heat, but if a tank becomes hot enough, it will rupture the burst disk in the valve. Constant stressing of the tank metal also may shorten the useful life of the cylinder. It is better to store tanks with a few hundred p.s.i. of air (7 to 14 bar) in them and to fill them just before use than to simply store them filled to their service pressure.

DIVING CAN HAVE PROFOUND EFFECTS ON YOUR SENSES

Diving can have some amazing effects on your senses while you are underwater. In particular, your vision and hearing will be dramatically affected; however, you will find dealing with these effects quite easy.

Objects Appear Bigger and Closer

The human eye is designed to focus light rays in air. This is why objects are blurry underwater unless an air space is placed in front of your eyes; divers use masks for this purpose. If you lose your mask, you can still see, but you will not be able to make out any details.

The refraction (i.e., bending) of light rays as they pass through water, and then through your face plate, causes magnification. Objects viewed underwater appear to be $\frac{4}{3}$ larger or closer than they do in air; things actually are further away than they appear to be. They also are smaller than they appear to be. Remember this when you report the sighting of an animal or object. People tend to exaggerate anyway, and coupled with the inherent visual magnification that occurs underwater, this trait results in some incredible diving stories.

It Is Difficult to Tell the Direction of a Sound

You determine the source of sound on land by subconsciously measuring the time difference between the sound reaching one of your ears and then reaching the other. While this interval is very short, you are able to distinguish it and can indicate the point or origin of a sound with your eyes closed. The exception occurs if the sound is directly in front or directly behind you, in which case it reaches both ears simultaneously.

Because of its density, water conducts sound very well. In fact, sound travels four times faster in water than in air. This makes it extremely difficult to determine the direction or origin of the sound (Fig. 3-21). Many interesting things can be heard beneath the surface, but you simply cannot tell the direction from which they are coming.

The sound of a boat's motor can be heard quite easily underwater, although it usually is impossible to tell the direction from which it is coming. Generally, you will only be able to tell if it is growing louder (i.e., approaching) or softer (i.e., departing). If you want to surface but hear a boat approaching nearby, remained submerged for as long as safely possible or until you can determine that the boat is departing. This is a primary reason why it is essential to fly the divers down flag and remain within its perimeter.

Other Senses

Your senses of smell and taste are restricted underwater. Touch is an important sense in the underwater world, but cold numbs this sense. In some situations, you may be able to feel things better by wearing bulky gloves that insulate your fingers. Also remember that cuts and scrapes that are acquired in water often go unnoticed until they are exposed to air after a dive. For these reasons, gloves are important and always should be worn.

Fig. 3-21. Sound travels faster in water than in air, but the direction from which a sound originates is difficult to determine underwater.

TEST THE DEPTH OF YOUR KNOWLEDGE

Ⓢee if your study on the effects of water was effective by answering the following questions:

1 Complete the following statement: When looking at objects underwater, remember that they appear to be _____ and _____ than they really are.

2 If you were to signal a nearby diver underwater by tapping on your tank with your dive knife, what might you expect to occur?

3 List two reasons why your sense of touch is reduced underwater.

THE DEEPER YOU DIVE, THE MORE AIR YOU NEED

Ⓣhe deeper you dive, the greater the surrounding pressure. The greater the surrounding pressure, the more dense the air that you breathe and the faster you empty your tank. The rate at which you consume the air in your tank is directly proportional to the depth of your dive. It should be easy to see that air will usually be consumed twice as fast at 33 feet (10 m) as at the surface, three times as fast at 66 feet (20 m), and so on.

Other factors also affect the rate at which your air is consumed. These include your activity level during the dive, mental state, body size, and the effectiveness of your thermal insulation.

Air Consumption Factors

Besides depth, physical activity has the greatest effect on your air consumption underwater. Exertion can cause you to use up to 10 times more air than relaxation will. Improving your air consumption is not the only reason to avoid exertion underwater, but it certainly is one that good divers keep in mind.

Beginning divers tend to be more active than necessary, but they also learn to relax underwater rather quickly. Air consumption rates usually decrease significantly during the first few dives after training, because divers learn to relax and "take it easy." With experience, these divers also learn to move through the water more efficiently. The sooner you can do this, the more enjoyable your diving will be.

As a diver, you need to think about developing a slow and relaxed breathing pattern as well as rate of breathing. The more you exert, the deeper and more frequently you will breathe and, hence, the more air that you will use. It is possible, however, to waste a great deal of air by poor breathing habits even when you are not exerting. You will learn more about breathing efficiency in the following chapter, but for now, be aware that shallow, rapid breathing (usually caused by unnecessary anxiety) wastes air and increases your air consumption. By limiting exertion and relaxing during your dive, you will be able to maintain a slow, deep pattern of respiration, with long inhalations and exhalations. This is the best way to breathe underwater.

Another factor in air consumption is your physical size. Large people, who have larger lungs, use more air than smaller people, who have smaller lungs. To compensate for these differences, larger divers generally use larger tanks. There usually is no reason for a small person to carry the same-size tank as a larger person unless it is needed for a specific purpose.

Body temperature also affects respiration. The colder you are, the more that you breathe. This is unfortunate, because heat is also lost through respiration. Therefore, this is yet another example of why it is important to wear the proper amount of insulation for the conditions where you dive.

These factors, or combinations of these factors, can significantly affect your breathing rate under different conditions. Through experience, you will learn to estimate the amount of air that you will use based on all of these factors.

Monitoring Your Air Consumption

As a practical matter, most sport divers do not calculate their air consumption before each dive. Instead, as they gain experience diving, they keep a record in their log books of how long their air lasts at different depths. This allows them to make rough predictions of the time they will be able to dive at a given depth. They monitor their submersible pressure gauges and dive computer, and they use the information from these instruments to advise them when to begin surfacing (Fig. 3-22).

Even if you calculate your air consumption mathematically, which is possible, any of the variables mentioned can change your predicted air consumption completely. If you work harder than planned or the water is colder than you thought, your air consumption will be greatly affected.

In certain advanced-diving situations, it is essential that you predict your air consumption to

Fig. 3-22. Always monitor your submersible pressure gauge carefully so that you know when it is time to surface.

avoid running out of air. This is especially important while deep diving, cave or cavern diving, or wreck diving. Anyone who does this type of diving must know exactly how much air they will need for any given dive.

Your rate of air consumption will change quite a bit during the first 10 to 20 dives that you make. Recording every dive in your log book will help you to estimate how long your air will last on most dives at different depths. This is a good practice to continue even beyond your early dives, because you will learn how much your usual rate is affected by exertion, temperature, and other factors. You will also be able to estimate not only the duration of your air supply for a given depth but will be able to adjust it for other factors as well.

TEST THE DEPTH OF YOUR KNOWLEDGE

See if your study of air consumption was effective by answering the following questions:

1 List two factors that affect your rate of air consumption underwater.

2 How do divers monitor their air supply underwater?

CHAPTER FOUR

YOUR BODY UNDERWATER

Whenever you go underwater, your body is affected by pressure and the effects of the water itself. This chapter discusses how specific parts of your body are affected by diving.

LEARNING OBJECTIVES

By the end of this chapter, you must be able to:

1. Name all of the air spaces in the human body.
2. State the name of the air sacs in the lungs as well as their function.
3. Explain why diving with congested sinuses is not safe.
4. Explain why you must be able to equalize the pressure inside your ears while underwater, and what happens if this is not done.
5. State the technique for equalizing pressure inside a face mask.
6. Explain the procedure for equalizing the pressure inside your ears while underwater.
7. Define the term "reverse block."
8. List two types of lung-expansion injuries.
9. Explain the most serious danger from a lung-overpressure injury.
10. State the name of the gas that controls your breathing rate.
11. Explain the proper technique for breathing underwater using scuba.
12. Define the term "hyperventilation," and explain how it relates to diving.
13. Describe how the human body reacts to overexertion.
14. Describe how the human body reacts to overheating.
15. Describe how the human body reacts to cold water.
16. Explain the proper techniques for rewarming a diver after exposure to cold water.
17. Explain why sport divers do not use pure oxygen while underwater.
18. Define the term "nitrox."
19. Explain why carbon monoxide is especially hazardous to divers who breathe it while underwater.
20. Explain the difference between nitrogen narcosis and decompression sickness.
21. State how to prevent and treat decompression sickness.
22. Describe how to prevent nitrogen narcosis.
23. Describe the best way to maintain fitness for diving.
24. List two reasons why street drugs and alcohol must be avoided before diving.

YOUR BODY HAS MANY AIR SPACES

The human body contains mostly fluids and solids; however, there are also air spaces. These include your lungs, sinuses, and middle ear, and they must be considered when diving. Pressure can affect these air spaces in dramatic ways, and these effects are considered to be the primary effects of pressure.

Your Lungs Play Several Vital Roles In Diving

The lungs are large air sacs within your chest cavity. When you breathe in, they expand, and when you exhale, they deflate. The inside of your lungs more closely resembles a sponge than a balloon (Fig. 4-1).

Inside the lungs are millions of tiny air sacs, which are called "alveoli." When you inhale, the alveoli inflate and fill with fresh air, which is absorbed through the walls of the alveoli. This air is then drawn into your circulatory system and transported throughout the body by the bloodstream. As the blood circulates throughout the body, it delivers oxygen to the body tissues.

Your body uses the oxygen you inhale, and it produces carbon dioxide along with other wastes. When you exhale, this CO_2 passes back out through the alveoli.

At rest, most people normally exchange a few pints of air with each breath. When you are active, however, your breathing rate increases. This is your body's response to the increased demand for oxygen created by activity. The harder you exercise, the more air that you breathe. Because the tanks that we wear for diving hold only a finite

Fig. 4-1. The inside of your lungs more closely resembles a sponge than a balloon.

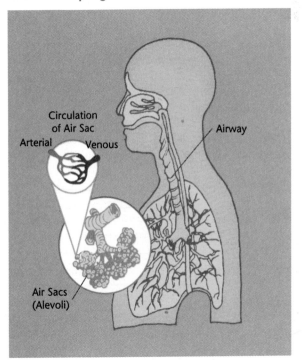

Circulation of Air Sac
Arterial   Venous

Airway

Air Sacs (Alevoli)

amount of air, it is easy to see how exertion uses up your air supply much faster than when you are relaxed.

Sinuses Also Hold Air

Sinuses are air cavities within your head that are lined with mucous producing membranes. Your head contains four sets of sinuses (Fig. 4-2).

Each sinus is connected by an air passage to the nasal airway. Under normal conditions, air passages to the sinuses are open. Sinuses can easily clog, however, when you have a cold or other head congestion, for example, because of allergies. Once a sinus becomes clogged, air can be trapped inside it. When this happens and you attempt to dive, you will feel pressure on your sinuses, because the air pressure inside the sinus does not equal the surrounding water pressure. Diving with a cold or other sinus congestion must be avoided for this as well as several other reasons.

In essence, the sinuses are air spaces that are surrounded by the bones of your head. Because it is solid, bone is not compressible. Therefore, if you continue to descend when the pressure within your sinuses is lower than the surrounding water pressure, the soft tissue surrounding the sinuses will be pushed into the sinus cavity. As you might imagine, this can be quite painful, but the problem is easily avoided by not diving when you suffer from congestion.

Fig. 4-2. The head contains four sets of sinus cavities that need to clear when diving. (Three sets are illustrated.)

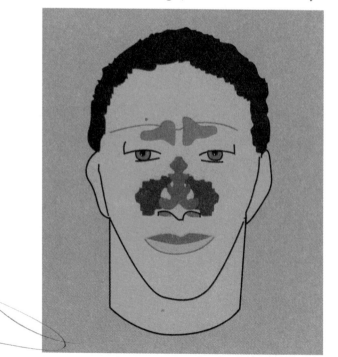

Under normal conditions, your sinuses will equalize by themselves.

Why Is There Pressure on Your Ears Underwater?

The air spaces inside your ears are especially important when you dive. You must be able to equalize the pressure inside your ears to dive.

The eardrum separates the outer ear from the middle ear, which is located within your head and is the area of concern. The middle ear has an airway leading to it from the back of your throat. This passage is known as the "Eustachian tube," and it allows air to move from your throat to your middle ear. This is how pressure is equalized inside the ears, by moving compressed air that you have inhaled from your lungs up through your Eustachian tube and into the middle-ear space.

For most people, equalizing the pressure inside their ears is not an automatic process compared with the effortless equalization of their sinuses. To pass air through your Eustachian tubes usually requires a deliberate effort to open the tubes and allow the air to flow through them. You will learn how to do this shortly.

The eardrum transmits sound vibrations to the hearing organ of the inner ear through a small series of bones in close contact with it. Your body's balance mechanism also is contained within the inner ear. Sudden changes in pressure or temperature inside one ear and not the other can cause dizziness to occur. This results from the different stimuli acting on the internal mechanism of the ears. This disorientation can be avoided, however, simply by keeping the pressure inside the ears in equilibrium (or "balance").

The eardrum can be stretched by pressure, but it will flex only slightly before it ruptures. When pressure inside an ear is not equalized, discomfort is felt immediately. This discomfort must be heeded and corrected to prevent damage to your ears. No discomfort or damage occurs when the air spaces of the ears are properly equalized.

Never use earplugs for skin or scuba diving. Earplugs trap air between themselves and the eardrum, and because there is no way to equalize this air space, the earplugs can be driven by the surrounding pressure into the eardrum. This is a painful and serious injury.

Do Not Forget There Is Air in Your Mask!

Although it might seem rather obvious, divers sometimes overlook the fact that their mask creates an air space attached to their body, and as expected, this air space is affected by pressure. When the pressure increases during your descent, the mask is pushed against your face, and the air inside the mask is compressed.

Because the mask is rather rigid, it will compress only slightly. If no air is added to it, a pressure imbalance will result, the pressure on the outside being greater than the pressure inside (Fig. 4-3). The effect of this low pressure inside the mask can cause the mask to suck tightly against your face, and the soft tissue of your face can be squeezed into the mask, causing tissue damage. This type of injury is known as a "mask squeeze."

This type of injury should never occur, because the pressure inside the mask can be equalized easily. Simply exhale a small amount of air from your nose into your mask every few feet as you descend. If you feel pressure on your face and eyes as you go lower, you need to exhale more air into your mask.

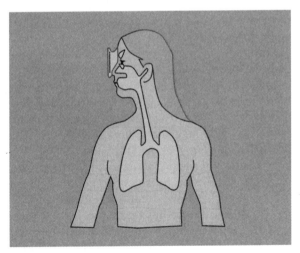

Fig. 4-3. Your body's air spaces include the lungs, sinuses, and ears. The mask is an attached air space that also requires pressure equalization.

TEST THE DEPTH OF YOUR KNOWLEDGE

Your ability to answer the following questions indicates that you have a good familiarization with the air spaces in your body:

1 Which air spaces in your body are affected by changes in pressure?

2 What problems might be expected if you attempted to dive with a cold?

3 What action should you take if you feel pressure on your face while descending?

HOW TO EQUALIZE PRESSURE AND BE COMFORTABLE UNDERWATER

Now that you know a bit about the air spaces, you should be able to understand how to equalize the pressure inside them.

Squeezes Must Be Avoided

While descending underwater, the pressure on your body increases at a rate of nearly 0.5 p.s.i. (0.03 bar) per foot of depth. If the pressure inside an air space does not equal the outside water pressure, the water pressure will squeeze that air space and try to compress it. Whenever the pressure outside an air space is greater than the internal pressure, the situation is called a "squeeze." Doctors refer to this type of injury as a "barotrauma," which means "pressure injury."

Divers can experience many different types of squeezes. Consequently, you must be specific when discussing this type of damage if people are to know what you mean. For example, there are ear squeezes, sinus squeezes, and mask squeezes. All of these injuries, however, can be easily avoided through proper equalization.

Squeezes of body air spaces can cause damage and must not be allowed to occur. The most common squeeze happens in the middle ear. If it is not corrected, an ear squeeze can result in a ruptured eardrum, leading to possible infection and, perhaps, even loss of hearing.

If an eardrum ruptures because you carelessly ignored the pain that signals an ear squeeze, water will enter your middle ear. Even if you are diving in the tropics, this water will be colder than the temperature inside your ear. When "cold" water enters your middle ear, it provides a shock to your balance mechanism and can cause dizziness (i.e., vertigo). If this occurs, hang onto any stable object that is close by, or hug yourself to provide some stability. You must allow time for the water that has entered your ear to warm to body temperature. This will happen quickly, however, and when it does, your sense of orientation and balance will return.

In the rare event that you suffer an ear squeeze, you must surface and immediately seek medical attention to avoid infection. Do not put anything in your ears. You will not be able to dive again until your eardrum has healed and your doctor permits you to get back in the water. Remember that this injury only occurs to divers who disregard pressure on the ears.

Sinus squeezes are also painful, but they can be easily prevented as well. If your sinuses are "clear" (i.e., not plugged with mucous from cold or allergy), they will equalize the pressure automatically. If the air passages leading to the sinuses are swollen and congested, clearing the sinuses will be difficult or impossible. Healthy sinuses are essential to diving.

Like an ear squeeze, the effect of a sinus squeeze is to push tissue into the air space to reduce its volume. As this tissue is damaged, small blood vessels in the sinus membranes rupture and, in effect, reduce the space inside the sinus by filling it with blood. This is obviously undesirable, and it is completely avoidable (Fig. 4-4).

You might be tempted to think that the obvious solution to sinus congestion lies in medication. Many sprays and tablets are available to help relieve stuffiness under ordinary circumstances topside. Some of these drugs perform well, but none is designed to work underwater. The effects of any drug may be modified under pressure, and very little is known about the potential problems that may occur when medications are used underwater.

A drug that causes drowsiness on land may be dangerous underwater. For this reason, consult a physician who knows about diving before using any medication during a dive. Also, be sure to avoid the influence of any medication that produces side effects.

All squeezes are painful, but they should not cause you undue concern. All can be prevented by pressure equalization or by ascending to a shallower depth. The extreme consequences of squeezes on your body's air spaces have been presented here only to familiarize you with their effects. By using the proper techniques also presented here, you should never suffer pain or injury from pressure increases during descent.

Fig. 4-4. The effect of a squeeze on a sinus is to fill the volume with associated tissue and blood in an attempt to equalize the pressure.

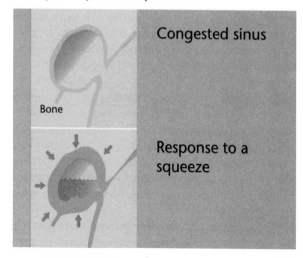

Congested sinus

Bone

Response to a squeeze

Equalization Techniques

You already know some equalization techniques from the information presented earlier. This section presents some additional equalization techniques that you must know and use.

The air space requiring the greatest attention is the middle ear. The air that fills the middle ear reaches this space through the Eustachian tube, which connects the middle ear to the back of your throat. While the opening of this tube usually is closed by a small flap of tissue, most people can open it easily by "flexing" the muscles at the back of their throat or jaw. If you listen closely while doing this, you normally can hear a slight crackling sound inside your head when you yawn, swallow, or jut your lower jaw forward; this sound occurs because the tubes are opening. Any of the actions just described (e.g., swallowing) can be useful for equalizing pressures when diving (Fig. 4-5).

Some divers are very fortunate and are able to clear their ears simply by jutting their jaw forward and exhaling into the mask. Most divers, however, require a bit more effort to open the tube and balance the pressure.

The most common method of equalizing pressure in the middle ear is known as the "Valsalva maneuver." In this technique, you close your mouth tightly, close your nostrils by pinching them firmly, and attempt to "exhale" firmly (but not forcefully). You may hear divers shorten the name to "Valsalva" (Fig. 4-6). As you build a slight pressure inside your head, you should hear the pressure open the tube by a gentle "pop," which signals that air has flowed into the Eustachian tube. You must never force this technique.

The Valsalva maneuver works well for most divers, especially when it is combined with jutting the jaw forward. The key to successful ear clearing is to keep the pressure difference between the water and middle ear to a minimum. This means that you must equalize early and often, starting on the surface even before you begin to submerge, and equalizing before the pressure on your ears ever has a chance to build.

If the pressure difference between the inside of your ears and the water becomes too great—and this can happen in just a few feet—pressure will hold closed the ends of the Eustachian tubes (Fig. 4-7). Once this happens, nothing that you can do at that depth will reopen them. Your only choice at this point is ascending a few feet, reducing the pressure difference until the tubes can be opened, and attempting to equalize again. In some cases, divers may need to return to the surface and begin their descent again from the beginning. This usually ends up wasting quite a bit of the air in their tank.

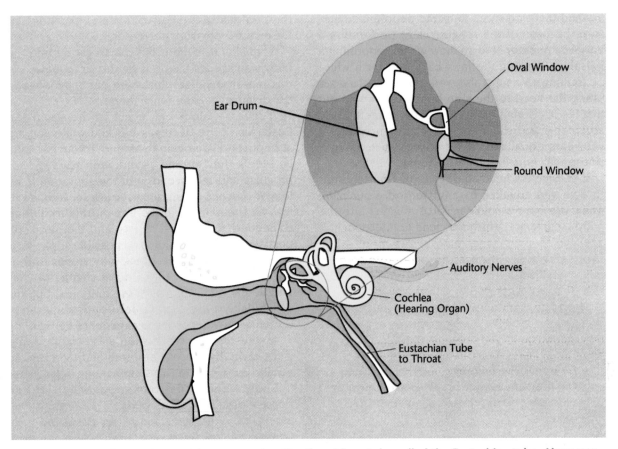

Fig. 4-5. The middle ear air space is connected to the throat by a tube called the Eustachian tube. Air passes through this space to equalize pressure in the air spaces in the ear.

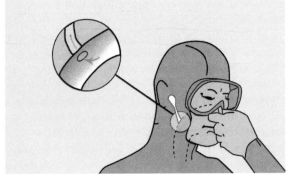

Fig. 4-6. The Valsalva maneuver is the most commonly used technique for equalizing pressure in the ears.

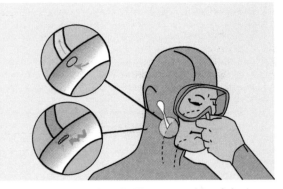

Fig. 4-7. The "trapdoor" effect caused by delaying ear clearing during descent. The pressure actually holds the end of the Eustachian tube closed.

It is much better to clear your ears continually during descent and go down in an uninterrupted manner than it is to "bounce" up and down, clearing your ears only occasionally. Most people have no problem if they begin clearing on the surface and then clear again approximately every 2 feet on the way down. Descending feet first also makes clearing much easier for most people. Remember, always equalize early and often.

Trying to equalize pressure in a squeezed ear by performing a very forceful Valsalva maneuver must not be done. Blowing hard against a closed nose and mouth will not open your Eustachian tubes if they are held shut by pressure. When these tubes have been closed by pressure, they actually will seal more tightly the harder you blow. Therefore, by blowing hard, you increase the pressure on your inner ear, which can damage both the mechanism and your hearing. Valsalva maneuvers must always be performed gently and never with extreme force.

Several other techniques may help you equalize the pressure in your ears more easily. One method that works well for some people is to elevate the base of the tongue while performing a Valsalva. Another is to swallow while performing a Valsalva. Wiggling the jaws back and forth while performing a Valsalva also works for some, as does tilting the head to the side opposite from an ear that is not clearing easily. Any of these methods is acceptable and should help keep the pressure in your ears equalized (while spaces such as your sinuses will equalize almost automatically).

If you have a head cold, you must not attempt to dive and equalize by any method. Equalizing when you have a cold can force mucous into the middle ear space, which may lead to infection.

TEST THE DEPTH OF YOUR KNOWLEDGE

It is essential that you understand the effects of pressure on your body. Check your knowledge by answering the following questions:

1 Complete the following statement: When the pressure outside an air space is greater than the pressure inside, the situation is called a _____.

2 List three possible consequences of failing to correct an ear squeeze.

3 What is the most likely cause of a sinus squeeze?

4 Which type of squeeze is the easiest to prevent?

5 In one sentence, describe the most commonly used technique for ear clearing.

6 Describe two ways that diving can cause hearing injuries.

SOME DIVING PROBLEMS CAN BE CAUSED BY AIR EXPANSION

On any dive, you must eventually surface when your air supply grows low. Just as increasing pressure can cause problems when you descend, decreasing pressure as you return to the surface can cause other problems.

What Is a Reverse Block?

A "reverse block" is the opposite of a squeeze, and it occurs when the pressure inside an air space is greater than the surrounding pressure. Blocks occur during ascent as the air that is trapped inside the ears or sinuses expands and the external pressure decreases.

Normally, it is more difficult to get air into the body's air spaces than it is for the air to leave. For this reason, reverse blocks are not common, and few divers ever experience them.

A reverse block can occur in the ear if the Eustachian tube becomes blocked while you are at depth and you begin to ascend. If your ear hurts and feels "full" during ascent, stop your upward progress and redescend until the sensation is no longer present. Then, jut your jaw forward, swallow, and reascend slowly. Repeat this technique as needed. If you must surface and the block still persists, come up as slowly as possible.

In some cases, the block may release all at once. If this occurs, the sudden change in your middle-ear pressure may cause dizziness, but this will quickly pass. Again, hold onto something, someone, or yourself if you experience vertigo.

A sinus block occurs when air is trapped in a sinus cavity by mucous at depth and then tries to expand during ascent. This can happen in two ways.

First, a sinus that was unequalized during descent usually fills with body fluids. Then, during ascent, the air in that sinus will try to expand to its original volume, but it cannot because of the fluid. In this case, pressure builds inside the sinus, and pain results.

Another way that a sinus block occurs is for a sinus that equalized normally during descent to become plugged or blocked at depth. The most common cause of this is a diver having used some type of cold or sinus medication before diving. As the effects of the drug wear off, the opening to the sinuses closes, which traps inside the air that entered under pressure. This situation is known as a "rebound effect." Once this air is trapped, it begins to expand inside the sinus as the diver ascends (Fig. 4-8). Relief will be obtained by redescending, but if you are running low on air, this may not be an option. Surface as slowly as possible if you are forced to ascend; this is your only choice in such a circumstance.

Prevention is the best way to avoid a sinus block. Avoid diving with a cold or other congestion. Also, do not dive if you must use medication to open your sinuses unless a diving physician has reviewed your medical situation and gives you the okay to do so.

Any gas that forms in your stomach or intestines while diving also will expand during ascent. This can cause discomfort by creating pressure on your stomach and bowels. To prevent this from happening, avoid eating gas-producing foods before diving. If you encounter problems from stomach

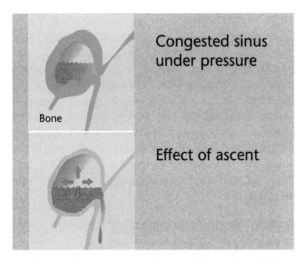

Congested sinus under pressure

Bone

Effect of ascent

Fig. 4-8. If sinus swelling closes a sinus while diving, pressure will develop inside the sinus during ascent.

gas while ascending, stop or slow your progress until the gas works its way out of your system.

Reverse blocks such as those described here are uncommon and easily avoided. By familiarizing yourself with them, you will be able to prevent, recognize, and handle them in the unlikely event one should occur.

Lung Expansion Injuries

Whenever you breathe compressed air under pressure, you are exposed to the risk of a "lung expansion" or "lung overpressure" injury. While these injuries are rare and most divers never experience these problems, you must understand both their causes and how to deal with them.

Under normal conditions while ascending from a dive, you breathe in and out in a relaxed manner, exhaling the compressed air from your lungs before it can expand as you rise through the water. You will suffer a serious injury, however, if you hold your breath and ascend.

With your airway closed, air expanding in your lungs will cause the air sacs (i.e., alveoli) to rupture shortly after they reach their full volume. Unfortunately, there is no sensation of discomfort that warns you when this is about to occur.

This type of accident most commonly occurs when a diver panics at depth, for whatever reason, and makes a rapid ascent while holding his or her breath. Running out of air is the usual cause of this problem. It is instinctive to hold your breath when you have nothing to breathe underwater; therefore, you must program yourself to vent your lungs in any situation that would force you to ascend with nothing to breathe. There are special techniques for dealing with this type of situation that your instructor will teach you, but the best is learning to avoid this situation in the first place (Fig. 4-9).

A lung expansion injury can occur in as little as 4 feet (1.1 m) of water. You must understand the importance of not holding your breath at any time while underwater. If a lung overpressure injury occurs, it is extremely serious and can be fatal. Fortunately, this type of accident normally can be avoided.

As the result of a lung rupture, a lung may collapse, which produces a condition known as "pneumothorax." In other circumstances, air from the lung may escape into the chest cavity, which results in another set of conditions known as "mediastinal emphysema," where continued expansion will cause further problems. Air also can become trapped under the skin; this condition is known as "subcutaneous emphysema."

The most serious result of a lung overpressure injury is a condition known as "air embolism." The word *embolism* means "plug," and an air embolism is a "plug" of air in the bloodstream. The greatest danger in this situation is that a plug of air will block the flow of blood to the brain. Air embolism can cause unconsciousness, paralysis, permanent brain damage, and even death. It is one of the most serious of all diving accidents.

Fig. 4-9. If the breath is held during an ascent, a lung can rupture and introduce air into the bloodstream. The air bubbles can block circulation to the brain. The blockage is referred to as an air embolism.

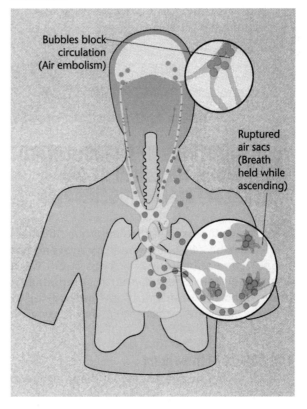

Bubbles block circulation (Air embolism)

Ruptured air sacs (Breath held while ascending)

At this point in your knowledge, it is natural to assume that it would be good to keep your lung volume as low as possible by forcefully blowing out all of the air that you can during ascent. In reality, however, forced exhalation while ascending is not the best thing to do. Some small airways in the lungs can collapse when your lung volume is too low, and air trapped behind such a closure can expand and still cause problems. The best technique is to maintain a normal lung volume during ascent (i.e., neither too full nor too empty). Normal breathing is the best and easiest prevention.

As long as you breathe normally during ascent, there is little danger of a lung overpressure injury. Therefore, it is essential that you always continue breathing whenever you are underwater using scuba equipment. You will learn a variety of techniques during this course for dealing with out-of-air emergencies that will help avoid this type of injury.

TEST THE DEPTH OF YOUR KNOWLEDGE

All divers must understand the importance of dealing with changes in pressure. Check how well you understand these important concepts by completing the following statements:

1 When the pressure inside a rigid air space is greater than the outside pressure, the condition is termed a _____.

2 Lung expansion injuries are caused by _____, _____, and _____.

3 Lung volume should be kept as _____ as possible during ascents when scuba diving.

YOUR BREATHING AND CIRCULATION MUST WORK TOGETHER AT ALL TIMES, ESPECIALLY UNDERWATER

Transporting oxygen through your body is a vital function of your circulatory system, and proper gas exchange in the lungs is critical to your underwater performance. It is important to understand the basics of these mechanisms to see how gases are exchanged in your body while diving.

The Basics of Breathing

Each breath begins when your diaphragm contracts and your chest muscles pull your ribs up, which expands your chest and draws air into your lungs. Oxygen in the air is absorbed through the thin walls of the air sacs in the lungs and then transferred to the blood. This oxygen-rich blood is pumped by the heart through the arteries to the body tissues, where some of the oxygen is used, creating CO_2 (a waste product) in the process. CO_2 then is transferred from the tissues to the blood, traveling through the veins to the heart and back to the lungs. The CO_2 is exhaled, fresh air is drawn into the lungs, and the cycle begins again (Fig. 4-10).

Carbon Dioxide Controls Your Breathing Rate

Your breathing rate is controlled by the amount of CO_2 in your bloodstream. The part of your brain that controls breathing senses the CO_2 level in the blood and then increases or decreases the muscular activity that controls breathing. The greater the amount of CO_2, the greater the stimulus to breathe. Some people mistakenly think that breathing is controlled by the oxygen level in your blood, but the primary stimulus for breathing is in fact CO_2.

Scuba Divers Must Learn to Breathe Slowly and Deeply Underwater

You breathe naturally on land and can do so underwater provided that your behavior is modified slightly and kept within certain limits. The pressure and density of air are different underwater, so your breathing must change somewhat to accommodate these differences. Generally, breathing should be deeper than normal when diving and kept at a slow pace by limiting your exertion (Fig. 4-11).

Fig. 4-10. The blood stream circulates oxygen to the tissues of the body and removes carbon dioxide.

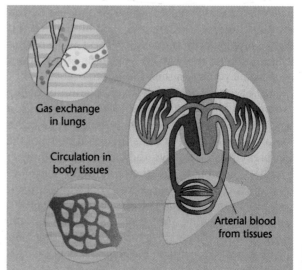

Gas exchange in lungs

Circulation in body tissues

Arterial blood from tissues

Fig. 4-11. Divers must breathe slowly underwater and a bit deeper than normal.

One mistake that divers make is to breathe too shallowly, not exchanging enough air with each breath. Only a small amount of CO_2 is eliminated with each shallow breath, and the more CO_2 in the lungs, the less that can come out of the blood and into the lungs. With more CO_2 in the blood, the desire to breathe increases. This desire can become even worse if the shallow breathing pattern continues.

A high level of CO_2 in the bloodstream stimulates a faster rate of breathing. This increased breathing rate, however, fails to lower the level of CO_2. This is because of the shallowness of each breath and the small amount of air that is consequently exchanged. The simple solution to this problem is deeper breathing; however, unless you are aware of this situation, you may not recognize the symptoms of shallow breathing. If you do not understand the problem, it is easy to become caught in a pattern of breathing faster and faster yet feeling as if you are not getting enough air.

While shallow, rapid breathing can be a problem, you also can get into trouble through deliberate, deep, rapid breathing. Such overbreathing is called "hyperventilation," and as you might suspect, it has an effect on CO_2 opposite that of shallow breathing. Hyperventilation lowers the level of CO_2 in the lungs and blood and can reduce it to well below normal levels if this pattern of breathing continues. Because CO_2 is the stimulus to breathe, you will feel less need to breathe following hyperventilation. If you have been breathing shallowly and feel some respiratory distress when it is not justified, deep breathing will flush CO_2 from your system and increase your breathing comfort.

Deliberate hyperventilation can be hazardous when it is followed by prolonged breath-holding for skin diving. If you hold your breath following excessive hyperventilation, your body will continue using oxygen past the point where the CO_2 in your body rises to a level high enough to trigger breathing. As a result, you can pass out from a lack of oxygen before you ever feel the need to breathe.

Moderate, purposeful hyperventilation can extend your breath-holding time without a high level of risk, but only if a few deep breaths are taken. You should use a maximum of only three or four deep breaths before any breath-hold dive.

"Skip breathing" is a technique used by some divers to extend the amount of time that a tank of air will last underwater. When a diver skip breathes, he or she holds each breath for an extended period of time rather than breathing normally. The danger in skip breathing is a buildup of CO_2 in your system. If this happens, you will be unable to breathe enough air for comfort in any situation that calls for you to exert yourself underwater; you will feel as though you are suffocating. In addition, it is common for divers who skip breathe to develop painful headaches. In short, skip breathing is very dangerous.

Because of the limitations on breathing imposed by some regulators, overexertion also must be avoided underwater. Even the best regulators have some breathing restrictions that limit the flow of air through them. When you work hard underwater, CO_2 can buildup within your body, even if you are breathing deeply. When this happens, you will feel starved for air and as if your regulator will not give you enough to breathe. Anxiety and panic can result unless you take prompt action to correct the problem. If this occurs, you must stop what you are doing, rest, and breathe slowly and deeply (with an emphasis on exhalation) until you gradually recover.

By taking it easy and learning the limits to exertion at various depths, you can avoid overexertion. By now, you also should understand why it is important to be in good shape, with a healthy heart and lungs, to enjoy scuba diving. You must learn to breathe slowly and deeply whenever you use scuba gear underwater.

Breathing Through a Snorkel Also Requires Practice

As a diver, you must have the ability to swim efficiently on the surface while wearing scuba gear and breathing through a snorkel. Without proper training, this can be difficult when surface conditions are rough (Fig. 4-12).

Snorkels also create resistance to breathing, so it is essential that you breathe slowly and deeply when using one for surface swimming. Shallow breathing through a snorkel can lead to a CO_2 buildup in your body as well.

Keeping your body horizontal when surface swimming while wearing scuba is essential. If you assume a vertical position and try to support the combined weight of your head and tank out of the water, without inflating your buoyancy compensator, you will quickly become exhausted. When you fail to inflate your compensator, your lungs are at a greater pressure than the air you are breathing through the snorkel, which makes it difficult to breathe. When you are on the surface, there always must be enough air in the buoyancy compensator to give you slight positive buoyancy for surface swimming.

What Happens When You Accidentally Inhale Water?

Any time you are in the water, whether you are diving or swimming, the possibility exists that you will get a mouthful of water when you least expect it. This commonly happens to swimmers, but it is much less frequent with scuba divers.

If this thought had not occurred to you yet, you will probably wonder what to do if you cough or sneeze underwater. Even a few drops of water can cause most people to choke or sputter. All of these problems, however, can be handled with the regulator in your mouth. Just keep the mouthpiece in place and cough or sneeze through it.

Fig. 4-12. Breathing through a snorkel requires practice, too.

Choking can almost be eliminated as a problem if you always inhale cautiously when taking your first breath after clearing the water from a snorkel or regulator. If you should happen to breathe in some water and begin coughing, do so through the regulator and speed your recovery by swallowing repeatedly.

Be sure not to ascend while choking or coughing. These actions cause your airway to close and could lead to a lung expansion injury.

Breathing is a natural thing, but you can control how you breathe when the need arises. Through the proper training in your Scuba Diver Certification course, breathing underwater will become something that you do naturally.

TEST THE DEPTH OF YOUR KNOWLEDGE

Check your level of understanding by completing the following statements:

1 Breathing occurs because of a stimulus to the brain. This stimulus is the level of _____ in the bloodstream.

2 The recommended breathing pattern for a diver using scuba underwater is _____.

3 If you feel starved for air while scuba diving, you should _____.

4 The main concept to recall if you cough, sneeze, or choke while diving is _____.

THERMAL CONSIDERATIONS UNDERWATER

Your body must remain within a rather narrow range of temperatures to function properly. Your well being is jeopardized if you become too hot or too cold, and both situations are possible in diving. You must know how thermal problems occur, how to recognize them, what to do if they happen, and how to prevent them.

Overheating Can Be a Big Problem

Most people tend to think about problems associated with keeping a diver warm in cold water rather than what happens when a diver overheats. Problems with overheating usually occur on land, however, when you are preparing to dive.

A diving suit protects you against heat loss in the water, but it also insulates you when you are topside. This can lead to serious problems of overheating both before and after the dive itself (Fig. 4-13).

Fig. 4-13. It is easy to overheat while wearing a diving suit when the weather is warm. Be sure to keep cool and avoid overheating.

Your body's first reaction to overheating is perspiration to lower body temperature by evaporation. Unfortunately, this does not work when you are covered head to toe by a dry suit, a wet suit, or other insulating garments.

If no action is taken to cool the body, the next symptoms that appear will be a pale, clammy appearance to the skin and a feeling of weakness, indicating heat exhaustion. At this point, measures must be taken immediately to lower the body temperature. Any further increase in your body temperature will cause your heat-resisting responses to shut down, and this can lead to an extremely serious condition known as "heat stroke." Hot, dry, flushed skin is a sign of heat stroke.

Common sense will help you to easily avoid overheating before and after diving. Avoid wearing a protective suit for long periods before or after a dive. If there will be a delay between the time you dress to dive and the time you will actually dive, stay out of the sun and get wet to cool off. Overheating usually is an avoidable problem.

Heat Loss Must Always Be Considered When Diving

Water conducts heat quite efficiently, and it can absorb a great deal with little change in its own temperature. When you are immersed in water

without proper thermal protection, heat will rapidly be drawn from your body.

Aside from heat lost by conduction, you should remember that heat also is lost underwater each time you take a breath and exhale. More heat is lost with each breath, and you can lose up to 20% of your body heat this way. This effect increases with depth, because the density of the air that you are breathing increases.

The deeper you dive, the greater the pressure that works to compress wet suits. This is unfortunate, because in most cases, the deeper the dive, the colder the water temperature. This is another good reason to limit recreational diving to relatively shallow depths. Diving is more fun, and safer, when you are warm.

As your body loses heat underwater, problems develop. Your muscles grow cold, numb, and lose their strength. Your ability to think clearly as well as your short-term memory are affected. If this process is allowed to continue unchecked, heat loss can create a serious medical emergency. Heart irregularities, unconsciousness, and death may occur. This condition is known as "hypothermia." Fortunately, there are many defenses against heat loss in the water. Some of these are natural, but others require deliberate action on your part.

Your body's first defense is to reduce the circulation of blood to your arms and legs. This conserves heat in the core of your body, where the vital organs are located. Once your "core temperature" (i.e., the internal temperature of the body) reaches a certain temperature, you will begin to shiver.

Shivering indicates chilling. Normally, the purpose of shivering is to produce heat, but shivering when you are underwater cannot keep up with your heat loss. Shivering must be taken as a signal to terminate all diving activities until you have recovered.

One positive action that you can take to generate heat is eating a well-balanced meal at least 2 hours before diving. This will give your body fuel to dive.

Your activity level while diving also plays a big role in the amount of heat your body generates. Remember, however, that heavy exercise is difficult underwater, and it requires you to use large quantities of air.

Your best defense in cold water is wearing the right amount of insulation for your needs (Fig. 4-14). If you grow cold while diving, you need to wear more insulation. If you are already wearing a full wet suit with hood, boots, and gloves and still grow cold, you may need a dry suit to keep warm. If you are wearing a dry suit and still are cold, you may need to use more insulation or a different

Fig. 4-14. You must wear proper insulation for diving in cold water. These divers are geared up for wreck diving off the East Coast and are wearing coveralls over wetsuits.

TEST THE DEPTH OF YOUR KNOWLEDGE

Thermal considerations always play a role in diving. Check how well you understand the need to adjust your insulation for each dive by answering the following questions:

1 What are the two principal means by which body heat is lost in the water?

2 What are two effects of cold water on divers?

3 What are two ways to prevent overheating before you dive?

4 What is one action that should be taken to rewarm after a dive and one that should be avoided?

type of underwear beneath your suit. It is especially important to cover high-heat-loss areas, including your head, torso, groin, and neck. With the proper insulation, you can stay warm in almost any diving environment.

If you become cold while diving, proper rewarming is essential. Get into warm, dry clothing as soon as possible. Warm drinks also may help, but avoid anything that contains alcohol or caffeine. In extreme cases, a warm or tepid bath may be advised, but such "active" rewarming must be performed under the supervision of trained medical personnel.

Warm baths are not recommended after deep dives, because these increase the possibility of decompression sickness. Similarly, warm baths are not recommended during advanced stages of hypothermia, where the body-core temperature has been lowered.

You must learn to recognize heat loss as a potentially serious diving problem, and you must either cease diving when cold or rewarm almost to the point of perspiring before resuming your dive. If you wear the right amount of insulation, dive wisely, recognize the symptoms of heat loss, and respond appropriately, you can avoid hypothermia. Learning to prevent underwater problems before they occur is one of the main purposes of this course.

WHAT ARE THE SECONDARY EFFECTS OF PRESSURE?

The primary effects of pressure are dramatic physical changes that are easy to see and experience, for example, the compression of a wetsuit. There are other, more subtle effects, however, that can be just as important to your safety underwater. These "secondary effects" have a direct impact on the gases in the air that we breathe while diving. Secondary effects also influence the oxygen and nitrogen in normal air.

Sport Divers Do Not Use Pure Oxygen

While oxygen is essential to sustain life, breathing pure oxygen at depths below 25 feet (7 m) can be deadly. Under such conditions, oxygen becomes toxic and is extremely hazardous.

Scuba tanks must never be filled with pure oxygen. The amount of oxygen that is found in ordinary air is not toxic within normal sport-diving depths (Fig. 4-15).

Some divers use special gas mixtures that have a percentage of oxygen and nitrogen different than that found in regular air. These mixtures usually are referred to as "Nitrox" or "enriched air." Nitrox is acceptable to use for sport diving, but it requires additional training and equipment (Fig. 4-16). Nitrox diving is beyond the scope of this NAUI Scuba Diver Certification course.

Carbon Monoxide Is Deadly

Carbon monoxide is a gas that is formed by the incomplete combustion of fuel such as gasoline or

Fig. 4-15. Sport divers don't use pure oxygen for diving.

Fig. 4-16. Nitrox is an acceptable gas to use for sport diving if you have been trained to use it.

diesel. This gas is potentially dangerous even in small concentrations, especially when it is breathed at depth.

Divers can encounter problems with carbon monoxide if exhaust fumes from a gasoline- or diesel-powered air compressor contaminate their air supply. This occurs when the intake for the air compressor is placed too close to the exhaust for the engine that drives the compressor. In this situation, gases from the engine exhaust are compressed along with the air. In addition, faulty air compressors can produce carbon monoxide, as will a good compressor that has been lubricated with the wrong oil.

Carbon monoxide is dangerous to divers. Once it is inhaled, it seriously interferes with the ability of the blood to carry oxygen. Symptoms of carbon-monoxide poisoning include confusion, headache, nausea, bright red lips and nail beds, and unconsciousness. Fresh air may be helpful, but pure oxygen and medical attention are needed for proper treatment. Carbon-monoxide poisoning also can be treated in a recompression chamber.

Although carbon monoxide itself is colorless, odorless, and tasteless, air that has been contaminated with it tends to taste and smell oily or foul. If the air from your tank seems suspect, do not use it. The facility that filled the tank must be notified of the problem as soon as possible so that they can investigate it.

Carbon-monoxide poisoning can be avoided by always filling your tanks at a professional dive facility, where the compressor is properly set up and maintained. Professional dive stores have their compressed air regularly analyzed for air quality and purity (Fig. 4-17).

People who smoke expose themselves to high levels of carbon monoxide. Therefore, it is unwise to smoke before diving.

Nitrogen Can Be a Problem in Two Quite Different Ways

Nitrogen is an inert gas with no effect on the human body under normal pressures. As depth and pressure increase underwater, however, nitrogen begins to affect your physiology.

At sea level, a certain amount of nitrogen is dissolved in your blood and tissues. As you breathe, some nitrogen molecules enter the bloodstream while others leave it; this occurs at a 1:1 rate of exchange. Because the net effect in this case is no increase in the amount of blood nitrogen, your system is in a state of "equilibrium."

The amount of nitrogen in your blood becomes unbalanced when the pressure of the air that you breathe increases. The deeper you dive and the longer the duration of your dive, the more nitrogen your body absorbs.

Problems can occur if you absorb a great deal of nitrogen and then ascend too quickly. It takes time

Fig. 4-17. Always have your tanks filled at a professional diving retailer's.

for nitrogen to enter your system, and it takes time for that nitrogen to leave as well.

If you ascend faster than the nitrogen can be eliminated through normal respiration, the excess nitrogen may form bubbles inside your body and produce an illness known as "decompression sickness" (DCS), or the "bends." If such bubbles are in your blood and tissues, they may impair the circulation, distort the tissues, and produce varying symptoms depending on their quantity and location. These symptoms range from skin rash, extreme fatigue, and painful joints to, in severe cases, paralysis and unconsciousness (Fig. 4-18).

As with all problems that may be encountered while diving, DCS can and must be prevented. Tables are available to provide time limits for various diving depths. These are called "no-decompression tables," and you will learn to use them during this course. You also can use a dive computer that performs similar functions to help avoid DCS. Remember, however, that no matter whether you use dive tables or a dive computer, a slight risk always exists that you may suffer DCS. Learning to dive is really a matter of learning to avoid potential problems that are imposed by the water environment. To avoid the bends, you must learn about decompression tables and how to use them correctly.

Treatment of DCS consists of recompressing a diver, which means putting him or her back under a pressure sufficient to cause the bubbles to

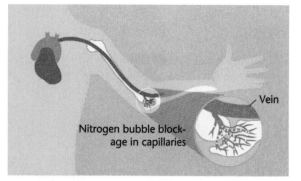

Fig. 4-18. Excess nitrogen can form bubbles in the blood stream which collect in the joints and cause an illness known as the bends. This is just one of the forms of decompression sickness.

return into solution. The diver then breathes high concentrations of oxygen, or even pure oxygen. This treatment must be performed in a controlled environment under medical supervision; it cannot be carried out in the water.

Special hyperbaric chambers are used in this treatment. These chambers are variously referred to as "hyperbaric chambers," "decompression chambers," "recompression chambers," or simply "chambers." You can use any of these terms; an experienced diver will know what you are talking about (Fig. 4-19).

A diver who shows any sign or symptom of the bends must never be taken back underwater. Information on the location of recompression chambers for the treatment of diving accidents is included in another chapter.

Fig. 4-19. Decompression sickness must be treated in a hyperbaric chamber like this one.

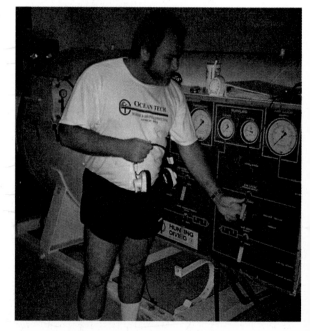

Even if a diver is promptly treated for DCS, permanent damage to the body can occur. Divers have suffered paralysis and other crippling injuries as a result. In rare but extreme cases, divers have died as a direct result of DCS.

Nitrogen under pressure also can produce another effect. At depths approaching 80 feet, this gas may be intoxicating. The narcotic effect of nitrogen at greater depths will produce impaired thought and judgment, and it will reduce a diver's physical ability. The danger exists that a diver could become unable to function well enough to ensure his or her safety.

Prevention of this problem, which is called "nitrogen narcosis" or "rapture of the deep," is simple: avoid deep dives. The symptoms of nitrogen narcosis increase in intensity with depth and time. Recovery is as simple as ascending to a shallower depth, where nitrogen has no effect. The symptoms leave as rapidly as they appear, and there are no after effects (Fig. 4-20).

TEST THE DEPTH OF YOUR KNOWLEDGE

Ⓟ roblems that are caused by the secondary effects of pressure are avoidable. Do you know how to avoid them? Check your knowledge by answering the following questions:

1 How can oxygen toxicity be prevented?

2 How can carbon-monoxide toxicity be prevented?

3 How can DCS be prevented?

4 How can nitrogen narcosis be prevented?

5 What is the correct reaction to symptoms of narcosis?

6 List two reasons to avoid deep dives.

Fig. 4-20. The effects of nitrogen narcosis can be similar to alcoholic intoxication.

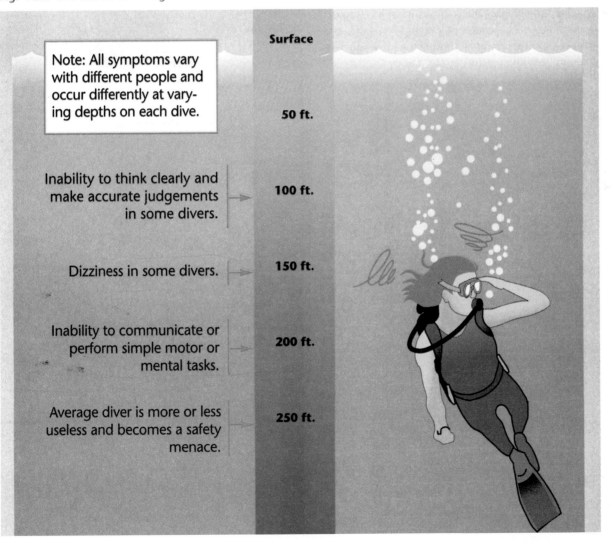

Note: All symptoms vary with different people and occur differently at varying depths on each dive.

Surface

50 ft.

Inability to think clearly and make accurate judgements in some divers. → 100 ft.

Dizziness in some divers. → 150 ft.

Inability to communicate or perform simple motor or mental tasks. → 200 ft.

Average diver is more or less useless and becomes a safety menace. 250 ft.

HEALTH AND FITNESS CONSIDERATIONS FOR DIVING

"Health" is the state of being sound in body and mind, and it is a prerequisite for diving. To engage in diving, you must have a sound heart and lungs, clear ears and sinuses, and freedom from any limiting disease or serious ailment.

At the beginning of this course, you completed a NAUI Medical History Form. If you indicated any problems that might affect your ability to dive, you were asked to have a medical examination and obtain medical approval before commencing your training. Even if no problems are identified on your medical history form, a physical examination by a doctor familiar with diving is a good idea.

Women have special health considerations because of menstruation and pregnancy. If a woman can engage in physical activities on land during menstruation, it usually is all right for her to dive (Fig. 4-21). If cramps or other effects of menstruation are bothersome, a woman should refrain from diving when such symptoms exist. Regarding pregnancy, not enough is known about the effects of pressure on an unborn child, so a woman must refrain from diving during pregnancy.

"Fitness" means the ability to meet the physical demands of a particular activity. You must be fit to dive. Initially, this means that you need good

Fig. 4-21. Menstruation does not usually pose a problem for most women divers.

aquatic ability, such as being able to swim at least 220 yards (200 m) nonstop without fins or other aids. This demonstrates the aquatic fitness that is needed to be comfortable in water. Later, you will need to develop fitness for using fins and performing other skills in the water.

Fitness for swimming may not necessarily mean fitness for diving, because different muscles are used in different ways. Playing sports such as baseball does not necessarily keep you fit for diving. To get into shape for a particular activity requires regular participation in that activity.

The best way to stay fit for diving is to dive regularly. An accepted alternative is to swim using a mask, snorkel, and fins. Remember that your ability to dive safely is decreased by inactivity. Before resuming diving after a layoff of 1 month or longer, your fitness should be re-established by pool workouts before any open-water dives. Refresher courses offered by NAUI instructors also afford opportunities to polish skills, add new knowledge of the basics, and help restore fitness and skill proficiency. These courses are recommended.

Just as good health and fitness are important for diving safety, use of recreational drugs can lead to problems underwater. Substances such as alcohol, marijuana, and cocaine, which alter your physiology or affect your ability to think clearly, must be avoided. Any street drug is extremely dangerous when taken before diving.

If you do not feel well enough to dive without using a drug, you must not dive, even if you feel fine with medication. The effects of drugs can be changed by pressure. Always refrain from using any drug for at least 12 hours before diving. Medication may mask the symptoms of your illness, but that illness still exists.

Divers take pride in their health and fitness. It is essential to maintain that health and fitness if you want to enjoy diving.

TEST THE DEPTH OF YOUR KNOWLEDGE

Consider the following questions on health and fitness:

1 Why is good health a prerequisite for diving?

2 When should a woman refrain from diving?

3 True or False: Only people with problems in their medical history should have a physical examination for diving.

4 Complete the following statement: The best way to maintain fitness for diving is to ____.

5 If you are not feeling well but medication helps you feel better, why should you refrain from diving?

CHAPTER FIVE

ENVIRONMENT

nderwater conditions vary significantly from one part of the world to another. Visibility, water temperature, waves, currents, and other factors all change in each dive area, and these differences influence both the way that you dress for a dive and what techniques are used.

No matter where you dive, you will discover special requirements pertaining to diving in that area. Before you go diving someplace you have never been before, you must learn about the environmental conditions that could affect your diving and how the local divers deal with them.

LEARNING OBJECTIVES

Before the end of this chapter, you must be able to:

1. List three different types of natural underwater dive sites.
2. Define the phrase "overhead environment" as it pertains to diving, and give two examples.
3. Explain how shore conditions can make diving difficult.
4. State the two water conditions that usually have the biggest influence on diving.
5. Define the term "thermocline."
6. List three factors that affect visibility underwater.
7. List and describe two different popular diving locations in the United States.
8. Define the term "tide," and explain two ways that tides affect diving conditions.
9. Explain the difference between standing and transitory currents.
10. Describe the technique for escaping a rip current.
11. List four different types of bottom terrain normally encountered by divers.
12. Describe the technique for escaping from an aquatic plant if you become entangled.
13. List two examples of common hazardous marine life that you might expect to see while ocean diving.
14. List two examples of common hazardous marine life you might expect to encounter while freshwater diving.
15. State the best time to take medication for motion sickness when you will be diving from a boat.
16. Explain how surf is created.

Along with the factors already described, other environmental and physical variations, such as the season of the year, the weather, dive-site characteristics, and shore conditions, also must be considered. The continental United States is a good example of a country with some of the most varied diving conditions in the world.

The underwater environments of the United States include such diverse conditions as oil rigs off Louisiana; tropical waters off the coast of Florida; cold waters in the Great Lakes, New England, and Alaska; and kelp forests off the coast of Southern California. Each of these environments is extremely different, and each requires certain skills, techniques, and equipment (Fig. 5-1).

Fig. 5-1. Diving environments and conditions vary widely. Many sport divers regularly dive off the oil rigs in the Gulf of Mexico.

This chapter begins by examining how dive-site characteristics and shore conditions affect your diving techniques in different areas. Then, it considers variations in temperature, visibility, and aquatic life. Your instructor will supplement this material with information on the local conditions and how they affect diving near your home.

PHYSICAL CHARACTERISTICS OF THE UNDERWATER SITE ARE IMPORTANT

Divers will dive almost anywhere there is water, but they generally are attracted to interesting underwater formations. These formations may be manmade, such as an artificial reef, oil rig, breakwater, jetty, or shipwreck. These sites can be as fascinating as any natural underwater formation. In particular, many divers find shipwrecks to be among the most exciting dive sites (Fig. 5-2).

Natural dive sites include submarine canyons with sheer dropoffs, lakes, rivers, caves, and both coral and rock reefs. Natural sites have the benefit of marine growth that may be thousands of years old. Specially trained divers also enjoy the thrill of exploring underwater caverns or diving beneath the ice of frozen lakes (Fig. 5-3).

Obviously, there are many types of dive sites, each offering new and different experiences. However, while there are numerous fascinating

Fig. 5-2. Shipwrecks are very popular with divers.

Fig. 5-3. Cave and cavern diving require special training and equipment.

places to explore underwater, many of them require special training beyond the Scuba Diver Certification course.

Any diving environment that does not allow direct vertical access to the surface is called an "overhead environment." Overhead environments include cave diving, "penetration" wreck diving (i.e., going inside the wreck), and ice diving. These environments are considered to be highly specialized, and they require additional equipment and training (no matter how much experience you have diving under other conditions) (Fig. 5-4). Even your instructor would need special training for these types of diving if he or she had no prior experience with these areas.

Fig. 5-4. Diving inside a shipwreck is not for the novice diver.

SHORE CONDITIONS CAN PRESENT THEIR OWN CHALLENGES

The easiest diving usually is that done from boats, and in many situations, boat diving offers some of the best diving available. Beach diving is a popular alternative for many divers, however, and can be extremely enjoyable.

Beach diving is quite different from boat diving. Beach diving generally is more strenuous than boat diving, and it presents varied and unique diving situations (Fig. 5-5).

One of the most challenging aspects of beach diving may be simply getting to the water's edge. Beach access may be difficult in areas with steep cliffs and rugged shores. To dive in some of the more rugged areas along the California coast, for example, you may need to walk or climb over rugged terrain, covering considerable distances either wearing or carrying your gear. This can be extremely exhausting and hazardous. To dive under these conditions, you must plan ahead as well as know your capabilities and limitations. When diving in these areas, also make sure that you have the energy to get back to your starting point after the dive.

As you enter the water, other problems can be created by the shoreline conditions. The shape of the bottom may affect currents and wave action. The bottom may slope gradually, drop off suddenly, or have scattered holes and rocks. The composition of the bottom will affect the way that you enter the water (Fig. 5-6).

Whenever you dive in a new area, you will need an orientation to the dive site. This can best be done by diving in new areas with a NAUI

Fig. 5-5. Beach diving is usually more strenuous than boat diving.

Fig. 5-6. Rocky shore entries can be hazardous and exhausting and must be done carefully.

Fig. 5-7. Whenever possible, make your first dive in a new area with an instructor or divemaster who has local diving experience.

TEST THE DEPTH OF YOUR KNOWLEDGE

Learning about the diving environment is one of the most interesting parts of diving. Check how well you have learned about dive sites by answering the following questions:

1   List five environmental factors that affect diving.

2   List two types of bottom conditions that may occur naturally.

3   List two different types of overhead environments that relate to diving.

4   Who is best qualified to provide an orientation to a new diving area?

Instructor, NAUI Divemaster, or other experienced local divers (Fig. 5-7). You will need to know what to look for, what to avoid, and any diving techniques that may be unique to that area. Always seek information about new dive sites from experienced divers. As you gain experience and participate in advanced courses, you will be able to explore new areas confidently and without supervision.

DIVING IS CONTROLLED BY THE WATER CONDITIONS

Water temperature and visibility probably are the two most important factors in determing how easy it is to dive. Diving in warm, clear water is relatively simple, because you must only wear a minimal amount of insulation and it is always easy to see where you are. Diving in colder, darker water is more difficult, because you must wear more insulation to be comfortable and it is not always possible to tell exactly where you are while underwater.

Water temperature can range from freezing to over 85° F (29° C). Diving in water that is colder than 75° F (24° C) normally requires that you wear some type of dive suit depending on the duration of the dive, your activity level during the dive, and your individual physiology. As a rule, the colder the water, the more insulation you will need to wear. Almost all diving requires some type of insulation, however, because the water temperature usually will be colder than your body-core temperature (Fig. 5-8).

Diving usually takes place in fairly temperate water, but because of water's great capacity to conduct and absorb heat, you will chill rapidly if you do not wear adequate protection. Water temperature always is a major factor to consider when planning a dive. In almost all cases, the deeper you dive, the colder the water temperature.

In freshwater, a phenomenon known as a "thermocline" will frequently appear. This is a sharp change in water temperature between the surface and the bottom. The two layers of water can vary in temperature as much as 20° F (6.7° C) and yet

remain distinctly separated and not mixing. If you are geared only for the surface-water temperature, you may find that this drastic temperature change at depth will force an early end to your dive. Thermoclines are commonly found in many lakes, but they also occur in the ocean (Fig. 5-9).

You must obtain information on the water temperature at the depths where you plan to dive to before entering the water. This information normally is available from local instructors, divemasters, or dive stores. You must select suitable thermal protection for both the water temperature and your individual physiological needs.

Another major factor affecting all dive operations is the underwater visibility, which can range from zero to well over 100 feet (30 m). Diving in water where the visibility is severely restricted can be hazardous, and zero-visibility diving requires special equipment, training, and procedures. If you arrive at a site and find that you cannot see anything underwater, you should postpone the dive until a day when the visibility is better. Zero-visibility diving is a necessary part of search-and-recovery training, but it is not fun when you are just learning to dive.

Underwater visibility is affected by the locale, season, weather, water movement, composition of the bottom, and other factors. For example, in California, visibility usually is best during the calm fall months and worst during the winter rains and storms. In New England, however, you can have good visibility during the winter months. Tidal

Fig. 5-8. The amount of insulation you will need to dive depends on the water temperature, your activity level during the dive, and your personal physiology.

Fig. 5-9. Temperature changes can be quite abrupt in thermoclines.

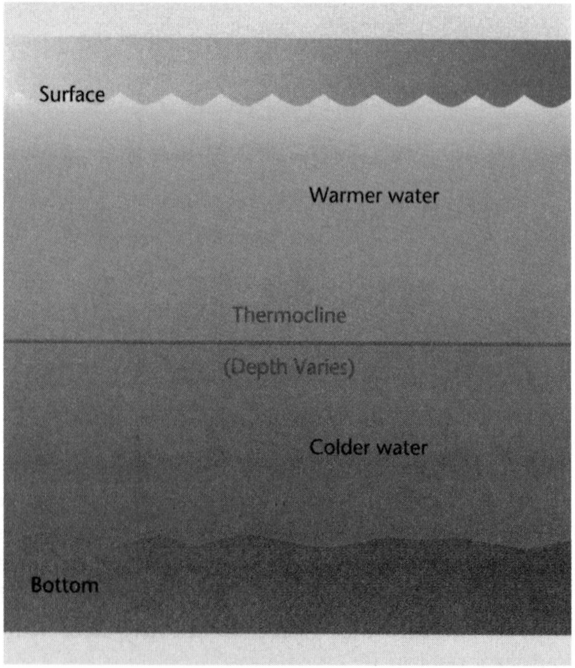

Surface

Warmer water

Thermocline
(Depth Varies)

Colder water

Bottom

changes also affect visibility and are discussed later in this chapter.

Several problems relate to visibility, and the most common is disorientation. With limited visibility, disorientation (and even dizziness) can result from a lack of visual references while you are submerged. You can avoid this by not diving in turbid water until you have been trained in the proper techniques. Entanglement in fishing line and other debris also can be a serious problem in low-visibility conditions.

There are special techniques for diving in limited visibility. Divers can hold hands to stay together or use a "buddy line." A buddy line is a short length of polypropylene line, usually no more than 6 feet (2 m) long, with a loop in each end (Fig. 5-10). Each diver in the buddy team holds one end of the line to maintain contact. Limited-visibility diving is a specialty area in diving, but your instructor will cover any special techniques that relate to visibility where you will be diving.

In extremely clear water, estimating distances can become somewhat difficult. When this happens, it is easy to exceed your planned depth, because some objects will be deeper and further away than they appear. Under these conditions, it is important to monitor your depth gauge even more frequently than normal.

Whether the visibility is good or poor, you can see why divers must stay close together underwater. In poor visibility, it is easy to become separated and lose track of each other, and if you are unable to find your buddy within 1 minute under these conditions, you must surface. In good visibility, it is easy to get too far apart, which means you will be unable to help your dive partner should he or she need assistance. It is essential to begin developing good diving habits from the very first time you go underwater. Learn to stay within touching distance of your partner, without getting in his or her way, if you want to be considered a good dive buddy.

WAVES AND SURF

Waves are created in the open ocean as the wind blows across the water; the energy from this wind is imparted to the ocean. With increasing wind or as the wind blows for a longer time, larger waves are formed.

In the open ocean, the energy from waves manifests as swells, where the ocean rises and falls. Unless the swells are quite large and the wind blows hard, waves usually do not break in the open sea.

Waves may travel across thousands of miles of ocean, but it is the energy of the waves and not the water itself that does the traveling. As waves enter shallow water and are affected by the bottom, they break and form surf. The larger the waves, the larger the surf.

In coastal areas where beach diving is popular, divers must contend with surf to enter the water. Chapter 9 provides an introduction to surf entries, and your instructor will cover this in more detail if such entries are common in your diving area. The "surf zone" is the area where surf forms and waves break.

"Surge" is the underwater movement of water you will experience when diving in areas close to a shore with wave action. When you are close to shore, in shallow water, and there are large waves, you will feel the effects of surge. As the waves move toward the shore, the surge will tend to push your body toward shore. As the waves recede from the shore, the surge will tend to push your body away from shore.

In most areas with large waves, surf, and heavy surge, visibility usually will be poor. Different beach conditions require different entry-and-exit techniques, so always get an orientation to any new diving area from a NAUI instructor or a qualified divemaster.

Fig. 5-10. Maintaining contact in low visibility conditions is frequently accomplished by using a buddy line.

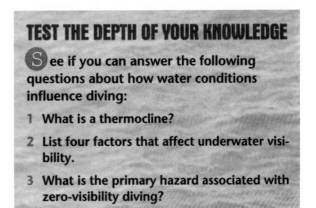

TEST THE DEPTH OF YOUR KNOWLEDGE

See if you can answer the following questions about how water conditions influence diving:

1 What is a thermocline?

2 List four factors that affect underwater visibility.

3 What is the primary hazard associated with zero-visibility diving?

EXAMPLES OF POPULAR DIVING AREAS

After completing this course, you will be able to dive on your own under conditions that are similar to those where you were trained. If you are like most divers, however, you will want to travel to other areas and experience new and different dive sites. Let us compare four different dive locales to give you an idea of the variety in diving that can be found across the United States and how diving can differ from one region to another.

Southern California

Southern California is one of the most popular diving areas in the world. With its mild year-round weather topside and good water conditions, diving is a favorite sport with many people in this part of the country.

Most diving in Southern California is concentrated among the giant kelp beds that are found offshore both along the coast and nearby islands, such as Catalina, San Clemente, and the Channel Islands off Santa Barbara. These kelp beds are home to numerous animals and fish, including harbor seals, many species of rockfish, lobsters, scallops, and thousands of other creatures. Diving in a kelp bed is like swimming through a redwood forest, with the light filtering down from the surface through the long kelp stalks (Fig. 5-11).

Fig. 5-11. The kelp beds of California provide a beautiful diving environment.

Visibility in Southern California may range from zero along the beaches to over 100 feet (30 m) at the islands, although the average visibility usually is between 30 and 50 feet (10 to 17 m). Water temperatures can be as low as 50° F (10° C) in the winter months to over 70° F (21° C) during the late summer and fall months. On average, water temperature usually is approximately 62° F.

The US Gulf Coast

The Gulf Coast of the United States contains a variety of diving locales, but a great deal is done at the offshore oil platforms. These platforms are located far from shore, so this type of diving normally is done from a boat.

The platforms act like artificial reefs, attracting many different kinds of fish and other animals that live on the structure. It is not unusual to see giant groupers weighing over 100 pounds (45 kg) at many of these sites.

Visibility at the offshore platforms is good for most of the year, with a low of usually not less than 30 feet (10 m) and, on some days, a high of as much as 150 feet (45 m) or better. Normal water temperatures during the summer months vary from the upper 70s (24° C) to the low 80s (29° C).

The US Great Lakes

The Great Lakes of the central United States offer some of the finest freshwater diving in the world. There are numerous shipwrecks located in these waters, most of which still are relatively intact because there is no salt to cause corrosion and no marine creatures that attack wood. Some of the wrecks in the Great Lakes are hundreds of years old yet still in excellent condition (Fig. 5-12).

Visibility in the Great Lakes can be very good, exceeding 50 feet (15 m) at some of the better dive spots. Most wrecks, however, are covered

Fig. 5-12. There are numerous shipwrecks located in the Great Lakes.

here with fine layers of silt that are easily stirred up, obscuring visibility. These waters are quite cold even during the summer months, and most divers wear dry suits.

Southern Florida

Southern Florida is another extremely popular diving destination. The reefs that lie offshore here provide excellent diving and are similar to those conditions found in the Caribbean. Visibility ranges from 40 to over 100 feet (13 to 30 m) on a good day. Water temperatures can dip into the high 60s (approximately 20° C) during the winter months, but they usually are well above 70° F (21° C).

Many colorful animals and fish can be seen in the Florida waters. The variety of marine life in coral reefs exceeds that found in colder waters, although the numbers of each different type of animal are fewer. In addition, marine life found here generally is more colorful.

MOVING WATER HAS TREMENDOUS POWER

Water is heavy. If you reflect a moment on the weight of a bucket of water, you can imagine the enormous potential energy that a large mass of moving water contains. It is useless to fight against strong water movement, such as a strong current, because you cannot swim against it. It is possible, however, to use the movement of the water to assist you in diving, and this is something that you will learn during this course.

You must understand what sets water into motion, how the water moves, and how to function effectively in moving water. This understanding will help you to cope with the movement of water and use it to your advantage (Fig. 5-13).

How Tides Affect Diving

One cause of water movement in many areas are "tides," which are caused by the gravitational attraction between the Earth, Moon, and Sun. The extent of tides range from negligible to a change in the water level of over 40 feet (12 m). Typically, the difference between the high and low tide is only a few feet of water.

Problems can arise because of changes in the water level at a dive site. Entry and exit conditions change because of such variations. For example, when the tide is "in," or "high," the water may extend onto the beach, covering rocks that are just outside the waves. This makes it easy to enter the water, because you can swim over the rocks. When

Fig. 5-13. When water moves, it has tremendous power.

the tide is "out," or "low," however, the water recedes, uncovering the rocks. If this happens while you are in the water, you may be forced to climb back over the rocks to return to the beach. This can be much more difficult and dangerous than swimming over them.

Another way that tides affect diving is if you are using a small boat that is docked or launched at a marina. As the tide recedes, dock and launch ramps can become quite steep. Launch ramps in particular can be extremely slippery, because they are exposed at low tide.

Tidal currents are a great concern to divers. When these currents pass through restricted areas, they can be quite strong, even strong enough to sweep you away no matter how hard you swim. Most divers cannot swim any faster than 1 knot (1.8 km/h) for longer than a few minutes. Many tidal currents, however, are 2 knots (3.7 km/h) or faster. In areas with strong tidal currents, it is essential to consult tide and current tables, which are readily available, to help plan your dives for slack-water periods (i.e., when there is no tidal current).

Water movement because of tides also can affect underwater visibility. The best diving conditions usually are during high tide. There are exceptions of course, and you will learn more about local currents from your instructor as part of your open-water training.

Currents

A "current" is the movement of water in a particular direction. Currents are like "rivers" or "streams" within the ocean.

Currents are caused by winds, gravity, and the Earth's rotation. You must consider currents whenever planning a dive, because attempting to swim against a strong current can lead to exhaustion.

Usually, you should begin a dive against the current, no matter how slight it may be. If your entry and exit points are the same, you can use the current to assist you to your exit point at the end of your dive by using this technique.

If you are diving from an anchored boat, a buoyed safety line of 100 feet (30 m) or more in length always must be trailed behind the boat (Fig. 5-14). This way, if you accidentally end up downcurrent from the boat, you still may be able to grab the line and pull yourself back in. In the NAUI Advanced Scuba course, you can learn how to "drift dive," using the current rather than fighting against it.

Currents can be separated into three general categories: 1) standing, 2) tidal, and 3) transitory. "Standing currents" are regular, steady currents that do not change very much (if they change at all). In many parts of the world, there are "long shore currents" that normally flow in one direction along the coast; this is a good example of a standing current. For example, the long shore current in California normally flows "down" along the coast from north to south. Rivers and streams are examples of standing currents. You must be aware of the speed and direction of any standing current that is present where you plan to dive and account for it in your dive plan.

"Tidal currents" are similar to those discussed in the previous section on tides. "Transitory currents" are those that may appear suddenly and, just as suddenly, disappear. A good example of such a current is a "rip current," which is a strong water movement that can cause problems for untrained divers.

Rip currents occur near the shore and are formed when water is pushed up onto the shore by wave or wind action and then funneled back out to sea through a narrow passage. This passage or restriction can be a narrow opening in a reef, sandbar, or other large formation blocking the return of water to the ocean. The offshore flow of this current is narrow and can be quite strong.

Fig. 5-14. Be sure to use a current line whenever you dive from a boat in areas where there are currents.

If you find yourself being carried away from shore or you are unable to make progress against the water when trying to return to the beach, you may be in a rip current. You can escape such a current by swimming parallel to the shore line on the downcurrent side of any long shore current. Once you have escaped the rip, you then can turn toward shore and swim in. If you try to swim out of the rip and into the oncoming long shore current, the long shore current will push you back into the rip (Fig. 5-15).

With experience, rip currents can be identified easily. If they occur in your area, your instructor will familiarize you with them and the areas where they appear.

While currents can carry you away from your entry point, they also can transport you to a planned exit point, which adds to the ease and enjoyment of your dive. If you live near the ocean and participate in NAUI advanced training, you will learn how to use currents to make ocean diving easier and more exciting. As a new diver, however, you must learn more about local currents and how to recognize them before you attempt to make unsupervised dives. The best way to accomplish this is by training with a NAUI instructor who has ample personal diving experience in your local area.

Even with experience, advanced divers should inquire about local currents and diving conditions from local divers whenever they plan on diving a new site. If you travel to a new area where conditions differ from those where you trained, get a local orientation. For example, if all of your diving has been in freshwater lakes, you will need an orientation to dive in the ocean, and vice versa. Similarly, if you learned in Florida but want to dive in the kelp forests of California, you also need a special orientation.

Fig. 5-15. Rip currents can be easily identified once you know what they look like.

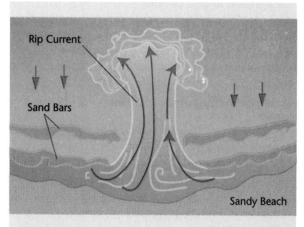

TEST THE DEPTH OF YOUR KNOWLEDGE

Ⓢee how much you have learned about currents by answering the following questions:

1   List three causes of water movement.

2   Briefly describe how to escape a rip current.

3   In which direction should you begin a dive: with the current, or against it?

Fig. 5-16. Rocky coasts provide good habitat for marine creatures.

DIFFERENT SITES HAVE DIFFERENT BOTTOM CONDITIONS

Ⓣhe bottom composition of the site also will affect your diving. This is true whether you dive in a quarry, lake, river, or ocean.

Usually, you can expect the underwater terrain at the dive site to be an extension of the shoreline. If the shore is rocky and rugged, similar underwater conditions probably will be found nearby. A wide, sandy beach generally indicates a vast expanse of sand offshore. There are exceptions, however, so it helps to check with other divers regarding an unfamiliar site whenever possible. Some information on bottom conditions also is available on navigational charts used for boating.

In most cases, the more vertical relief there is to a dive site and the more aquatic plants present, the greater the amount of marine life in that area. Flat stretches of bottom tend to be barren compared with kelp forests and coral reefs. Divers tend to seek areas with abundant life, which makes for the most interesting diving.

Many different terrains can be found underwater. These include mud, silt, clay, sand, pebbles, rocks, and coral.

Mud and silt bottoms are stirred easily, which can reduce visibility to zero because of suspended sediment. Sand bottoms offer somewhat better visibility, but these tend to be underwater deserts. Rocky bottoms provide a good base for marine plants and provide many holes and crevices that aquatic animals use as homes (Fig. 5-16).

Aquatic plants do not grow well in tropical waters, but coral thrives in these waters and makes for excellent diving. Barnacles, rocks, and other underwater formations have sharp edges, so gloves are required to prevent cuts and scratches while diving areas with these features.

Varying bottom compositions require different diving techniques. You must learn one technique for a beach entry on a sandy bottom that provides good footing and yet another for a muddy bottom, which can pose an entirely different set of problems. Once you have entered the water, you will find that careful movement is required to avoid stirring up a muddy or silty bottom. Mud also can be very slippery when you are entering or exiting the water.

Sandy bottoms do not cloud the water as easily as muddy or silty bottoms. Coral and rock reefs usually provide the best visibility as well as many interesting things to see (Fig. 5-17). Once you begin diving in open water, you will find that bottom composition is yet another element that affects your dive.

Fig. 5-17. Coral reefs usually have excellent visibility for diving.

TEST THE DEPTH OF YOUR KNOWLEDGE

See how much you have learned about bottom conditions by answering the following questions:

1 List three types of bottom conditions that may be found underwater.

2 List four aspects of diving that can be affected by bottom composition.

3 Describe two problems that can arise when diving in an area with a muddy bottom.

DIVING WITH POTENTIALLY DANGEROUS MARINE LIFE

The many different types of life in the underwater world make diving interesting. There are thousands of animals and plants to capture your interest and amaze you. There is beauty and color to be discovered that surpasses anything you can imagine.

Given the dramatic portrayal of dangerous marine life found in movies and television, it is natural for you to be concerned about dangerous animals and plants. As you will learn, however, these dramatic portrayals usually are gross exaggerations of the dangers posed by these creatures. Most divers look forward to encounters with underwater life.

Of course, there are potentially dangerous animals and plants underwater, just as there are potentially dangerous animals and plants on land. You probably know how to avoid attracting or agitating bears or snakes if you go camping, or even how to handle aggressive dogs in your own neighborhood. By reading or through training and experience, you have learned how to recognize and avoid dangerous animals so that you can go hiking, camping, or walking around your neighborhood without undue apprehension.

Going underwater is similar to going hiking or camping. There are aquatic animals that can be just as harmful as a snake or a bear, but as you learn more about them, you will look forward to seeing them, without apprehension or fear.

Aggressive animal behavior is rare underwater. Any injury that you might receive from an aquatic animal almost certainly would result from a defensive action on the part of that creature. Remember that nearly all animals will attack if they feel cornered or threatened.

You also may injure yourself by accidentally coming into contact with an animal or disturbing it.

Avoid potential problems with hazardous marine life by learning to identify those creatures in your area. Do not touch animals that you know can harm you or those you cannot identify.

Each region has its own hazardous animals. There are creatures that can bite, some that can stick you, others that can sting, and even a few that can create an electric shock. Identification and avoidance are your keys to safety.

How do you recognize the dangerous animals in your area? Someone who is knowledgeable and experienced must show you which creatures to avoid. Not only must you know which animals to avoid, however, you also must know where you are likely to meet them.

During this course, your instructor will teach you about the animals in your area, but you must seek out similar information when visiting other regions. Learning what marine life lives in a given area is one of the main reasons for obtaining a formal orientation to diving in an unfamiliar region.

New divers frequently are concerned about becoming entangled in large plants (e.g., kelp), fishing nets, and fishing line underwater. If you overreact when snagged and twist or fight to get free, this can be a serious problem. The correct response is to stop, analyze the situation, and get assistance from your buddy or slowly take steps to free yourself. As long as you have air and you have not exceeded your allowable bottom time, there is no urgency to free yourself. Take your time, and sort the problem out logically. Usually, you will find a way to solve the problem by yourself. With experience and confidence, you will find that diving in dense growths of aquatic plants can be exciting and beautiful; you also will find that snagging your equipment is only a minor nuisance that can be dealt with quite easily.

The largest predator you are likely to meet underwater is another diver. Also, remember that your greatest enemy while diving is panic.

Common Hazardous Marine Life

In saltwater, the most common form of hazardous marine life probably is the sea urchin (Fig. 5-18). These are small, spiny creatures that are covered with sharp, needle-like spines all over their bodies. They are found in almost every ocean. Sea urchins are extremely slow-moving creatures, and they do not attack divers. Divers are injured when they bump into or step on these creatures and break off the spines below their skin. This type of injury usually can be avoided.

Jellyfish are slimy, gelatin-like creatures that swim by "pulsing," or contracting, their bodies. They feed on small fish and other tiny creatures

Fig. 5-18. Sea urchins. (From 1980 edition, Jeppesen Open Water Audiovisual Components).

Fig. 5-20. Stingrays are normally docile creatures.

that float in the water. There are many different species of jellyfish, and they also are found in most oceans (Fig. 5-19).

Like sea urchins, jellyfish are slow-moving animals and do not attack divers. These creatures cause injuries through a diver's accidental contact with their stinging cells, which are located in the jellyfish's tentacles. Almost any diving suit will help to protect you from the sting of a jellyfish. In addition, it frequently is possible to see these creatures from some distance and thus avoid them.

Stingrays are just one example of a fish with an external body spine that can cause injury (Fig. 5-20). Most fish with defensive spines such as these inject a toxin into the wound when they respond to a threat. Also like most of the other fish with

Fig. 5-19. Jellyfish are capable of inflicting painful stings. (From 1980 edition, Jeppesen Open Water Audiovisual Components).

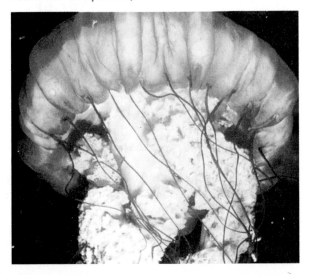

spines, however, stingrays normally are docile creatures that lie on the bottom much of the time. They will "attack" only when they are provoked, usually because a diver has stepped on them. The best way to avoid this type of injury is to always look carefully at the bottom before walking or putting down your hands.

Freshwater also contains hazards, such as alligators in the southeastern United States, snakes, and snapping turtles. It is rare, however, for a diver to have a negative encounter with these animals. In most cases, they will avoid divers if possible.

These are just a few examples of the more common forms of hazardous marine life, and from these descriptions, you should know that most marine life poses little threat to divers. You can avoid most of these creatures quite easily, and they should provide you little cause for concern when diving.

What About Sharks and Other Large Fish?

Most new divers are very concerned about encountering the larger, more aggressive animals in the ocean, such as sharks, barracudas, and killer whales. While these animals occasionally create problems for divers, even seeing such a large animal is extremely rare (Fig. 5-21).

Statistically, your chances of encountering a large shark that would injure you are much lower than having a traffic accident on your way to the dive site. Because shark attacks occur so infrequently, they are much more emotionally dramatic than traffic accidents. In fact, many divers pay substantial amounts of money to go on diving trips specifically to see sharks, because sighting one on an ordinary dive is so rare.

Fig. 5-21. Professional underwater photographers will "bait" sharks to draw them close enough to shoot photos. This is not an activity for the novice diver.

Fig. 5-22. Barracudas are extremely curious and have sharp teeth.

Fig. 5-23. Killer whales are highly intelligent creatures. (From 1980 edition, Jeppesen Open Water Audiovisual Components).

Barracudas are large, curious fish with a somewhat menacing appearance, and these fish occasionally do attack divers. While a barracuda can cause a painful bite, there has never been a recorded case of a barracuda injury killing a diver. Barracudas are curious creatures and will follow divers for long periods of time. They are attracted by bright, shiny objects such as jewelry. In most situations, however, a barracuda will back away or leave the area if you swim toward it (Fig. 5-22).

Killer whales are large marine mammals and among the most intelligent creatures in the ocean. While they readily attack seals and sea lions, they are not known to attack divers. Many of the larger marine parks have killer whales on display, and divers regularly enter the water with them without problems. If you do see a killer whale in the ocean, however, it would be wise to leave the area, because even though it is unlikely, a diver could be mistaken for a marine mammal (i.e., prey) (Fig. 5-23).

TEST THE DEPTH OF YOUR KNOWLEDGE

See how much you have learned about marine life by answering the following questions:

1 True or False: Injuries from aquatic life usually stem from offensive behavior by an animal.

2 List three rules for avoiding injury by aquatic animals while diving.

3 List two ways that an orientation to a new diving area can help you avoid injury from underwater animals.

BOAT DIVING PRESENTS SOME OF THE BEST DIVING OPPORTUNITIES

Many of the best diving sites in the world are in remote locations and can be reached effectively only by boat. To enjoy this experience, you must learn the proper procedures for diving from boats. Boat diving requires some unique skills whether you dive from small or large vessels (Fig. 5-24).

Commercial charter boats depart at a set time, so plan to arrive at least 30 minutes before your departure time. Sign in when you board the boat, and stow your equipment as directed by the crew. Tour the vessel for orientation, and ask questions to familiarize yourself with its layout.

Fig. 5-24. Boat diving offers excellent opportunities to travel to remote dive sites.

If you are prone to seasickness, suitable medication may be advisable before departure. No matter what type of medication you use, however, it must not produce adverse side effects, such as drowsiness or dizziness, that would endanger your safety underwater. Testing the medication on a day when you do not plan to dive or conduct any other critical activities, such as driving a car, is essential.

While nonprescription medicine is effective for most people, some divers can function on a boat only when they take prescription medications for motion sickness. Whether you take a prescription or a nonprescription drug, consult with a physician who understands diving regarding the suitability of any medication you plan to use while underwater.

If you wait until the boat is moving to take medication for motion sickness, it will be too late. Any medication that you use must be taken a minimum of 1 hour before the boat departs. If you forgot to take your medication before departure, get fresh air, watch the horizon, and stay near the center of the boat. Lying down with your eyes closed may bring relief as well. If you do get sick and must vomit, go to the back of the boat and do so over the side. Do *not* go into the boat's bathroom, or "head," to vomit.

Many divers who get mildly seasick find that they usually feel better when they are underwater. Most people develop their "sea legs" fairly quickly. You must not dive if you are actively vomiting or extremely nauseated, however, because of the danger of inhaling vomit while breathing through a regulator. This can cause you to choke, and the acid in the vomit can injure your lungs.

It is important to acquaint yourself with the procedures for diving from a charter boat. Go with an experienced diver or group to learn the correct techniques. You must know how to enter, exit, get your tank filled, keep your gear together, and all of the other procedures used for boat diving in your area.

Diving from a small boat requires that you learn yet another set of procedures. Because of space limitations created by the size of the vessel, you must learn how to manage your gear in as compact an area as possible. For example, you may need to don your dive suit on shore, board the boat, and ride out to the site.

Procedures for entering and exiting the water vary depending on the size and configuration of the vessel. On a small boat, care may be required to keep the boat balanced as you enter or exit; it often is helpful in such a case to don and remove your scuba equipment in the water rather than aboard a small boat. Some means to get back aboard the boat also must be available.

Additional safety procedures also are necessary for small boat diving. A written plan, called a "float plan," of your destination and expected time of return must be left with someone ashore so that help can be summoned if you do not return within a reasonable time. Good seamanship is important, and more than one person aboard the boat must be trained to operate it competently. Be sure to take a US Coast Guard Auxillary or US Power Squadron course in small boat handling if you plan regular dives from such a craft.

After the anchor is set, it must be checked at the beginning of the dive to make sure that it is secure and at the end to ensure that it is clear for lifting. In addition, someone who can operate the boat should remain aboard during all dives.

Whether you dive from a large or small boat, you must remain near the vessel and upcurrent from it during your dive. A trail line with a float behind the boat also is essential whenever the possibility of a current exists.

There is much to learn and practice to dive properly from boats. As with any new aspect of diving, training is essential, followed by initial participation with an experienced diver. This is particularly true for specialized diving activities, such as drift diving. Learning about diving from someone more experienced helps to greatly reduce embarrassment, frustration, and unpleasant incidents.

TEST THE DEPTH OF YOUR KNOWLEDGE

Boat diving presents special opportunities, but you also must know the special techniques that are involved. See how carefully you have read the preceding material by answering the following questions:

1 To dive safely from a boat, what are the first two actions that you should take?

2 List three steps that you can take to help prevent seasickness.

OTHER CONSIDERATIONS TO HELP ENSURE ENJOYMENT

Some divers take chances in unfavorable diving conditions simply because they have traveled a long way to reach a particular site. This is extremely dangerous and must be avoided. A good idea is to always have a contingency plan that includes an alternate dive site—or even a nondiving activity. There will always be another day to go diving, and the risks that bad conditions create are not worth any potential rewards.

Along with the factors already discussed, a few others also can influence your dive. Sunlight is a good example of an often overlooked "ingredient" in any dive, particularly if you plan an activity such as underwater photography. The sun's intensity varies in different parts of the world, and from a purely physical standpoint, its rays are much more intense in tropical than in temperate areas. Divers must take extra precautions to avoid sunburn, because it can easily ruin a diving vacation. It is easy to become sunburned between dives or while snorkeling on the surface. Keep in the shade as much as possible, cover up with light clothing, and use sunscreen.

Many times at popular dive sites, there also are submerged obstructions that cannot be seen from the surface. Cautious divers always watch for anything that can lead to an entanglement underwater. Such items might include fishing line, hooks and nets, wire and cable, trees, or brush. Just knowing that such hazards may be present and looking out for them can aid greatly in preventing difficulties. Plan in advance how you will cope with these possible nuisances.

Boat traffic is a consideration that deserves special attention. To caution boaters and let them know that divers are underwater in the immediate area, special flags, known as "divers down flags," are flown from all dive vessels. In most states, these signal boaters to remain at least 100 feet (30 m) clear of a circular area surrounding the flag, and they must be flown only when divers actually are in the water.

To be protected by the flag, you must surface close to it. Not all boaters know or respect the dive flag, so be prepared for those who trespass into the supposedly protected area. It always is a good idea to pause before surfacing and listen for the sound of approaching vessels. Any type of watercraft, whether it is a powerboat or a sailboat, poses a serious threat to divers in the water, so be sure to exercise caution.

The infinite variety of underwater environments makes scuba diving a lifelong recreational activity. Once you explore new dive sites, you will want to explore others. Every site is different.

Diving activities as well as the underwater environment vary from region to region and site to site. Learning more about the special qualities of the diving environment increases your enjoyment and safety underwater. One of NAUI's specialty courses is the Underwater Environment; ask your Instructor about it.

TEST THE DEPTH OF YOUR KNOWLEDGE

Check your knowledge by answering the following questions:

1 List three ways to avoid sunburn during a tropical diving vacation.

2 List three precautions for avoiding an entanglement in underwater obstructions.

3 List three practices that divers use to avoid being struck by a boat while in the water.

CHAPTER SIX

CONSERVATION

As a diver, you have a profound effect on the underwater world. If you are a careful and conscientious diver, you can help ensure that the reefs where you dive today will be there for your children tomorrow. A careless or uncaring diver, however, can destroy hundreds of years of coral growth in a single dive.

Most divers would not deliberately do anything to hurt the creatures in the underwater world. If you do not know or understand the delicate nature of certain fish or animals, however, it is easy to hurt them. This chapter discusses some of things that you can do to help protect the underwater world.

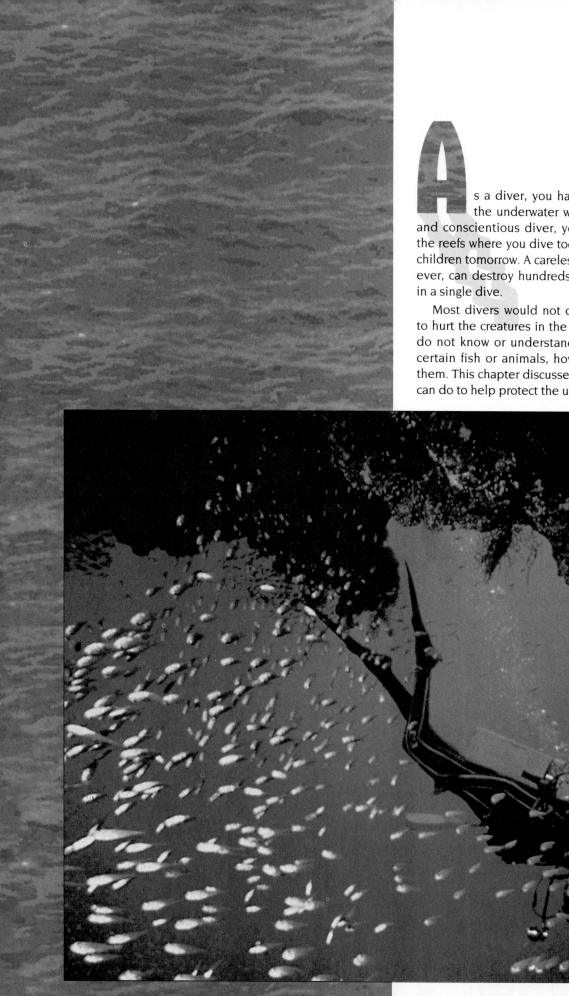

LEARNING OBJECTIVES

By the end of this chapter, you must be able to:

1. List two ways that coral reefs can be damaged, and explain how divers can prevent this.
2. State two reasons why fish must not be handled.
3. Explain why it is preferable to collect dead rather than live shells.
4. List two reasons why divers must obey Fish and Game laws.
5. State two reasons why divers must not remove artifacts from shipwrecks.
6. List two reasons why plastic trash must not be dumped at sea.

MOST SMALL MARINE CREATURES ARE QUITE DELICATE

When you first dive in a coral reef, it can be difficult to imagine that the hard coral structures actually are thousands of delicate animals called "polyps." If you are careless about your buoyancy control, it is very easy to break off pieces, and once broken, the coral will die (Figs. 6-1 through 6-3).

Fig. 6-1. Avoid touching coral or other marine creatures.

Fig. 6-2. Dangling gauges and other equipment can kill or injure marine life.

Fig. 6-3. Responsible divers keep their gauges and other gear fastened out of the way.

Silt or sand landing on top of corals also can be extremely destructive. The tiny polyps that live within the hard coral structure are filter feeders and eat the tiny microscopic plants and animals floating in the water. If your buoyancy control is poor and you stir up large clouds of sand or silt, any sand or silt that lands on the corals can choke the polyps and keep them from feeding properly (Fig. 6-4).

While this information applies to coral reefs, animals that live in colder waters also can be damaged through accidental contact. For example, a rare form of purple coral grows at only a few dive sites in California. This coral is extremely beautiful, but it also is delicate and slow growing. It is easy to break and must not be handled.

Fig. 6-4. Good buoyancy control helps to prevent silt and sand from destroying coral reefs.

Certain types of fish and other creatures are slow moving and easily caught, and this tempts some divers to handle and examine them, or to hold them while another diver photographs them. This also must be avoided for several reasons. Like coral, most fish have a protective layer of slime that covers their body. When this slime is removed by human handling, it makes the fish extremely vulnerable to harmful parasites. In addition, handling a fish may damage its internal organs, killing the fish.

SHELL COLLECTORS MUST ONLY COLLECT DEAD SHELLS

Many thousands of beautiful shells live under the sea, both in tropical and in colder waters. Divers can observe these creatures in their native habitats, so shell collecting is a natural activity that is enjoyed by many divers.

Every shell that lives underwater is formed by some type of marine animal. If you collect shells with living animals, you are removing that animal from the population and destroying its chances to reproduce. Conscientious divers only collect shells that are dead. Check that nothing is living inside the shell. It usually is possible to find a good specimen of the shell that you want without resorting to collecting a live animal.

UNDERWATER HUNTERS MUST OBEY ALL APPLICABLE LAWS

If you speak with any diver having over 20 years of experience, they probably will tell you about "the good old days," when game was plentiful and reefs were brimming with life. Sadly, with the impact of divers, commercial as well as sport fishermen, and pollution, many areas are not as healthy as they were in the past.

Divers must take responsibility for protecting the world's underwater resources for generations to come. If you hunt or take game underwater, you must be familiar with the fishing regulations in your area. You must know which species legally can be taken, the closed and open seasons, catch and size limits, legal methods of take, and any other pertinent information. Divers who violate fishing regulations give all divers a bad name, and they encourage governments to invoke further regulations that affect all diving.

Even if the fishing regulations in your area are generous, allowing substantial bag limits of a particular species on any given day, you must resist taking more game than you need for your personal consumption. Take only what you can use fresh and not "extra" game that must be frozen. Some bag limits exceed what a normal individual can use, but you certainly do not need to take everything that you can get.

Most marine species are overused, and fishing regulations in most areas have not kept pace with the increasing demands placed on them by all groups. Most areas have a serious competition between sport and commercial fishermen for the same species. The ultimate losers, however, are the animals being harvested.

BE CONSERVATION CONSCIOUS WITH SHIPWRECKS

Most divers enjoy the thrill of exploring a sunken ship, whether it is a fishing boat that sank a few years ago, a Japanese destroyer sunk during World War II, or a British mail steamship wrecked during the 1800s. Little can compete with the excitement of finding a new, unexplored wreck.

Many divers like to collect artifacts from shipwrecks to decorate their homes. Unfortunately, when you do this, you generally destroy part of the wreck to remove the item from it. When this happens, it takes away from the "atmosphere" of the wreck. If enough people remove artifacts, the wreck can be reduced to a pile of rubble on the sea floor (Fig. 6-5).

In many areas, removing artifacts from shipwrecks is illegal, and violators can lose all of their dive gear and face severe fines. Several years ago, a group of divers received stiff fines for illegally removing artifacts in a marine park. One of the divers was fined more than $70,000 and prohibited from diving in the park for 1 year.

Fig. 6-5. Shipwrecks are easily destroyed if every diver who visits them tries to take a piece of the wreck home with them.

NEVER DISCARD YOUR TRASH AT SEA OR AT THE BEACH

Many types of trash can be harmful to marine creatures, so it is essential that you do not dump trash overboard when diving from a boat or carelessly discard it at the beach. Synthetic materials such as plastics can survive for years in the marine environment and harm numerous animals.

If you buy soft drinks in six-packs with plastic rings holding the package together, these rings must be cut open. This helps avoid the possibility of a marine mammal or bird becoming entangled in them if the plastic is lost over the side. These rings must be recycled whenever possible (Fig. 6-6).

Plastic trash bags are especially harmful to sea turtles. These animals regularly feed on jellyfish as part of their diet, and a plastic bag floating in the ocean resembles a jellyfish closely enough that a sea turtle will eat it. Unfortunately, these bags cannot be digested by turtles and become trapped in their digestive systems, thus killing the turtles.

Trash must be disposed of properly on shore and recycled where possible. Looking at trash underwater is not a fun part of diving.

TAKE CARE OF THE UNDERWATER WORLD

You can do many things to help take care of the underwater world. The information presented here is merely a portion of what you must know to help

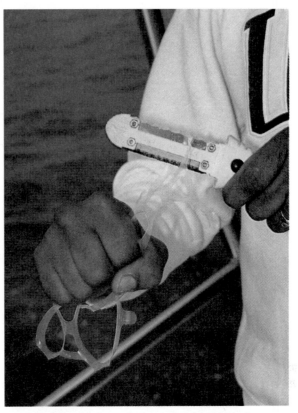

Fig. 6-6. Plastic six pack rings should always be cut open to avoid the danger that a marine mammal or bird can become entangled in them if they are lost over the side of the boat.

protect marine life. You will learn important conservation measures that pertain to your specific diving area from your instructor. As you travel to other areas, local conservation tips will be part of the orientation that you receive from local instructors and divemasters.

TEST THE DEPTH OF YOUR KNOWLEDGE

You can have a tremendous impact on marine life. Measure your understanding of how to help protect the animals and plants in our lakes, rivers, and seas by answering the following questions:

1 Name two different ways that coral is sensitive to damage.

2 If you are a shell collector, what is the best type of shell to collect?

3 Plastic trash bags are mistakenly eaten by what type of marine creature?

4 What should be done to a plastic six-pack ring to prevent it from harming marine life?

CHAPTER SEVEN

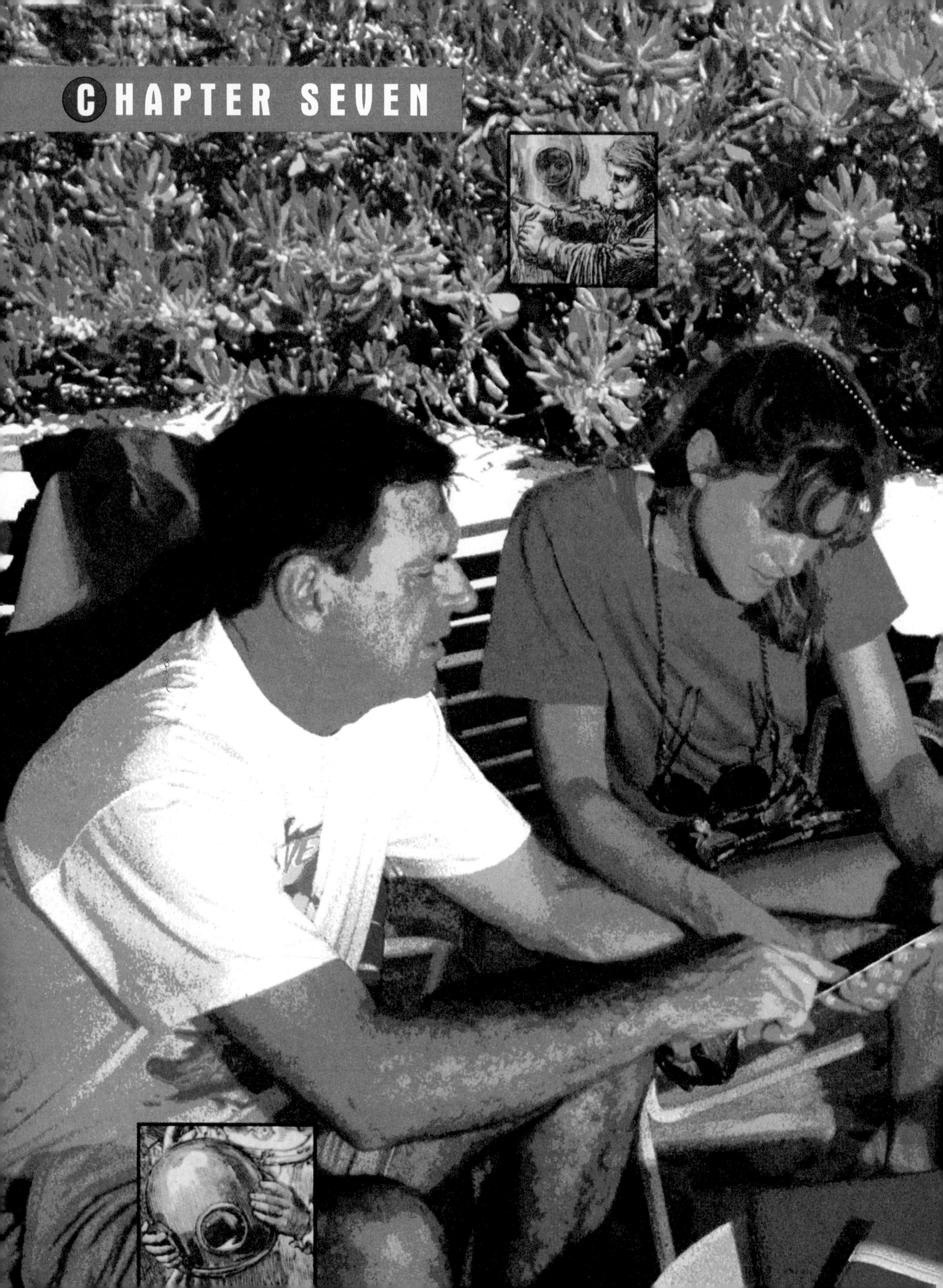

he length of time that you can stay underwater depends directly on the depth of your dive and both the number and depth of any dives you have made during the previous 24 hours. This chapter provides the basis for these limitations, introduces dive computers, and discusses how to use the NAUI Dive Tables. By using dive tables or a computer, you will learn how to plan your dives with the correct time and depth limits.

The various gases of the air that you breathe dissolve into your body tissues according to the concentration of each gas in the air. Air is primarily a mixture of nitrogen and oxygen. The oxygen you inhale is partly consumed by your body with each breath, and it is used by all of the body's tissues.

When planning dives to avoid the need for decompression, nitrogen is the gas about which you are concerned. A certain amount of it is dissolved in your blood and tissues at all times. When you breathe at sea level, nitrogen molecules in the air are exchanged for previously dissolved nitrogen molecules in our bodies. The exchange rate between "new" and "old" nitrogen is constant, and the amount of nitrogen in solution within your bloodstream remains constant as long as you remain at sea level.

LEARNING OBJECTIVES

By the end of this chapter, you must be able to:

1. Explain how the absorption of nitrogen in the body limits the time that a diver may spend underwater.
2. Define the term "ingassing."
3. Define the term "outgassing."
4. Define the term "decompression sickness."
5. List three factors that contribute to a diver's susceptibility to decompression sickness.
6. Define the term "dive time limit."
7. Define the term "residual nitrogen."
8. Explain the concept of a multilevel dive and how a dive computer is used in this situation.
9. Explain the difference between a decompression stop and a precautionary decompression stop.
10. Define the term "surface interval time."
11. Define the term "repetitive dive."
12. State the maximum ascent rate for use with the NAUI Dive Tables.
13. Explain why on any day you must always make your deepest dive first.
14. Explain why you must always use your exact depth or next greater depth when using the NAUI Dive Tables.
15. State the minimum time for a surface interval.
16. Explain why you must never dive right up to the no-decompression limit.
17. Explain the information provided by NAUI Dive Table 1 (the End-of-Dive Letter Group).
18. Explain the information provided by NAUI Dive Table 2 (the Surface Interval Table).
19. Explain the information provided by NAUI Dive Table 3 (the Repetitive Dive Timetable).
20. Compute the letter group for single dives to any depth.
21. Compute the letter groups and residual nitrogen times for a series of up to five repetitive dives.
22. Explain how to plan surface intervals to obtain the maximum allowable dive times for successive dives in a series.
23. Explain how limiting the depth increases your bottom time on a dive.
24. List the special equipment needed for a decompression stop.
25. Explain the procedure for an omitted decompression.
26. Explain the procedure for a dive that is cold and/or strenuous.
27. Explain the procedure for flying after diving.
28. State the maximum altitude at which you may dive without using special procedures for altitude diving.

INGASSING OF NITROGEN

As you descend underwater and subject your body to increasing pressure, the balance of nitrogen absorption and elimination in your body is upset. Under increased pressure, the air that you breathe is denser and the number of nitrogen molecules you inhale with each breath is increased. Consequently, more nitrogen molecules are in the air that you breathe than there are in your body. The result of this is an "ingassing" of nitrogen into the body until a state of equilibrium (i.e., balance) is achieved between the amount of nitrogen inhaled and that dissolved in your body.

This ingassing occurs rapidly at first but then proceeds more and more slowly until equilibrium is reached many hours later (assuming that the pressure remains constant). No negative effects are experienced by divers when nitrogen ingassing occurs at moderate depths.

The different tissues of the body (e.g., fat, muscle, bone, and so on) absorb nitrogen at different rates when you are underwater. Nitrogen is absorbed quickly by muscle but quite slowly by bone. There are different ingassing rates for each kind of tissue, and the cumulative effects of these various rates involve complex mathematics. Fortunately, these varying rates are considered by dive computers, tables, and calculators, thus eliminating the need for you to make complex calculations.

OUTGASSING OF NITROGEN

After spending time underwater, your body has absorbed a quantity of nitrogen from the air you breathe on scuba that is greater than that found in your body at sea level. When you ascend and reduce the pressure on your body, this balance between the nitrogen in your system and the amount being breathed once again becomes unequal. When this occurs, there is a greater concentration of nitrogen in your blood and tissues than in the air that you are breathing. The result is an "outgassing" of nitrogen from your body until a state of equilibrium is again reached.

The excess nitrogen passes from the body tissues into the blood, from the blood into the lungs, and is then exhaled. This process occurs rapidly during the first few minutes after ascent, but it takes many hours for your body's nitrogen level to return to normal.

If the reduction in pressure from the depth of your dive to the surface is not too rapid for the amount of nitrogen you have absorbed, this outgassing can occur without a problem. If the change in pressure is sudden, however, the nitrogen may come out of solution so rapidly that bubbles form in your body. These bubbles can damage tissues and cause a painful condition known as "decompression sickness," "DCS," or the "bends."

A bottle of soda can illustrate the principle of decompression sickness. Carbon dioxide is dissolved in the soda under pressure, and it remains in solution until the pressure is suddenly reduced by opening the sealed container. This rapid drop in pressure causes the carbon dioxide to form bubbles within the liquid, and the drink foams. If the pressure in the container were relieved very slowly, no bubbling would occur (Fig. 7-1).

To lessen the chance of bubbling within your body, you must control both the amount of nitrogen that is absorbed while diving and the rate at which it is eliminated from your body. This is the purpose of the information provided by dive time planners, which include dive computers, dive tables, and dive calculators.

Several factors can increase the chance of suffering decompression sickness in situations where it might not normally occur. These include old age, obesity, fatigue, injuries, dehydration, and the effects of drugs or alcohol. You must be fit for diving, and you must dive conservatively.

A specific reduction in pressure is required for bubbles to form. If you dive deeper than approximately 20 feet (6 m) and then ascend, the pressure change may be sufficient for bubbles to form if the amount of absorbed nitrogen is suffi-

Fig. 7-1. This bottle of soda was sealed under pressure. When the bottle is opened, bubbles form because of the sudden drop in pressure inside the bottle. The carbon dioxide that was dissolved in the liquid forms the bubbles.

ciently high. If you dive to depths of 20 feet (6 m) or less, decompression sickness is not likely to occur unless you further reduce the pressure by going to altitude and thus increasing your body's outgassing.

For depths of 21 feet (6.4 m) or greater, time limits called "dive time limits" or "no-decompression limits" have been established. The time spent at a given depth is not to exceed these limits, or decompression sickness could be experienced either during or after your ascent from the dive.

Time limits for various depths have been established by the US Navy based on field tests of military divers. Physiologic research and accident analysis, however, have resulted in the recommendation by many highly qualified experts that shorter time limits than those in the US Navy Tables be used for recreational diving. Reduced time limits have been incorporated into the NAUI Dive Tables and Dive Time Calculator to reduce the risk of decompression sickness during recreational diving. Most dive computers allow less bottom time than the US Navy tables for a single dive at a constant depth.

Divers who use time limits in excess of those currently recommended recognize and accept the

TABLE 7.1 DIVE LIMITS DEPTH	NAUI LIMIT	U.S.N. LIMIT
0-20' (0-6 m)	No limit	No limit
21-40' (6.4-12 m)	130 mins.	200 mins.
41-50' (12.5-15 m)	80 mins.	100 mins.
51-60' (15.5-18 m)	55 mins.	60 mins.
61-70' (18.6-21 m)	45 mins.	50 mins.
71-80' (21.6-24 m)	35 mins.	40 mins.
81-90' (25-27 m)	25 mins.	30 mins.
91-100' (27.6-30 m)	22 mins.	25 mins.

increased risk that is associated with these longer dive times. You must be aware, however, that all dives carry the risk of decompression sickness (Table 7-1).

Diving to depths of greater than 60 feet (18 m) is discouraged for entry-level (NAUI Scuba Diver Certified) divers. Intermediate divers are qualified for a maximum depth of 80 feet. NAUI Advanced Scuba Divers are qualified for a maximum depth of 100 feet (30 m). NAUI Deep-Diving Specialty divers are qualified for a depth of 130 feet (39 m), which is the maximum depth limit for recreational diving.

You need not memorize the dive time limits. Most are included in your NAUI Dive Tables and the NAUI Dive Time Calculator. These times are presented here merely to acquaint you with the typical time limits for diving. Note, however, that the allowable time decreases as the depth increases. If you are using a dive computer, it will probably have time limits that are different from these.

Nitrogen outgassing occurs at different rates for various body tissues, so the outgassing from different tissues becomes the controlling factor for time limits of various depths. You should be familiar with this concept, because if forms the basis for computations performed by dive computers and the time limits established by different dive tables and calculators. At this point in your diving education, however, it is not necessary to understand thoroughly the principles that apply to outgassing. You will learn more about the theories behind dive time calculations in the NAUI Master Scuba diver course.

RESIDUAL NITROGEN CHANGES IN A SERIES OF DIVES

To understand the use of dive computers, tables, and calculators, you must be familiar with the concept of "residual nitrogen." As you know, many hours are required to either fully absorb or fully eliminate nitrogen into or out of your system. Therefore, if you absorb nitrogen at depth,

ascend to the surface, and then descend again within 24 hours of your first descent, there will still be nitrogen remaining in your body from the first dive.

Nitrogen from the second dive will be added to the nitrogen remaining from the first dive. The net result is that after the second dive, you will have more nitrogen in your system than if you had not made a prior dive. You must always take account for any nitrogen remaining in your system from dives made within the previous 24 hours, and this "residual nitrogen" reduces your allowable dive time for any given depth on each subsequent dive (Fig. 7-2).

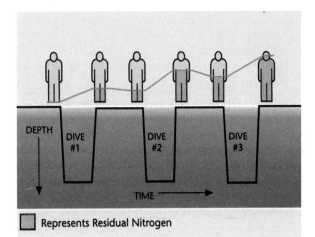

Represents Residual Nitrogen

Fig. 7-2. Residual nitrogen is the nitrogen that remains in your body from dives made within the past 24 hours. It accumulates from dive to dive.

TEST THE DEPTH OF YOUR KNOWLEDGE

You must have a good understanding of dive time limits to prevent decompression sickness when you dive. See how well you understand these basic concepts by answering the following questions:

1 Briefly describe "ingassing" as it relates to diving.

2 What causes bubbles to form during "outgassing?"

3 What is the deepest depth to which you can dive with no dive time limit?

4 According to Table 7-1, what is the no-decompression limit for a dive of 52 feet?

5 In one sentence, define the term "residual nitrogen."

DETERMINING TIME LIMITS FOR SPECIFIC DIVES

There are three ways to determine how long you may dive and then ascend within the dive time limits. The most popular and easiest is using a dive computer. This also is the most expensive way to monitor your bottom times, but it is used by more divers than any other method. You can also use information from the NAUI Dive Tables or Dive Time Calculator.

Each method of computing your dive time offers certain advantages, and each has certain limitations. You should be familiar with each method so that you can minimize the risk of decompression sickness by the proper use of any option.

As previously mentioned, different body tissues absorb and release nitrogen at different rates. Mathematical models have been developed to estimate ingassing and outgassing for various tissues, and dive computers with such mathematic programs continuously calculate the amount of nitrogen in different "theoretic tissues" for any given depth. This information is used to determine time/depth limits, which are displayed for the diver. Remember that both dive tables and computers are only models of what happens inside the human body. No method of calculating your dive time that is presently available accurately accounts for your individual age, body type, fitness, fatigue, drug or alcohol use, and so on.

Dive tables provide time limits in increments of 10 feet (3 m) of depth and assume that the entire dive is spent at the deepest depth. This is one disadvantage to the use of tables compared with a computer. A dive computer calculates both ingassing and outgassing in increments of 1 foot (0.3 m) and only for the depth at which you are diving, even as that depth varies during your dive.

With a dive computer, you are not penalized by being required to count all of your dive time as having occurred at the deepest depth. When you spend part of the dive in shallower water than the maximum depth, a dive computer considers this. The computer calculates only the amount of nitrogen that a mathematic model predicts is absorbed or eliminated at each depth. The result of a dive with progressively shallower depths (called a "multilevel dive") using a dive computer is longer dive time limits. Also, there is less time penalty for residual nitrogen than when the fixed-calculation dive tables are used.

Besides the expense of a dive computer, however, it is an electronic device that can fail without warning. Most dive computers are highly reliable, but this possibility must always be considered. When a dive computer fails, your only option is to surface promptly—after making a precautionary stop in the water at 15 feet (5 m) for 3 minutes—and refrain from diving for 24 hours. This must be done, because there is no way to recalculate your previous dive or dives using tables or starting with a "fresh" computer.

Dive tables are available that can compute multilevel dives. The manual planning and execution of multilevel dives are complex, however, and not recommended for recreational diving (Fig. 7-3). If you wish to receive time credit for reduced nitrogen absorption during multilevel dives, obtain and use a dive computer, but only after becoming proficient in using dive tables.

The overview of dive tables later in this chapter will prepare you to learn how to use the NAUI Dive Tables and Dive Time Calculator. A "letter group" designation is used in the tables as a simple means to express the amount of residual nitrogen within your body. The letters range in sequence from "A" to "L." A very small amount of nitrogen is represented by "A," and the amount increases as the letters progress toward "L." When you dive, the amount of nitrogen that you have theoretically absorbed during that dive is designated with a letter group from the tables. As you spend time on the surface between dives, you are assigned to lower letter groups as you outgas nitrogen.

When you dive again to a given depth, your letter group at that time is used to determine the time that represents the residual nitrogen in your system. This time is subtracted from the normal dive time limits, which results in a reduced time limit for your repetitive dive. The residual nitrogen time from your previous dive also is added to the

Fig. 7-3. Multilevel dives involve diving at progressively shallower depths during a dive.

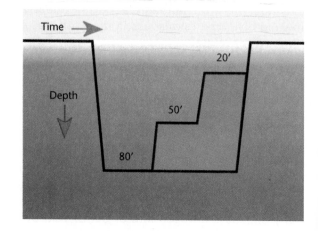

time that you actually spend diving, and that total time is used to determine a new letter group.

Manual dive calculators are based on the dive tables, but manual calculators eliminate the calculation tables that are required to determine letter groups when more than one dive is made. A dive calculator also reduces the errors that often are made in reading dive tables. It is easy to learn how to use a dive calculator, but this should be done only after you are familiar with the procedures for planning dive time limits using the dive tables. A dive calculator may not always be available, but dive tables usually are (Fig. 7-4).

It is important to know and understand that a variety of dive tables and computers exist and that the information they provide varies. Some are more conservative than others. Always use the type of table, calculator, or computer with which you are familiar. If your dive buddy is using a different type, you should agree to abide by the most conservative dive planning information.

DIVE TABLE TERMS AND RULES

To use the NAUI Dive Tables and Dive Time Calculator properly, you must be familiar with certain terms and rules that must be followed.

NAUI Dive Table Terms

The following terms apply to the NAUI Dive Tables. Be aware that if you use different tables or a dive computer, the terminology used may not be the same, or the same terms may have different meanings (Fig. 7-5). These terms include:

Fig. 7-4. As a diver, you must understand how to use dive tables.

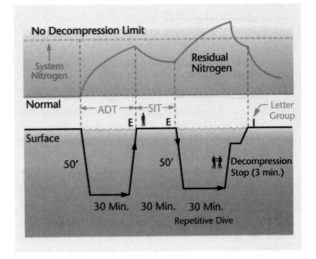

Fig. 7-5. This chart provides a visual representation of dive table terms.

1. *Dive Schedule*: The schedule of a dive is an abbreviated statement of the depth and duration of that dive, and it is expressed as depth/time (e.g., 70 ft/40 min = 70 ft for 40 min, or 21 m for 40 min).
2. *Maximum Dive Time*: The time that may be spent at a given depth without being required to stop during ascent to prevent decompression sickness. This sometimes also is referred to as the "Maximum Allowable Dive Time."
3. *Decompression Stop*: The time that a diver stops and waits at a specified depth during ascent from a dive to allow for nitrogen elimination before surfacing.
4. *Precautionary Decompression Stop*: Three minutes spent at a depth of 15 feet (5 m) as a safety precaution even though the Maximum Dive Time has not been exceeded. This procedure should be followed at the end of every dive. Time spent decompressing is considered to be "neutral" time and is not part of dive time.
5. *Required Decompression Stop*: The amount of time specified by dive tables, calculator, or computer to be spent at a specified depth whenever the Maximum Dive Time Limits are exceeded.
6. *Actual Dive Time*: The time from the moment you begin your descent until the time you return to the surface. (Time spent doing precautionary decompression may be excluded.)
7. *Letter Group Designation*: A letter symbol that designates the amount of excess nitrogen in your system. The closer to the beginning of the alphabet, the less residual nitrogen in your system.

8. _Surface Interval Time_: Time spent on the surface between dives. During this time, excess nitrogen is eliminated from your body and your letter group designation changes, moving closer to the beginning of the alphabet.

9. _Residual Nitrogen_: The nitrogen remaining in your system from a dive (or dives) made within the past 24 hours.

10. _Repetitive Dive_: Any dive that is made within 24 hours of a previous dive.

11. _Residual Nitrogen Time_: The amount of time on repetitive dives that you must consider as having already spent at a given depth for a planned dive. This time is based on residual nitrogen that remains in your system from a previous dive. The Residual Nitrogen Time is obtained from a table and is based on your letter group designation following your Surface Interval Time.

12. _Adjusted Maximum Dive Time_: For repetitive dives, the Adjusted Maximum Dive Time is the Maximum Dive Time for the depth of the dive minus the Residual Nitrogen Time for the dive.

13. _Total Nitrogen Time_: The sum of your Residual Nitrogen Time and your Actual Dive Time following a repetitive dive. This total is used to obtain a new letter group after the repetitive dive. The Total Nitrogen Time is expressed as RNT + ADT = TNT.

TEST THE DEPTH OF YOUR KNOWLEDGE

Use the NAUI Dive Tables to solve the following problems:

1 What is the Dive Schedule for a dive to 60 feet (18 m) for 30 minutes?

2 Identify the Surface Interval Times in the following series of dives: 50 ft/35 min (15 m/35 min), 1:25, 40 ft/35 min (12 m/35 min), 2:20, 30 ft/40 min (10 m/40 min).

3 If your Residual Nitrogen Time is 36 minutes and your Actual Dive Time 19 minutes, what is your Total Nitrogen Time for the dive?

4 How is the amount of nitrogen that remains in your system after a dive expressed in the dive tables?

5 Complete the following: According to the NAUI Dive Tables, you should decompress at a depth of _____ feet (_____ m) for _____ minutes following dives in which Maximum Dive Times are reached.

NAUI Dive Table Rules

The following rules apply to the NAUI Dive Tables. If you use different tables or a dive computer, a different set of rules will apply. You must understand these rules completely as they apply to any new set of dive tables or dive computer that you might use to calculate your dive times.

1. During any dive, ascend no faster than 30 feet (9 m) per minute. This is only 1 foot (0.3 m) every 2 seconds, and this slow pace is the maximum rate of ascent. A timing device and depth gauge (or a dive computer) is required to measure your rate of ascent.

2. Use the exact or next greater number when referring to the dive tables. If a number in a table is exceeded, use the next greater number. For example, for depths of between 40 and 130 feet (12 to 39 m), numbers in the dive tables increase in 10-foot increments. Consequently, a dive to 41 feet (12.3 m) is considered to be a 50-foot (15-m) dive and a dive to 61 feet (18.3 m) is counted to be a 70-foot (21-m) dive.

3. When determining the dive schedule for a dive, use the deepest depth that you attain during the dive. If part of the dive was spent at 60 feet (18 m) while the majority was at 40 feet (12 m), the dive must be considered to have been spent entirely at 60 feet (18 m).

4. When making a series of dives, always make your deepest dive first. Plan repetitive dives to shallower depths than your previous dives. This allows you to outgas nitrogen on progressively shallower dives instead of carrying a large amount of residual nitrogen on deeper repetitive dives.

5. Consider all dives made at depths shallower than 40 feet (12 m) as 40-foot (12-m) dives when planning repetitive dives.

6. A Surface Interval Time of at least 10 minutes is required before use of the Surface Interval Timetable; however, NAUI recommends a minimum of 1 hour between dives.

7. If a dive is particularly cold or strenuous, use the next greater actual dive time.

8. Avoid dives that take you right up to the no-decompression limit for any given depth/time combination. If you accidentally overstay your bottom time or exceed your ascent rate on such a dive, you could be in a decompression situation or suffer decompression sickness. Always allow yourself enough time to make a slow, comfortable ascent with plenty of air (Fig. 7-6).

Fig. 7-6. A general rule with dive tables is to use the deepest depth reached during your dive.

TEST THE DEPTH OF YOUR KNOWLEDGE

Apply the rules for using NAUI Dive Tables to the following questions:

1 Complete the following: When using the NAUI Dive Tables, ascend from all dives at a maximum rate of _____ feet per minute, and allow a minimum of _____ minutes between dives.

2 Arrange the following dives into the preferred sequence: 30 ft/40 min (10 m/40 min), 60 ft/30 min (18 m/30 min), 50 ft/20 min (15 m/20 min).

3 Complete the following: A dive of up to 25 feet (7.6 m) for 40 minutes should be considered as a dive schedule of _____ when planning a repetitive dive.

FINDING YOUR TIME LIMITS FOR SINGLE AND REPETITIVE DIVES

Now that you know the ideas behind the tables, the terms used for them, and the rules for their use, you are ready to learn how to refer to the NAUI Dive Tables. This section covers the general organization of these tables and how they are used to determine Dive Time Limits for both single and repetitive dives (Fig. 7-7).

General Organization of the Dive Tables

The NAUI Dive Tables are based on the US Navy Decompression Tables, and they have been designed by NAUI specifically for recreational diving. These tables are configured so that each one flows into the next. You begin with Table 1, which is called the "End-of-Dive Letter Group" table. Not

only does this table give you a letter group designation at the end of a dive, it also contains the Maximum Dive Time information for depths between 40 and 130 feet (12 to 39 m). Look at Table 1, and note that the Maximum Dive Times are circled for each depth (Fig. 7-8).

Table 1 is entered horizontally from the left. The numbers in the table represent bottom time in minutes. Find the row for the appropriate depth, and move to the right along that line until you find

Fig. 7-7. The NAUI Dive Tables are simple to use.

Fig. 7-8. NAUI Dive Table 1: the "End-of-Dive Letter Group" Table.

TABLE 1 - END-OF-DIVE LETTER GROUP

START DEPTH M	FEET												
12	40 ▶	5	15	25	30	40	50	70	80	100	110	⦶130	150 / 5
15	50 ▶		10	15	25	30	40	50	60	70	⦶80		100 / 5
18	60 ▶		10	15	20	25	30	40	50	⦶55	60 / 5		80 / 7
21	70 ▶		5	10	15	20	30	35	40	⦶45	50 / 5	60 / 8	70 / 14
24	80 ▶		5	10	15	20	25	30	⦶35	40 / 5		50 / 10	60 / 17
27	90 ▶		5	10	12	15	20	⦶25	30 / 5		40 / 7		50 / 18
30	100 ▶		5	7	10	15	20	⦶22	25 / 5			40 / 15	
33	110 ▶			5	10	13	⦶15	20 / 5			30 / 7		
36	120 ▶			5	10	⦶12	15 / 5			25 / 6	30 / 14		
39	130 ▶			5	⦶8	10 / 5					25 / 10		

Legend: ⦿ MAXIMUM DIVE TIME (MDT)   ▮ DIVE TIME REQUIRING DECOMPRESSION / NO. MINUTES REQUIRED AT 15' STOP (5M)

a bottom time that meets or exceeds your dive time. Now look down that column. At the bottom of the column, below the table, find the letter group designation indicating the amount of nitrogen that remains in your system following a dive. For example, someone diving to 50 feet (15 m) for 30 minutes would have a letter group designation of "E."

When using the tables, you should use a straight-edged object, such as a ruler or pad of paper, to line up the numbers and work your way from table to table. Align the straight edge along the far side of the column or the bottom of the row that you need to follow. If you try using a finger to trace your path through the tables, it is easy to slide into another row, especially if you are on a rocking boat.

The longer you remain out of the water, the more excess nitrogen you eliminate. Crediting you with this nitrogen loss is the purpose of Table 2, the "Surface Interval Time Table." This table consists of blocks containing two numbers, which represent the minimum and maximum times for a given time interval. The lower number in each box is the minimum surface interval time for a particular group; the higher number is the maximum time. These times are expressed as hours and minutes (Fig. 7-9).

The Surface Interval Time table is entered vertically coming down the column from Table 1, and it is followed downward until you find a range of times in which the length of your surface interval falls. Then, follow that row horizontally to the left,

exit the table, and receive a new letter group designation. For example, if you enter the table with an "E" designation and have a surface interval of 3 hours, you will exit the table on the third horizontal line and receive a new letter group of "C." Note that the maximum time in this table is 24 hours. All excess nitrogen is considered to be eliminated after 24 hours, so a dive after that time is not a repetitive dive.

Table 3 is the "Repetitive Dive Timetable" (Fig. 7-10). It provides your Residual Nitrogen Time (RNT) based on your current letter group and planned depth for the next dive. It also provides Maximum Dive Times that are reduced by the amount of your RNT. Your Actual Dive Time (ADT) must not exceed the Adjusted Maximum Dive Time (AMDT). In addition, your RNT must be added to your ADT to obtain your Total Nitrogen Time (TNT). This formula is illustrated in the upper left corner of your NAUI Dive Tables.

To use Table 3, enter it horizontally from the right on the row that represents your letter group designation after your Surface Interval Time. Now, follow the table to the left until you intersect the column that corresponds with the depth of your planned repetitive dive. Be sure to align a straight edge beneath the row to ensure that you stay in the correct row.

Depths are listed across the top of Table 3. At the coordinates of the depth and the letter group, you will find two numbers. The top number repre-

Fig. 7-9. NAUI Dive Table 3: the "Repetitive Dive Timetable."

Fig. 7-10. NAUI Dive Table 2: the "Surface Interval Time" Table.

M. / FT.	12 / 40	15 / 50	18 / 60	21 / 70	24 / 80	27 / 90	30 / 100	33 / 110	36 / 120	39 / 130	NEW GROUP
	7 / 123	6 / 74	5 / 50	4 / 41	4 / 31	3 / 22	3 / 19	3 / 12	3 / 9	3 / 5	◄ A
	17 / 113	13 / 67	11 / 44	9 / 36	8 / 27	7 / 18	7 / 15	6 / 9	6 / 6	6	◄ B
	25 / 105	21 / 59	17 / 38	15 / 30	13 / 22	11 / 14	10 / 12	10 / 5	9	8	◄ C
	37 / 93	29 / 51	24 / 31	20 / 25	18 / 17	16 / 9	14 / 8	13	12	11	◄ D
	49 / 81	38 / 42	30 / 25	26 / 19	23 / 12	20 / 5	18 / 4	16	15	13	◄ E
	61 / 69	47 / 33	36 / 19	31 / 14	28 / 7	24	22	20	18	16	◄ F
	73 / 57	56 / 24	44 / 11	37 / 8	32	29	26	24	21	19	◄ G
	87 / 43	66 / 14	52	43	38	33	30	27	25	22	◄ H
	101 / 29	76 / 4	61	50	43	38	34	31	28	25	◄ I
	116 / 14	87	70	57	48	43	38				◄ J
	138	99	79	64	54	47	AVOID REPETITIVE DIVES OVER 100 FEET				◄ K
	161	111	88	72	61	53					◄ L

TABLE 3 - REPETITIVE DIVE TIMETABLE

A	B	C	D	E	F	G	H	I	J	K	L
24:00 / 0:10	24:00 / 3:21	24:00 / 4:50	24:00 / 5:49	24:00 / 6:35	24:00 / 7:06	24:00 / 7:36	24:00 / 8:00	24:00 / 8:22	24:00 / 8:51	24:00 / 8:59	24:00 / 9:13
	3:20 / 0:10	4:49 / 1:40	5:48 / 2:39	6:34 / 3:58	7:05 / 4:26	7:35 / 4:50	7:59 / 5:13	8:21 / 5:41	8:50 / 5:49	8:58 / 6:03	9:12 / 6:03
		1:39 / 0:10	2:38 / 1:10	3:24 / 1:58	3:57 / 2:29	4:25 / 2:59	4:49 / 3:21	5:12 / 3:44	5:40 / 4:03	5:48 / 4:20	6:02 / 4:36
			1:09 / 0:10	1:57 / 0:55	2:28 / 1:30	2:58 / 2:00	3:20 / 2:24	3:43 / 2:45	4:02 / 3:05	4:19 / 3:22	4:35 / 3:37
				0:54 / 0:10	1:29 / 0:46	1:59 / 1:16	2:23 / 1:42	2:44 / 2:03	3:04 / 2:21	3:21 / 2:39	3:36 / 2:54
					0:45 / 0:10	1:15 / 0:41	1:41 / 1:07	2:02 / 1:30	2:20 / 1:48	2:38 / 2:04	2:53 / 2:20
						0:40 / 0:10	1:06 / 0:37	1:29 / 1:00	1:47 / 1:20	2:03 / 1:36	2:19 / 1:50
							0:36 / 0:10	0:59 / 0:34	1:19 / 0:55	1:35 / 1:12	1:49 / 1:26
								0:33 / 0:10	0:54 / 0:32	1:11 / 0:50	1:25 / 1:05
									0:31 / 0:10	0:49 / 0:29	1:04 / 0:46
										0:28 / 0:10	0:45 / 0:27
											0:26 / 0:10

TABLE 2 - SURFACE INTERVAL TIME (SIT) TABLE

sents the RNT for that depth; the bottom represents the AMDT for that depth. Comparing the totals of the AMDT with the RNTs for any depth, you will find that all total the Maximum Dive Time Limit for that depth as given in Table 1. The AMDT is found by subtracting the RNT from the Maximum Dive Time for a given depth; Table 3 has already done this work for you. Remember, your ADT must not exceed your AMDT during a repetitive dive.

An example of using Table 3 is a "C" letter group diver who plans a dive to 50 feet (15 m). At the coordinates of "C" and 50 feet, you find the number 21 over the number 59. This means that the diver has 21 minutes of RNT and the ADT must not exceed 59 minutes. This diver proceeds with the dive, keeping the ADT within the 59 minute AMDT. Then, the diver adds the ADT to the 21 minutes of RNT and uses the dive schedule of 50 ft/TNT (15 m/TNT) to reenter Table 1 and obtain an End-of-Dive letter group. Note how the cycle has been completed with the three tables. For each successive repetitive dive, you continue to cycle through the NAUI Dive Tables in this fashion. Even if you use a dive computer, record the depth and time of each dive as well as your surface interval between dives.

EXERCISES

Use the NAUI Dive Tables to find the Dive Time Limits for both single and repetitive dives:

1. What is the Maximum Dive Time for a dive to 60 feet (18 m) for your first dive of the day? *55 Minutes*
ANSWER: *Because you have no residual nitrogen, you are allowed the Maximum Dive Time for the depth: 55 minutes.*

2. What is your letter group designation following a dive to 55 feet (16.7 m) for 39 minutes? *G*
ANSWER: *Remember, when you exceed the numbers in the tables, you use the next greater number. There is no 55-foot (16.7-m) depth in Table 1; therefore, you use the 60-foot (18-m) schedule. The first time that does not exceed 39 minutes in the 60-foot (18-m) row in Table 1 is 40. Thus, the dive schedule for a 55 ft/39 min (16.7 m/39 min) dive is actually 60 ft/40 min (18 m/40 min) in the tables. Following the 40-minute column to the bottom of the table, you find that your letter group designation following this dive is "G."*

3. If your initial letter group is "G," what is your new letter group after a surface interval of 1 hour? *F*
ANSWER: *The correct answer is "F." To obtain this, enter Table 2 vertically at the group "G" column, and follow it down until you find the time range (0:41 to 1:15) corresponding with your surface interval. At this point, follow that row to the left and obtain your new letter group.*

4. With an "F" letter group, what is the AMDT for a dive to 50 feet (15 m)? *33 Minutes*
ANSWER: *Table 3 is the Repetitive Dive Timetable, providing the AMDT information. As an "F" diver going down to 50 feet (15 m), the AMDT is 33 minutes. This is found as the lower number at the coordinates of "F" and 50 feet (15 m) in Table 3. Remember, your ADT must not exceed this time.*

5. What is the RNT of a diver making a 50-foot (15-m) dive with an "F" letter group designation? *47*
ANSWER: *Table 3 also provides the RNT times. At the 50-foot (15-m) and "F" coordinates, the top number (i.e., 47) is the RNT.*

6. Given an ADT of 32 minutes on a dive to 50 feet (15 m) with a letter group of "F," what is the TNT of the dive? *RNT= 47 ADT 32 TNT 79*
ANSWER: *The TNT is the sum of the ADT and the RNT, so the TNT in this instance is the 32 minutes of ADT plus 47 minutes of RNT, resulting in a TNT of 79 minutes.*

7. What is the End-of-Dive letter group for the dive in question six? *J*
ANSWER: *The dive schedule is 50 ft/79 min (15 m/79 min). This information is taken from Table 1 to obtain the End-of-Dive letter group. For a depth of 50 feet (15 m), the first time that is not exceeded by your TNT is 80 minutes. The letter group for a total time of 80 minutes is "J."*

Looking Back

Having just used the NAUI Dive Tables, you are acquainted with their arrangement. You should now be able to determine the Maximum Dive Time for both single and repetitive dives, and you also should be able to determine your correct letter group designation following a dive. Next, you will learn how to use the tables so that your combined dive plans do not exceed the Dive Time Limits.

DIVE TABLE PLANNING

When making repetitive dives, you will be unable at times to dive to the depth and/or the duration that you would like. This is because of the AMDTs imposed on you by residual nitrogen. This section shows you three ways to plan dives within the Dive Time Limits.

Limiting Your Actual Dive Time

The first way to keep within the Maximum Dive Time is easy: limit your ADT. Your first dive of the day must not exceed the Maximum Dive Time for the depth of that dive, and your repetitive dives must not exceed the AMDT for your planned depth. As you will see, this can be rather restrictive.

Suppose you wish to make three 25-minute dives to a depth of 60 feet (18 m). Assume a surface interval time of 1 hour between dives and an ADT of 25 minutes for the first dive. Following the first dive, your letter group designation is "E."

After a surface interval of 1 hour, your letter group changes to "D." According to Table 3, your AMDT for the second dive is 31 minutes. If you repeat the ADT of your first dive (i.e., 25 min), your TNT for the second dive is your ADT (i.e., 25 min) plus your RNT of 24 minutes, for a total of 49 minutes. Your End-of-Dive letter group following this second dive is "H."

One hour after surfacing from the second dive, your letter group is "G." A "G" diver who plans a dive to 60 feet (18 m) is limited, according to Table 3, to a maximum ADT of 11 minutes. You can see that making three back-to-back dives to depths of 60 feet or more can be quite limiting if you want to spend the maximum amount of time in the water. Now, use this three-dive example to find other ways of allowing you to spend more time underwater.

Planning Your Surface Intervals

A good way to control your residual nitrogen and your AMDT for a repetitive dive, is with the surface interval. The longer that you remain on the surface between dives, the less nitrogen remains in your system and the longer you can stay underwater on the next dive. You must be able to determine exactly how long a surface interval is required to carry out a planned dive without nearing the no-decompression limits.

Use the third dive from the previous example of three dives in series. After the second dive, your letter group designation was "H." To plan the third dive, start with Table 3 and the bottom time that you want for the planned depth, then work backwards. For a desired ADT of 25 minutes at 60 feet (18 m), find the first group in the 60-foot (18-m) column with an AMDT of 25 minutes or longer. The group with this is "E," which has an AMDT of 25 minutes. You now have one half of this problem solved.

At this point, you must determine how long it will take for you to change from letter group "H" to "E," and Table 2 quickly provides this information. Look at the coordinates of letter group "E" horizontally (i.e., the ending group) and of "H" vertically (i.e., the starting group), and find the minimum time that is required (i.e., 1:42). By waiting just 42 minutes longer between your second and third dives, you can give the third dive a duration of 25 minutes. Therefore, planning your surface interval is the second way to plan your dives (Fig. 7-11).

Limiting Your Depth

Your third option in dive planning is increasing your bottom time by limiting your depth. If you were not able to extend your surface interval

Fig. 7-11. In this dive profile, the dive time of the third dive is quite limited because of residual nitrogen from the previous dives. Note: Precautionary decompression time (3 minutes @ 15' or 4.6m) is NOT included in Actual Dive Time (ADT)

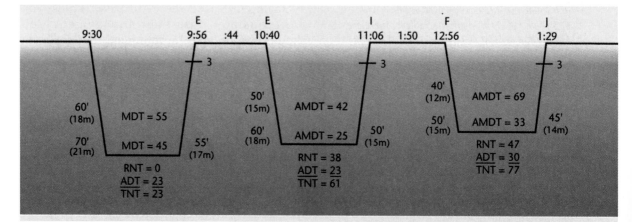

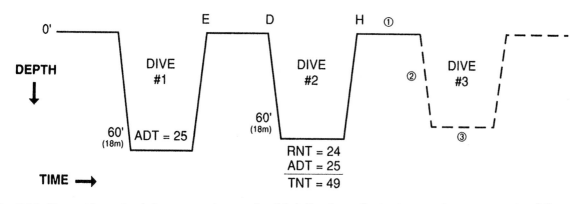

Fig. 7-12. To avoid required decompression on the third dive from the text example, you can extend the surface interval (#1), limit the depth (#2), or limit the Actual Dive Time (#3).

between the second and third dives in the previous example and did not want to make a short-duration dive, you could dive to a shallower depth and spend more time there.

Again, assuming that you have a letter group designation of "G" following a 1-hour surface interval after your second 25-minute dive to 60 feet (18 m), refer to Table 3. Look for the maximum depth that will permit a 25-minute dive with a letter group of "G." Enter Table 3 on the "G" line, and follow it to the left until you find an AMDT of 25 minutes or longer. In this instance, the time is 57 minutes and the depth 40 feet (12 m). Therefore, by diving 20 feet (6 m) shallower on your third dive, you can make a 25-minute dive. This is making good use of the dive tables (Fig. 7-12).

TEST THE DEPTH OF YOUR KNOWLEDGE

You now know three ways of using the dive tables to plan your dives within the Dive Time limits. Your instructor will provide more information on planning procedures, but for now, see if you can solve the following problems:

1 After a dive to 65 feet (19.8 m) for 28 minutes and a surface interval of 2 hours, what is the maximum time that you can dive on a second dive to a depth of 60 feet (18 m)?

2 After a dive to 70 feet (21 m) for 30 minutes, what is the minimum surface interval that will allow you to repeat that dive without exceeding the AMDT?

3 With a letter group designation of "E" following a series of dives, what is the maximum depth to which you can dive for at least 20 minutes?

USING THE NAUI DIVE TIME CALCULATOR

The NAUI Dive Tables are the basis for the Dive Time Calculator, which eliminates the calculations that are required with the tables. Once you are familiar with the NAUI Dive Tables, learning how to use the NAUI Dive Time Calculator is easy (Fig. 7-13).

General Organization

On the Dive Time Calculator, NAUI Dive Tables 1 and 3 are combined on the baseplate. Letter group designations appear around the circumference, and ADTs in minutes appear in the window. End-of-Dive letter groups appear to the right of the ADT numbers in the disc window. Dive Table 2 (i.e., the Surface Interval Timetable) is printed on the disc.

Dive Planning Using the Calculator

For your first dive of the day, find the "No Group" section on the baseplate. Align the depth

Fig. 7-13. The NAUI Dive Time Calculator is easier to use than dive tables.

arrow on the edge of the disc with the planned depth of your dive. The Maximum Dive Time for that dive appears as the largest number in the window. For example, a "No Group" diver who plans a dive to 60 feet (18 m) would have a Maximum Dive Time of 55 minutes.

Assuming that your first dive of the day was to 60 feet (18 m) and your ADT was 23 minutes, your next step would be determining your letter group designation following that dive. Align the disc as described previously, reading bottom times from the center of the disc outward, and find the first time that you do not exceed. For our schedule of 60 ft/23 min (18 m/23 min), the first time not exceeded on the first dive is 25 minutes. The End-of-Dive letter group appears to the right of the window next to 25: "E."

Changes in the letter group with surface intervals are determined the same way in the NAUI Dive Tables. After a surface interval of 1 hour, an "E" diver would have a letter group designation of "D."

For planning repetitive dives, find your new letter group on the circumference of the baseplate and align the depth arrow on the disc with the planned depth of your repetitive dive. If, as a "D" diver, you wish to return to 60 feet (18 m), you will find in the window that your ADT should not exceed 31 minutes. If you then made a second dive of 23 minutes as a "D" diver, your End-of-Dive letter group would be found beside the first ADT number in the window that is not exceeded. In this instance, that ADT would be 26 minutes, and your End-of-Dive group would be "H."

Note that the calculator design eliminates the AMDT. It also eliminates the need for adding the RNT to the ADT to obtain the TNT when determining your End-of-Dive letter group. All of this is made unnecessary by the design of the calculator; however, the answers that you obtain with it are exactly as those calculated from the dive schedules using the NAUI Dive Tables.

Dive Planning with the Calculator

The same three methods of dive planning that are used with dive tables also can be used with the Dive Time Calculator. You may limit your bottom time to the maximum number indicated for a given depth and group, extend your surface interval to obtain a lesser group letter, or dive to a shallower depth.

For example, assume that a group "F" diver wishes to dive for at least 25 minutes. Looking in the window below group "F" on the calculator, you find that by moving the window back and forth, you may dive for up to 19 minutes at 60 feet (18 m) and up to 33 minutes at 50 feet

(15 m). Thus, to avoid exceeding the Maximum Dive Time, the group "F" diver must dive no deeper than 50 feet (15 m) and remain no longer than 25 minutes.

If you wanted to dive to 60 feet (18 m) for 25 minutes but could not because you were a group "F" diver, you would need to determine the letter designation allowing you to make the dive and the minimum surface interval required to achieve that letter group. To determine the group allowing a 60 ft/25 min (18 m/25 min) dive schedule, align the depth arrow with 60 feet (18 m) in group "F." Then, work back one group at a time, realigning the depth arrow with 60 feet (18 m) for each group, until you find a Maximum Dive Time of 25 minutes or longer. In this instance, the first letter group allowing a Maximum Dive Time of 25 minutes is "E."

In some instances, the words "DO NOT DIVE" appear in the calculator window. This means that you have too much residual nitrogen to permit a dive at the depth selected for a particular letter group. You will need to extend your surface interval to dive at that depth, or you will need to select a shallower depth where diving is allowed.

As you can see, using the Dive Time Calculator is easier than using dive tables.

EXERCISES

Using the NAUI Dive Time Calculator, find the Dive Time Limits for both single and repetitive dives and plan repetitive dives in the following answer:

1 What is the Maximum Dive Time for a dive to 60 feet (18 m) for your first dive of the day?

ANSWER: *You have no letter group designation for your first dive. Align the depth arrow of the disc with 60 feet (18 m) under the "No Group" section of the baseplate. The Maximum Dive Time shown is 55 minutes.*

2 What is your letter group designation following a first dive to 55 feet (16.7 m) for 39 minutes?

ANSWER: *As with dive tables, use the next larger number whenever a number is exceeded. There are no 55-foot (16.7-m) depths on the Calculator, so you must use the 60-foot schedule. The first number under 60 feet (18 m) that is greater than 39 in the "No Group" section is 40 minutes. The dive schedule then becomes 60 ft/ 40 min (18 m/40 min), and the letter group is found to the right of the window beside 40. That letter group is "G."*

3 One hour after your first dive, your letter group is "F." With this new group designation, what is the Maximum Dive Time for a dive to 50 feet (15 m)?

ANSWER: *Align the depth arrow on the disc with 50 feet (15 m) in the group "F" section of the baseplate. The Maximum Dive Time shown in the window is 33 minutes.*

4 If a group "F" diver makes a 32-minute dive to a depth of 50 feet (15 m), what is that diver's End-of-Dive letter group designation?

ANSWER: *Align the depth arrow on the disc with 50 feet (15 m) in the Group "F" section of the base plate. Find the first time not exceeded by a 32 minute dive. In this case, that number is 33 minutes. Find the End-of-Dive group letter, which is "J," on the disc next to 33 in the window.*

5 As a group "H" diver, what is the minimum surface interval what will allow diving to a depth of 60 feet (18 m) for 25 minutes without exceeding the Dive Time Limits?

ANSWER: *A group "H" diver may not dive to 60 feet (18 m), as is stated in the window of the calculator, because a diver with this letter designation has a large amount of residual nitrogen. Moving the depth arrow to 60 feet (18 m) at lower letter groups on the baseplate shows that the time limits for groups G, F, and E are 11, 19, and 25 minutes, respectively. This means that you will need to attain letter group "E""before you can dive for at least 25 minutes without exceeding the Maximum Dive Time. Because you are in group "H" and know that you must attain group "E," determining the surface interval is merely a matter of referring to the Surface Interval Timetable. How long does it take to move from the "H" to "E" group? At the coordinates "H" and "E" on the Surface Interval Timetable, the minimum time is 1:42.*

Referring to the dive table examples that you did previously, you will find that you have just solved the same problems using the Dive Time Calculator as you did using the dive tables. The solutions are identical!

HOW TO USE THE DIVE PLANNING WORKSHEET

You must systematically keep track of depth, bottom time, surface intervals, letter group designations, and other information when working with the Dive Tables or Dive Calculator. On the back of your NAUI Dive Tables is a Dive Planning and Recording Worksheet. This section explains how to use this worksheet, which is essential for preventing of errors and any resulting problems. This method of calculating your dive times is known as the "profile method."

The NAUI Worksheet on your dive tables can be written on with a standard pencil and erased or scoured clean without damaging the tables. It is intended to be used frequently, so take a pencil when you go diving and write the dive information directly onto your NAUI Worksheet. Your NAUI Dive Tables also are waterproof, so you can record information on them in the water or refer to planning information that you previously entered.

The concept of the worksheet is quite simple (Fig. 7-14). Time is plotted horizontally and to the right and depth vertically and downward. Four simple rules make this worksheet easy to use, and these rules are:

1. Enter the appropriate time (T) on the top corner of each dive profile. Include the appropriate letter group (LG) designation in the blanks above the times.
2. Enter the maximum planned depth (PD) for each dive profile (on the left side) before a dive and the actual depth (AD) after the dive (on the right side).
3. Enter either the Maximum Dive Time (MDT) or Adjusted Maximum Dive Time (AMDT) for each dive profile. The reason for MDT and AMDT being listed twice at the bottom of each profile is that the time limit for both the intended maximum depth as well as the next greater depth must be included for contingency planning.
4. Enter the formula for the Total Nitrogen Time (RNT + ADT = TNT) beneath each repetitive dive profile.

Fig. 7-14. The concept of the NAUI Dive Planning Worksheet is simple.

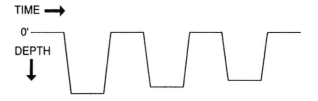

The first step is planning your first dive by entering the planned depth and Maximum Dive Time on the first dive profile. Enter the Maximum Dive Times along the bottom line of the profile, as shown in the example. Then, record the time at the beginning of your descent on the upper left corner of the profile. When you return to the surface, the elapsed time, along with your end-of-dive letter group, is recorded in the upper right corner. The deepest depth of your dive should be recorded on the right side of the dive profile (Fig. 7-15).

When planning a repetitive dive, the procedure is nearly the same. The difference is that you use the AMDTs at the bottom of the repetitive profile and, unless using the Dive Calculator, add your RNT to your ADT at the bottom of the profile to obtain the TNT.

When precautionary decompression is carried out, the time spent decompressing is shown next to a short horizontal line that is drawn through the ascent side of the dive profile. (This appears as the number "3" in Figure 7-16.)

Now record a series of dives on a worksheet as an example (Fig. 7-16). You then will be given another series of dives to record for practice.

Fig. 7-15. Basic rules for the use of the worksheet. *AD*, Actual depth; *LG*, Letter group; *PD*, planned depth; *SIT*, surface interval time. (The remaining terms have been previously defined in the text).

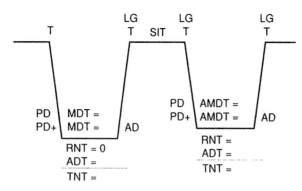

Fig. 7-16. Example of a completed worksheet.

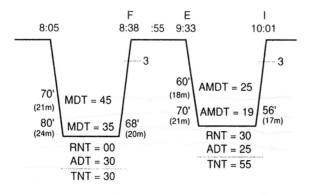

Sample Worksheet Problem

Your first dive of the day is planned for a depth of 60 feet (18 m), begins at 9:30 AM, and lasts for 23 minutes. The actual depth of the dive is 55 feet (16.7 m). You make a precautionary decompression stop at 15 feet (5 m) for 3 minutes, you surface at 9:56 AM and remain out of the water until 10:40 AM.

Your next dive is to a depth of 50 feet (15 m) for 23 minutes. You make a precautionary decompression stop at 15 feet (5 m) for 3 minutes. You surface at 11:06 AM, and have a surface interval of 1:50.

At 12:56 PM, you begin your third dive to a planned depth of 40 feet (12 m), but you end up reaching a depth of 45 feet (13.7 m) with an ADT of 30 minutes. You make a precautionary decompression stop at 15 feet (5 m) for 3 minutes, and you surface from the third dive at 1:29 PM.

Note that when the worksheet is used in conjunction with the calculator, "RNT + ADT" for a sum of "TNT" is disregarded. Only the depth and the ADT are required to determine "End-of-Dive" letter groups when using the Dive Time Calculator (Fig. 7-17).

Exercise Problem

Record the following dives on the worksheet, and take them to class for review with your instructor. Work the exercise once using the NAUI Dive Tables and once using the NAUI Dive Time Calculator. Compare your results; they should be the same.

Your first dive of the day begins at 8:00 AM and is to a depth of 60 feet (18 m) for 31 minutes. You make a precautionary decompression stop at 15 feet (5 m) for 3 minutes. The time at surfacing is 8:34 AM, and the surface interval time is 1:31.

The second dive begins at 10:05 AM, is to a depth of 55 feet (16.8 m), and lasts for 24 minutes. You make a precautionary decompression stop at 15 feet (5 m) for 3 minutes. The time at surfacing is 10:32 AM.

The third dive, which begins at 12:36 PM, is to a depth of 50 feet (15 m) for 31 minutes. What is the time of surfacing from this dive and the End-of-Dive letter group?

Do not rely on your memory to keep track of dive times, maximum depths, or surface intervals. This information must be recorded, and the NAUI Worksheet provides an easy and convenient way to accomplish this. Get into the habit of recording your dives on the worksheet, and it will become easy to keep track of your diving. This will also make it easier to complete your log book at the end of the day.

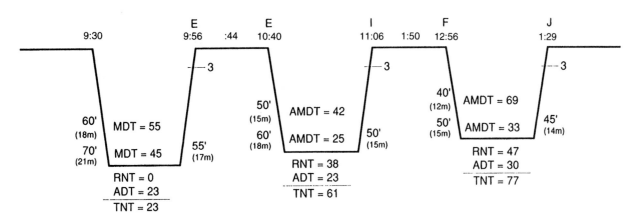

Fig. 7-17. Sample worksheet problem.

SPECIAL RULES AND SAMPLE PROBLEMS

There are a number of special rules and procedures you also must learn to be able to handle special situations. How long do you decompress if the Maximum Dive Time is exceeded? What is the procedure for decompression? How can you keep from getting decompression sickness if you are to fly after diving? What if you want to go diving at an altitude above sea level? How do you handle a cold or strenuous dive? These answers follow.

Decompression

Intentionally exceeding the Maximum Dive Time is unwise, unsafe, and discouraged. As you will learn in advanced or specialty training for deep diving, many requirements must be met to carry out decompression dives properly, and even if these requirements are met, dives requiring decompression are still discouraged. The long-term effects of decompression diving even now are not understood clearly; therefore, it is deemed to be inappropriate for recreational divers.

Some divers engage in what is known as "technical diving," which is extremely advanced diving beyond the scope of recreational diving. Technical diving typically involves decompression dives. You must have special equipment and training as well as extensive diving experience to participate in this. In addition, this type of diving is much more hazardous than recreational diving, and the risk of decompression sickness is much greater.

If you accidentally exceed a Maximum Dive Time, you must decompress. This involves stopping at a depth of approximately 15 feet (5 m) during your ascent and remaining there for a specified time to allow your body to expel excess nitrogen.

During a decompression stop, physical activity must be kept to a minimum (Fig. 7-18).

You must have some means of support that will help you maintain a constant depth during decompression stops. An ascent line, a decompression "bar" suspended from a boat, or the contour of the bottom in shallow water are all examples of such support. Without something to grasp, it is difficult to remain at one depth in shallow water. Swimming and hovering decompression are possible, but these are not easy. If you think that you may need to decompress, have some means available to help you remain at a constant depth of approximately 15 feet (5 m).

Fig. 7-18. Decompression diving is not recommended.

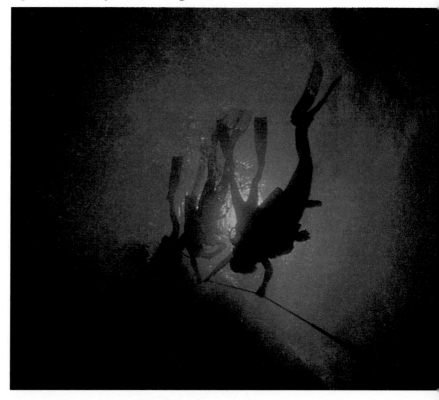

For an idea of the time involved in decompression, refer to NAUI Dive Table I. You already are familiar with the Maximum Dive Time for each depth, and to the right of the MDT are split squares containing two sets of numbers. The top number represents dive time and the lower number the decompression time that is required for that dive time. This decompression information tells you how long to remain at a depth of approximately 15 feet (5 m) to avoid decompression sickness if you should mistakenly exceed the Maximum Dive Times. For example, if your TNT on an 80-foot (24-m) dive was 45 minutes, a 10-minute decompression stop would be required.

Required decompression information is handled differently using the NAUI Dive Time Calculator than with the Dive Tables. A separate Decompression Timetable is provided. To use this table, look in the first column for the depth of your dive. Next, look in the second column for the first time that equals or exceeds your ADT in excess of the Dive Time limit for your depth. Finally, decompress at 15 feet (5 m) for the time that is indicated in column three.

Even when decompression stops are not required, you still want to stop at 15 feet (5 m) for 3 minutes at the end of every dive, just as safety precaution. While not required, such "precautionary stops" are a good idea. Taking this action is recommended both to help prevent decompression sickness and to maintain control of your ascent near the surface.

You may wonder how to document time spent decompressing, but this is simply "neutral" time. For example, if you had an ADT of 45 minutes on a dive to 70 feet (21 m), you should stop at 15 feet (5 m) for 3 minutes. Determine your End-of-Dive letter group by using the schedule 70 ft/45 min (21 m/45 min). Including this decompression stop time as part of your ADT also may be done as an added precaution.

To document either precautionary or required decompression stops, enter the decompression time on the worksheet next to a short horizontal line drawn through the ascent line of the dive profile, as shown in the example. If decompression is required, refrain from further diving activities or flying after diving for at least 24 hours.

Omitted Decompression

If you surface and discover that you omitted your required decompression, discontinue diving, rest, breathe oxygen (if available), drink plenty of fluids, and watch for symptoms of decompression sickness. If you suspect that you may have the

bends, contact the Divers Alert Network at their 24-hour emergency telephone line: (919) 684-8111. They will advise you of the procedure to follow for obtaining treatment.

If you have omitted decompression, refrain from diving for at least 24 hours no matter how well you feel. Do not re-enter the water to make up for the omitted decompression.

Cold and/or Strenuous Dives

If you grow cold and/or work hard during a dive, use the next greater time for your dive schedule. For example, a first dive to 60 feet (18 m) for 40 minutes is considered to be a 50-minute dive.

Flying After Diving

Decreasing pressure to below that at sea level following diving can lead to decompression sickness. You must know how long to delay flying after diving to avoid such problems. The following are guidelines for going to altitudes of up to 8000 feet (2438 m) after diving.

Commercial airliners pressurize their cabins to maintain an altitude equivalent to 8000 feet (2438 m) or less. So, after recreational diving, NAUI recommends that you wait from 12 to 24 hours before flying.

If you make dives that require decompression (which you are advised not to do) or if the required decompression is omitted, wait more than 24 hours before flying. Some dive computers may allow you to fly after a shorter surface interval, but this is not recommended.

Diving at Altitude

Atmospheric pressure decreases with altitude, which means that the rate of change in pressure is greater when descending into water at altitude than it is at sea level. To account for this difference, special altitude dive tables are used and special procedures followed.

The maximum rate of ascent changes with altitude, as do depths for decompression stops. Before diving at altitudes above 1000 feet (304.8 m), you must be trained in using the special tables and procedures. If altitude diving is common in your area, your instructor may provide additional information as part of your training there. Otherwise, he or she may recommend that you participate in a high-altitude specialty training program before you receive NAUI Scuba Diver Certification.

High-altitude training is beyond the scope or purpose of this textbook. Do not attempt high-altitude diving without first completing an appropriate high-altitude training program.

TEST THE DEPTH OF YOUR KNOWLEDGE

Ⓢee how much you have learned about special situations by answering the following questions:

1 When is it appropriate to make a precautionary decompression stop?

2 How much decompression is required for a Total Dive Time of 50 minutes spent at a depth of 80 feet (24.4 m)?

3 Complete the following: The dive schedule for a first dive of the day to 80 feet (24.4 m) for 21 minutes is _____ if you grow chilled during the dive.

4 As a rule of thumb, how long should you wait before flying after conservative diving?

5 Special diving procedures should be followed above what altitude?

SAMPLE DIVE TABLE PROBLEMS

Ⓨou have learned a great deal about the NAUI Dive Tables, Dive Calculator, and their uses. Now it is time to apply what you know to typical diving situations. The following problems contain all aspects of using dive tables and dive calculators that you will need to know for recreational diving. Explanations are included. When you understand how to correctly work problems such as these, you will be able to plan your dives to help avoid decompression sickness.

Use the worksheet provided for all problems, and include a 3-minute precautionary stop at 15 feet (3 m) for all dives. Do not include the decompression time as part of the dive time.

❶ The first dive is to 60 feet (18 m) for 30 minutes, and it is followed by a 30-minute surface interval. The second dive is to 50 feet (15 meters) for 30 minutes. What is the End-of-Dive letter group after the second dive?

ANSWER: *60 ft/30 min (18 m/30 min) results in group "F." After a 30-minute surface interval, the letter group remains "F." A diver in group "F" who uses the dive tables and goes to 50 feet has an RNT of 47 minutes, which is added to the ADT of 30 minutes, for a TNT of 77 minutes. A schedule of 50 ft/77 min (15 m/77 min) results in an End-of-Dive letter group of "J."*

In this problem, note that addition of the RNT to the ADT is not required when using the NAUI Dive Time Calculator. Simply look up the ADT of 30 minutes under 50 feet (15 m) in the group "F" section, and then note that the End-of-Dive letter group is "J."

❷ The first dive is to 55 feet (16.8 m) for 31 minutes, followed by a surface interval of 1 hour. The second dive is to 51 feet (15.5 m). What is the Maximum Dive Time for the second dive, and what is the End-of-Dive letter group if the AMDT is reached?

ANSWER: *55 feet (16.8 m) for 31 minutes actually is a 60 ft/40 min (18 m/40 min) schedule, resulting in a letter group of "G." A 1-hour surface interval leads to group "F," and a diver in that group going to 51 feet (60 ft [18 m] on the dive tables) has a RNT of 36 minutes. The AMDT for a group "F" diver at 60 feet (18 m) is 19 minutes.*

Remember that your AMDT must include your ascent time, which is approximately 1 minute for this dive, so you will need to begin your ascent either at or before 18 minutes of bottom time. If your ADT is 19 minutes, your TNT is 36 minutes (RNT) plus 19 minutes (ADT), for a total of 55 minutes. The dive of 51 ft/55 min (15.5 m/55 min) is a 60 ft/55 min (18 m/55 min) schedule, producing an End-of-Dive letter group of "I."

❸ After the second dive in problem 2, how long a surface interval is required to make a 25-minute dive to 50 feet (15 m) without exceeding the AMDT? Also, what is your End-of-Dive letter group following the third dive if your ADT is 25 minutes? (Use the worksheet from the previous problem.)

ANSWER: *To plan the minimum surface interval using the Dive Tables, refer to Table 3 and determine the letter group that is required to allow the dive to be made. In this instance, you must achieve a group "F" designation, which has an AMDT of 33 minutes, to make a 25-minute dive to 50 feet (15 m). When you know the needed letter group to make this dive, go to the Surface Interval Timetable and work it in reverse to determine the minimum time to achieve the necessary letter group. Because you want the new group to be "F" and your starting group is "I," the minimum time that is required is 1:30.*

Now determine the End-of-Dive letter group. Your ADT (including your ascent time) is 25 minutes, and your RNT as a group "F" diver to 50 feet (15 m) is 47 minutes, producing a TNT of 72 minutes for a schedule of 50 ft/80 min (15 m/80 min) and a letter group of "J." Note that when planning dives, you sometimes may need to use the tables in reverse order.

To solve this problem using the Dive Time Calculator, begin at the group "I" section on the baseplate. Move the depth arrow from one entry for 50 feet (15 m) to the same-depth entry for the next lesser letter group until the desired time of 25 minutes is permitted. In this instance, the first group allowing a 25-minute dive to 50 feet (15 meters) is letter group "F." The Surface Interval Timetable on the calculator is used in exactly the same way as that described for the NAUI Dive Tables. A dive schedule of 50 ft/25 min (15 m/25 min) as a group "F" diver produces an End-of-Dive letter group of "J."

4 Complete the Worksheet for three dives to 52 feet (15.9 m) for 25 minutes each with a surface interval of 1-hour between dives.

ANSWER: *This problem is tricky, both because it does not ask you to plan the dive to avoid required decompression and because decompression is required. This illustrates what can happen if you do not document your dive schedules and do not use the tables to plan your dives. The first dive places you in letter group "E," and a 1-hour surface interval leads to group "D." A group "D" diver returning to 52 feet (15.9 m) has a RNT of 24 minutes.*

The TNT for the second dive is 49 minutes, so the dive schedule is 60 ft/50 min (18 m/50 min) and results in an End-of-Dive letter group of "H." One hour later, the new group designation is "G," and a group "G" diver going to 52 feet (15.9 m) has an AMDT of 11 minutes (which is exceeded) and a RNT of 44 minutes. Although you should not exceed the AMDT, it is exceeded during this dive of 25 minutes. The TNT is 44 minutes (RNT) plus 25 minutes (ADT), for a total of 69 minutes. Therefore, you are required to decompress for 7 minutes, as indicated by the tables, when the TNT is greater than 60 minutes and equal to or less than 80 minutes.

To use the Dive Time Calculator in determining the decompression requirement, go to the timetable and find at the bottom of the disc the exact or next greater time in excess of the time limit for the dive, then determine the decompression schedule. In this example, the ADT was exceeded by 14 minutes. Seven minutes of decompression are indicated for dive times at 60 feet (18 m) that exceed the limits by more than 5 minutes and up to 25 minutes.

By working with the Dive Tables and the Dive Calculator, you will soon feel very comfortable with their use, and your instructor will be glad to help you with any difficulties you may have. Remember the importance of recording and planning your dives to help prevent decompression sickness.

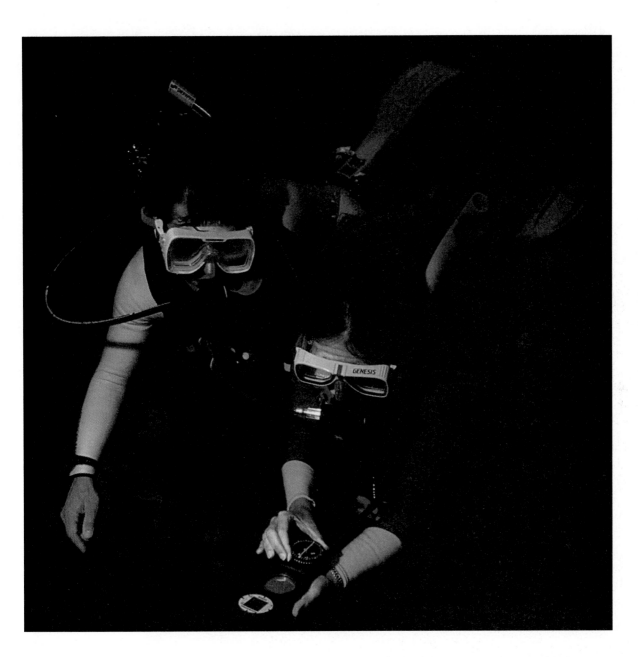

CHAPTER EIGHT

USING DIVE COMPUTERS

If you are like most divers, one of your first purchases will probably be a dive computer. This instrument allows you more dive time because of its capability to continuously calculate multilevel dives, only considering the nitrogen that you actually absorb. You also will find that dive planning is easier, because you do not need to make calculations yourself. You must not become totally dependent on a computer, however, because electronic devices do sometimes fail.

LEARNING OBJECTIVES

By the end of this chapter, you must be able to:

① **Define the term "ceiling" as it applies to dive computers.**

② **Define the term "scrolling" as it applies to dive computers.**

③ **State the nine rules for using a dive computer.**

④ **Explain why reverting to use of the Dive Tables normally is not possible if your dive computer fails.**

⑤ **State the proper time to turn on a dive computer and why.**

⑥ **Define the term "air-integrated dive computer."**

⑦ **Explain the risk of violating an ascent rate given by the dive computer.**

⑧ **Define the dive computer term "OUT OF RANGE."**

⑨ **State the procedure for planning a dive using a dive computer.**

The models of dive computers differ greatly. Each offers various features, and different mathematical models are used by different manufacturers. This results in dive schedules ranging from the conservatism of the NAUI Dive Tables to other, more liberal profiles. Because dive computer designs and features are subject to change, NAUI does not recommend any particular type. You should discuss the types and features of these various computers with your instructor and your retailer, and you should choose the model that best suits your own diving style and needs (Fig. 8-1).

COMPUTER TERMS YOU MUST KNOW

Ⓨou must be familiar with certain terms to use a dive computer.

Ceiling

Most dive computers do not use the standard depths for decompression stops. Instead, they calculate the shallowest depth to which you may ascend without risk of forming bubbles in your system. This minimum depth is called your "ceiling," and it must not be passed, or "violated." Whenever a computer displays a ceiling, you have entered a decompression situation. To help avoid decompression sickness, you should dive with a computer in such a way that you prevent a ceiling from becoming established.

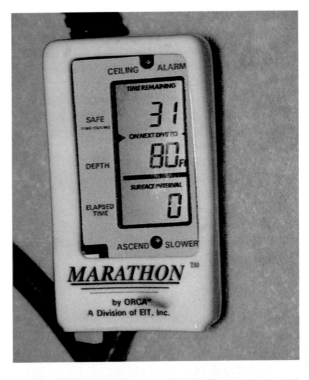

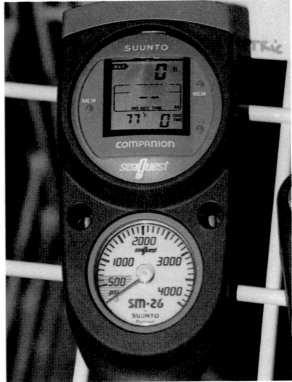

Fig. 8-1. There are many different types of dive computers.

Scrolling

Before you dive, a computer will continuously flash the Maximum Dive Times in sequence for various depths. This feature is an aid for dive planning, and it is called "scrolling."

BASIC COMPUTER USAGE

A dive computer can become the "ultimate instrument" for diving activities. Some combine information that usually would require several instruments and present that information on a single digital display. A computer also may be able to display several, or even all, of the following:

1. Current depth.
2. Maximum depth attained.
3. Elapsed bottom time.
4. Surface interval time.
5. Water or air temperature.
6. Minutes remaining within Dive Time Limits.
7. Minutes remaining based on your remaining air supply and consumption.
8. End-of-Dive letter group designation.
9. Rate of ascent.
10. Dive number.
11. Profile of the dive.
12. How soon it is acceptable for you to fly after your last dive.
13. Scrolling of Dive Time Limits.
14. Ceiling.

In addition, the following rules must be followed when using a dive computer:

1. Each diver who is relying on a computer must have a separate unit; one computer may not be shared by a buddy team. A dive computer that is used by one diver may not be used by another for a subsequent dive until the time required by the computer for complete outgassing has elapsed.
2. The dive computer instruction manual must be studied carefully and the computer used in accordance with the manufacturer's instructions. Completion of a dive computer specialty course is strongly recommended.
3. If a dive computer fails at any time during a dive, that dive must be terminated and appropriate surfacing procedures (i.e., precautionary decompression) initiated immediately.
4. You must not dive for 24 hours before using a dive computer.
5. Once a dive computer is in use, it must not be turned off until it indicates that complete outgassing has occurred or 24 hours have elapsed (whichever comes first).
6. When using a computer, nonemergency ascents must be at the rate specified for the make and model of the dive computer being used. Most computers specify ascent rates that are slower than those used in the Dive Tables.
7. A 5-minute precautionary decompression stop is recommended for all dive computer repetitive dives to 60 feet (18 m) or greater, even if the computer does not indicate a ceiling.
8. Repetitive divers must start the series of dives at the maximum planned depth, followed by subsequent dives of shallower depths. Mutlilevel divers also must begin their dive at the maximum planned depth, followed by shallower depths.
9. Repetitive dives to depths greater than 100 feet (30 m) must not be made.

Some suggest planning dives with the Dive Tables or a dive calculator as a contingency plan for computer diving. Because of the computer's capability for multilevel calculating, however, this practice usually is not feasible, although it is possible with some computers. Generally, you cannot revert to the Dive Tables if the computer fails or is accidentally switched off. Your only options in this case are to discontinue diving for 24 hours or to limit any subsequent dives during that day to depths of 20 feet (6 m) or less.

Computer diving is easier than diving with manual calculations, but you must always be able to use the Dive Tables and Dive Calculator if a computer is not available.

TEST THE DEPTH OF YOUR KNOWLEDGE

See how much you have learned about dive computers by answering the following questions:

1 Complete the following: A "ceiling" display on a dive computer indicates the depth to which you may _____.

2 If a computer is shut off or fails between dives, what is the maximum recommended depth for any repetitive dive?

3 What is the maximum recommended depth for a repetitive dive using a dive computer?

4 True or False: Planned dives using a dive computer should be calculated in advance with the Dive Tables.

HOW TO INTERPRET COMPUTER DISPLAYS

Although many different dive computers are available, all perform many of the same basic functions. Additionally, while the layout of the display screens on most computers is somewhat different, these screens display much of the same information.

This section presents a "typical" dive computer and explains the most common screens and functions. Remember that your computer may be quite different, may not function in the same way, and the meaning of some of the data may be different. You must read and understand the manual that is supplied with your personal dive computer. Also, the illustrations presented here are general examples only, and they do not apply to all computers.

What Happens when You First Turn the Computer On?

When a dive computer is first turned on, it must "initialize" itself. This is the process where the operating program is loaded into the computer's memory. When this happens, the computer typically runs through a self-diagnostic test, checking all of its functions. The computer display will "fill" during this sequence, and any alarms will usually flash or sound. This is a normal procedure with most computers.

Most computers must be turned on before you enter the water. Some turn on with a switch; others turn on automatically when you enter the water. Air-integrated computers normally turn on when the regulator is connected to a tank and the air flow is turned on.

If your computer is turned on manually or when you turn on your air flow, it must be initialized before you begin your dive. Do not turn on a computer at depth after you have started your descent, or your dive will not be recorded accurately. In addition, some computers may be damaged if they are turned on after descent.

Scrolling

As mentioned previously, all computers scroll before diving. They do this when they are first turned on, after they have initialized, and between dives while you are topside. The computer accounts for your residual nitrogen and the time that you have been on the surface, and it gives you a reading of your Allowable Maximum Dive Time for the next dive at different depths.

Most computers will scroll continuously while you are on the surface. Once they have finished scrolling through the maximum dive depths that they are able to calculate, they show your last dive or series of dives.

What Does the Computer Look Like in Dive Mode?

While in normal dive mode, most computers will display your current depth, maximum depth, water temperature, bottom time, and time that you have left at your current depth (Fig. 8-2). In

addition, some also show a graphic representation of how much nitrogen is in your body.

An air-integrated dive computer will indicate the air pressure in your tank. It also may indicate how much bottom time you have left based on your present air consumption. Some dive computers are sophisticated enough to compare your remaining air supply with your remaining dive time and display whichever is the shorter, limiting factor (Fig. 8-3).

As your bottom time diminishes and you approach decompression status, some computers give you a warning to "GO UP!" When this occurs, you must begin your ascent immediately (Fig. 8-4).

You Should Never See the Ceiling Display

When your dive computer displays a "ceiling," it means that you have an obligation to decompress. The ceiling depth is the depth of your first decompression stop. Whenever a ceiling is displayed, you must not ascend above the depth of that ceiling. You can be 1 or 2 feet deeper than the ceiling, but you must not be shallower (Fig. 8-5).

If you have more than one decompression stop, your computer will display another ceiling at a shallower depth than the first. You must complete this stop as well as any others until your computer displays a "zero" ceiling or indicates no ceiling at all.

Fig. 8-2. At depth, most dive computers will display your depth and your bottom time as well as your remaining allowable bottom time.

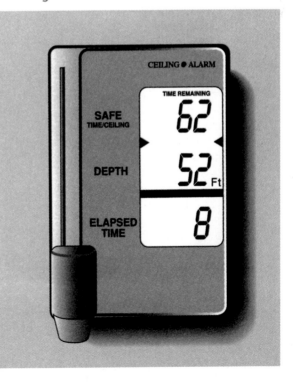

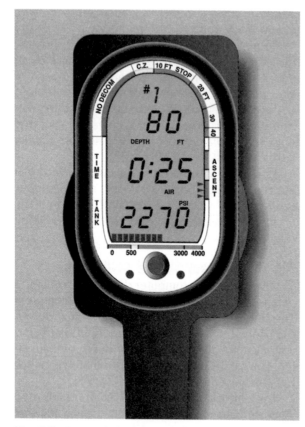

Fig. 8-3. Some air-integrated dive computers will display your remaining bottom time based on your air consumption or remaining no-decompression time, whichever is shorter.

Fig. 8-4. This dive computer is signaling that the diver is close to decompression status.

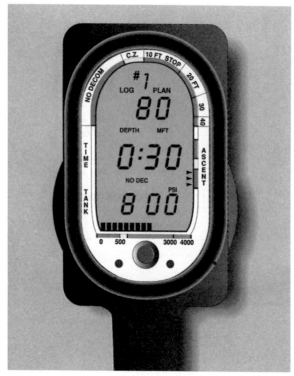

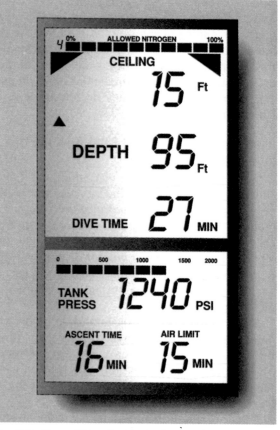

Fig. 8-5. The ceiling display indicates that you must make a decompression stop.

What Happens when You Violate Your Ascent Rate?

Most dive computers require that you use an extremely slow ascent rate, while some models require different rates for different depth ranges. The rate of ascent, however, varies from model to model.

All dive computers give a warning when you have exceeded the ascent rate and provide some type of signal. Some computers warn you with a flashing screen that says "ASCEND SLOWER" or "SLOW DOWN," while others flash a red warning light. Still other models warn you audibly with a beep or a synthesized voice. Whatever signal is given, however, you must slow, or possibly even stop, your ascent depending on your model of computer until you are cleared to continue (Fig. 8-6).

Remember that any time you violate the ascent rate that your computer requires, you increase the risk of suffering decompression sickness. Always carefully monitor your dive computer during every ascent.

What Happens if I Exceed the Computer's Maximum Depth?

If you are foolish enough to exceed the maximum depth capability or bottom time of your dive computer, most of them will warn that you are

Fig. 8-6. Most dive computers will warn you if you violate the ascent rate required by the computer.

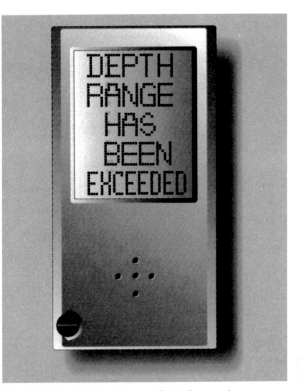

Fig. 8-7. If you dive deeper than the maximum depth capability of your computer you will either get a warning that you are "OUT OF RANGE" or you will be "locked out" of using the computer.

"OUT OF RANGE" or provide some similar message. When this occurs, you must begin your ascent immediately.

In most of these cases, the computer provides you with enough information to complete your decompression but then locks you out of using it for 24 hours. You should never dive in such a way that you see the "OUT OF RANGE" message (Fig. 8-7).

HOW TO PLAN YOUR NEXT DIVE WITH A COMPUTER

Between dives, you must monitor the computer to plan your next dive. Check the computer as it scrolls. As your surface interval lengthens, you will see that the Allowable Maximum Dive Time for your next planned dive increases. Wait until you have enough time to make your next dive comfortably and you are rested and ready to go.

HOW TO RECORD INFORMATION IN YOUR LOG BOOK

If your computer does not automatically display information from your last day, you can call up that information by accessing the computer's "log

mode" (Fig. 8-8). On most computers, the log mode can be called up manually by simultaneously pressing a series of buttons. This usually is accomplished by licking two fingers and placing them on the appropriate contacts to complete the circuit.

HOW DO YOU KNOW WHEN IT IS "SAFE" TO FLY AFTER DIVING?

The display of most computers will tell you when it is safe to fly based on the mathematic model that is programmed into that computer. The computer will either say "TIME-TO-FLY" or show an icon of an airplane with a display of hours and minutes beside it (Fig. 8-9).

NAUI and most diving medical authorities recommend that you be conservative in flying after diving, particularly if you have been on a multiday diving trip. It is best to refrain from diving for 24 hours before flying in any aircraft.

Dive computers are becoming extremely common in diving, and there probably will be a time when divers no longer use the Dive Tables. If you want to be a knowledgeable diver, it is important that you understand both the Dive Tables and the principles of dive computer use.

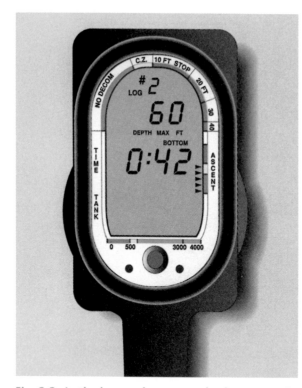

Fig. 8-8. In the log mode you can check your previous dive(s). Different computers will store varying numbers of prior dives.

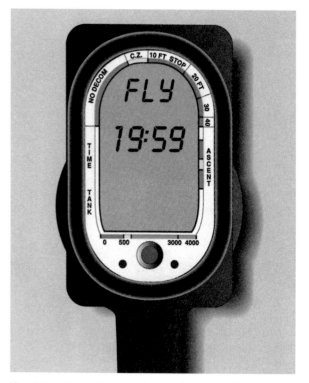

Fig. 8-9. Many dive computers feature a "time-to-fly" indicator.

No matter which computer you choose, you must be completely familiar with its operation. Read the manual until you understand it thoroughly, and carry a copy of the manual in a waterproof bag in your dive bag so that you can refer to it if needed while on a dive trip.

Remember that no matter which dive computer you use, you can still suffer decompression sickness, even if you have used the computer exactly as the manufacturer intended. Always make a precautionary decompression stop at the end of every dive, and be conservative in the use of your dive computer (Fig. 8-10).

Fig. 8-10. Always make a precautionary decompression stop at the end of every dive.

TEST THE DEPTH OF YOUR KNOWLEDGE

Dive computers make diving easier and more convenient. See if you can answer the following questions regarding their use:

1 When you first turn your dive computer on, what cycle must it complete before it can be used?

2 When a dive computer reads out each allowable depth and time while you are on the surface, what is this process called?

3 What is the main risk if you ascend above the ceiling that a dive computer indicates?

4 What are two ways that a dive computer may inform you when you have exceeded your ascent rate?

CHAPTER NINE

DIVING GEAR

t is one thing to use your diving gear in a swimming pool or other confined water environment, but exploring open water is what scuba diving is all about. To enjoy diving, you must be able to combine your knowledge of the underwater environment with the ability to handle your equipment under a variety of conditions. You must have the confidence and ability to operate your gear by feel, because the dive mask will restrict much of your vision. You also must be able to judge diving conditions as they change so that you can decide when it is a good time to dive and when it is time to get out of the water. In this open water course, you learn the basics of diving, but you can become a knowledgeable diver only through additional experience and further training.

LEARNING OBJECTIVES

By the end of this chapter, you must be able to:

1. State the procedure for preparing a new dive mask for use.
2. State the correct location to don snorkeling gear when you are preparing to enter the water.
3. Explain the correct procedure for walking while wearing fins.
4. Explain the procedure for clearing water from the dive mask while you are underwater.
5. Explain the difference between the blast and displacement methods of snorkel clearing.
6. List two types of kicks that are used to swim underwater.
7. Explain the technique that is used for a head-first dive.
8. State the order in which most diving suits are donned.
9. State the correct procedure for assembling a scuba unit, including buoyancy compensator, tank, and regulator.
10. State the correct procedure for donning a scuba unit.
11. State the equipment that must be checked before entering the water while wearing scuba, and explain how each item must be checked.
12. List three types of water entries that may be used for diving, and explain how each is performed.
13. State the most important safety precaution for using a ladder to exit the water.
14. Explain the single most important precaution that you must take whenever the regulator is removed from your mouth underwater.
15. State the preferred and alternate methods of sharing air with another diver.
16. State the technique for breathing from a freeflowing regulator underwater.
17. Explain the two techniques for recovering a regulator that has been knocked out of your mouth underwater.
18. List the steps in disassembly of a scuba unit, including buoyancy compensator, tank, and regulator.
19. List the steps in testing a diver's buoyancy on the surface of the water.
20. State the procedure for a proper descent at the start of a dive.
21. List the steps that are required to make a normal ascent at the end of a dive.
22. List two different types of assisted ascents.
23. Define the term "independent emergency ascent."
24. State the most and least desirable types of dependent ascent.
25. List three factors that affect your buoyancy underwater.
26. Explain why venting air from your buoyancy compensator or dry suit as you ascend from a dive is essential.
27. List one example of a situation where you might need to remove your tank in the water.
28. Explain the procedure for donning a weight belt while you are in the water.
29. Explain the procedure to follow if you become separated from your dive buddy while underwater.
30. List three items that may assist you with natural navigation underwater.
31. Define the term "lubber line" as it applies to using a compass.
32. Define the term "reciprocal course" as it applies to using a compass.
33. State how often you must monitor your air supply on a dive to 30 feet (10 m) or less.
34. State the minimum tank pressure that you must have when ascending from 60 feet (18 m) or less.
35. State the minimum tank pressure that you must have when ascending from 60 feet (18 m) or greater.

If your training is occurring during the winter months in an area where the weather is very cold, you still have the option of completing your open water training immediately. This can be accomplished through NAUI's referral program, where you will complete your training at a tropical resort under the direction of another NAUI instructor. Ask your local instructor for details on this exciting program.

USING YOUR MASK, FINS, AND SNORKEL

Developing good skills with your mask, fins, and snorkel is fundamental to being a good diver. You must know the proper use of these most basic pieces of gear.

Preparing Your Mask, Fins, and Snorkel for Use

Almost all new diving gear requires some preparation before it can be used. This is especially true of masks, because when you buy them, they normally will have a thin film of lubricant still on them from the manufacturing process that will cause them to fog. This film must be removed before you use the mask, otherwise the mask will continually fog and significantly reduce your vision. Thoroughly scrub the inside of the lens with a mild, liquid, dishwashing soap or toothpaste. This will remove any lubricant.

Once the oily film coating a new mask has been removed, the lens usually can be kept free of condensation by applying a commercial defogger or saliva to the inside surface before you enter the water. Saliva is readily available and free, but commercial defoggers usually are more effective. Coat the inside of the lens, and dunk the mask briefly in the water before you put it on your face.

A snorkel must be attached to the left side of your mask strap (Fig. 9-1). Some snorkels use a rubber snorkel-keeper, while others have plastic clips. When properly attached, the snorkel should hang so that the mouthpiece may comfortably reach your mouth. Your instructor will show you the best way to attach a snorkel to your mask.

All you must do to prepare your fins for use is adjust the straps for a snug, comfortable fit (Fig. 9-2). If you plan to use booties with your fins, be sure to wear them when making your adjustments. If the fin straps are "oily" or slippery, which can occur because of a lubricant used in manufacturing, you must wash the straps with a mild solution of soapy water to remove the oils. If this is not done, the straps may slip in the water and become loose, which might cause you to lose your fins.

Donning Your Snorkeling Gear

When you are ready to get in the water, your gear must be donned at the water's edge, not at a distance from your entry point. If you will be wearing booties, these are the first pieces of gear that you must don. It is best to sit down while donning booties to avoid falling, especially if you are aboard a rocking boat.

Fig. 9-1. Your snorkel must be attached to the left side of your mask.

Fig. 9-2. Make sure that your fins are adjusted properly.

Your booties and feet must be either totally wet or completely dry for the booties to slip on easily. If only one or the other are moist, it can be difficult to don your booties (depending on their design).

Your fins must be donned at the water's edge as well. If possible, sitting is preferred, because again, you will be less likely to fall. Wet the inside of the foot pocket in the fins and also your feet (or booties) to make the fins easier to don.

Fig. 9-3. Don your fins at the water's edge.

Fig. 9-4. If you must stand while you don your fins, be sure to lean on your buddy.

If you are able to sit down, grasp each fin with both hands on either side of the blade, and shove the fin onto your foot as far as possible (Fig. 9-3). To comfortably reach your foot, you will need to cross one leg over the other as you are donning each fin. Then, slide the heel strap over your heel. Never pull the fin onto your foot by only pulling on the heel strap, becauase this will stress the strap and could cause it to break.

If you must stand while donning your fins, brace yourself with one hand against your dive buddy or another stable object (Fig. 9-4). In this situation, the easiest way to don your fins is to put them on the deck and have your buddy stand on the blades. Kick your foot into one of the fins until it is solidly in the foot pocket. Then, have your buddy remove his foot from the blade so that you can raise your foot with the fin on it, crossing the leg on which you are donning the fin over the leg you are using to stand. Slip the heel strap over the rear of your foot, and repeat the procedure for the other foot.

Avoid walking while you are wearing fins, because you can easily lose your balance and fall. If you must move short distances while wearing fins out of the water, shuffle your feet backward or sideways rather than trying to walk forward (Fig. 9-5).

Your mask and snorkel are donned last so that you will not restrict your vision while you are out of the water. Once the mask is on your face, it usually

Fig. 9-5. Walk backward when you are wearing fins out of the water.

is difficult to see downward. Place the mask on your forehead, and position the strap high on the back of your head. Next, slide the mask down onto your face, and readjust the mask strap to a lower position (i.e., across the middle of the back of your head). This method works both with and without a hood (Figs. 9-6 through 9-8).

Fig. 9-6. When donning a mask, first hold it against your face.

Fig. 9-7. While holding a mask against your face, slide the strap over your head to don the mask.

Fig. 9-8. Your mask must have no hair trapped beneath it, or the mask will leak.

Place the snorkel in your mouth, and adjust its position so that the snorkel's mouthpiece remains in your mouth even when your mouth is open wide. If you cannot adjust the snorkel for this exact position, get it as close as you can. The idea is to eliminate or minimize tension on your mouth that is caused by the snorkel (Fig. 9-9).

Fig. 9-9. The snorkel must be adjusted properly so that it is comfortable in your mouth.

How to Clear Water from a Mask If It Floods Underwater

It is not uncommon for some water to enter a diver's mask while he or she is underwater. This can happen for a variety of reasons. For example, if your mask fogs while underwater, the easiest way to remove the fog is to allow some water to enter it. Also, diving sometimes can be funny, and if you find yourself laughing underwater, the muscles of your face create channels that will let water enter the mask. In addition, your mask occasionally may be knocked sideways on your face through the careless movement of a buddy. In any of these situations, you must know how to get the water out of your mask.

When you are skindiving and water seeps into your mask, you can simply wait until you surface and pour it out. You also can clear the mask underwater, although this requires you to exhale some of the air in your lungs. Clearing a mask underwater as a skindiver holding your breath is a rather advanced skill. If you can do it, great, but it is not considered to be essential.

To clear water from your mask, you must replace that water with air (Fig. 9-10). When you force air into the top of the mask, the water flows out the bottom. To clear the mask, you must exhale air into it from your nose. At the same time as you exhale into the mask, you also must tilt your head back (toward the surface). Apply pressure to the top of the mask frame with the heel of your hand, preventing air from escaping out the top.

Fig. 9-10. Clearing water from a mask is something that every diver must be able to do.

If you are breathing from scuba and using the air that you have breathed from the tank to clear your mask, these actions must be quite deliberate. You must consciously think about what you are doing, and you must concentrate on inhaling through your mouth and exhaling through your nose. This pattern is different from that of normal breathing, and it is different from using scuba under normal conditions as well. If you do not concentrate on what your are doing, it is easy to forget and inhale the water through your nose, which will cause you to cough and choke.

You must begin exhaling before you tilt your head back so that the water will not run up your nose. A single, steady exhalation is more effective than short, strong bursts of air, which tend to escape instead of remaining inside the mask (Fig. 9-11).

In a purge-valve mask, the water flows out a one-way valve in the nose area. To make the purge valve work properly, you must tilt your head forward during the clearing process.

Fig. 9-11. When clearing water from a mask, the water literally is "poured out" as air displaces it. This is why tipping the head back is important during the clearing.

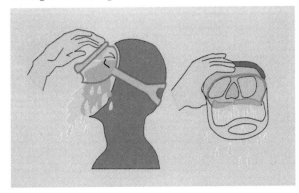

It does not take much air to clear a mask completely. When you become proficient at mask clearing, you should be able to clear your mask several times on a single breath of air.

When your mask floods in cold water, there is a natural tendency to "gasp" or quickly inhale as the cold water hits your face. This also can cause you to inhale water through your nose if you do not consciously brace yourself for it.

Removing water from your mask is one of the most important of all diving skills. You must repeat this skill many times until you are completely comfortable with it and can execute it automatically. Initially, your instructor will have you practice this skill in shallow water, where it is acceptable to overweight yourself slightly so that you do not have to fight your own buoyancy as you practice.

How to Clear Water from Your Snorkel

A snorkel allows you to conserve both your energy and the air in your tank while at the surface. It is a valuable piece of diving equipment. Once you have mastered the skills of snorkel use, you also will have developed useful skills for scuba diving. Snorkel breathing and clearing techniques will help you to learn to use your regulator more effectively.

The ability to snorkel swim comfortably on the surface while wearing scuba gear is another of the most important diving skills that you can master. Many diving accidents occur on the surface, because of fatigue, and involve divers who do not know how to pace themselves or handle a long snorkel swim. Good snorkel-swimming skills are essential to your success as a diver.

Water can enter the open end of a snorkel as you breathe through it at the surface. This can result from wave action or if you accidentally dip the end of the snorkel below the surface. Many modern snorkels have special valves that automatically clear themselves if a small amount of water enters the snorkel in this way. Others do not have these valves, however, and if you own one of these, you must be able to clear water from the tube so that you can continue breathing.

There are three ways to clear a snorkel at the surface. Removing the mouthpiece and pouring the water out is the most obvious technique, but it also is the least efficient. Lifting your head to pour the water out and get a breath requires considerable energy and, if done repeatedly, can rapidly lead to fatigue. On some snorkels, this method will not remove water because of the shape of the mouthpiece and tube. Using this method identifies you as a novice diver, because it is the least preferred method for clearing a snorkel at the surface.

Another method is known as the "blast method." This technique involves exhaling a short, forceful breath of air that blasts the water from the snorkel tube. The technique is similar to that used to launch a pea from a pea shooter (Fig. 9-12).

After blasting water from the snorkel, inhale cautiously through it. If any water remains, you usually can inhale past it if you do so slowly. A deep breath at this point, however, usually causes you to inhale water. The blast can be repeated forcefully to rid the snorkel of any that remains. This is another skill that becomes automatic with practice.

When you ascend from a breath-hold dive, you can use yet another snorkel-clearing technique, one that uses the least amount of energy yet rids the snorkel of water with a single breath. This technique is called the "displacement method," and it is easy to perform (Fig. 9-13).

Fig. 9-12. One strong exhalation will clear most of the water from your snorkel.

Fig. 9-13. More efficient than blast clearing, displacement clearing takes advantage of air expansion and gravity to reduce the effort that is needed to clear a snorkel.

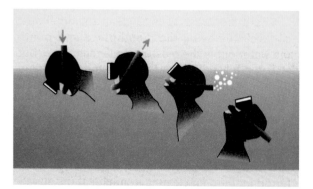

To use the displacement method, tilt your head far back as you ascend from a breath-hold dive. This must be done on every dive anyway so that you can watch the water above you for obstructions as you rise. With your head tilted back, your snorkel will be inverted.

As you near the surface, exhale a small amount of air into the snorkel. This air will expand as you ascend and "displace" the water inside the tube. When you surface, rapidly tilt your head forward, continue to exhale gently, and your snorkel will be empty. If you have done this properly, you can inhale immediately without needing to clear any further water from your snorkel. Once you learn this technique, you will be amazed at how easy it is to clear a snorkel when ascending as a skindiver.

Getting the Most from Your Fins

Fins provide divers with thrust and stability in water. When fully equipped for diving, we must use the powerful muscles of our legs for propulsion, not only to overcome resistance to movement but to free our hands for other purposes as well. Imagine trying to take photographs underwater or pursue some other activity if you needed to swim with your hands. Obviously, it is quite difficult to do both.

Fins can be moved in a variety of ways to create propulsion. The principles, however, are always the same. Your legs should be extended and the blades of the fins pointed behind you. Thrust against the water slowly and powerfully during each stroke.

The flutter kick is the most commonly used, and it is illustrated in Figure 9-14. Note how little the knees are bent. If the knees are bent too much and pulled up toward the stomach, the fins will merely slip back and forth in the water and produce little or no thrust. Your fins should sweep the water away behind you, and with most, the power

Fig. 9-14. A slow, relaxed kick, such as the flutter kick shown here, normally is used underwater.

portion of your kicking stroke will occur during the downward motion. Normally, speed is not the objective; moving steadily and without overexertion usually is your goal.

When moving at the surface, you need to modify the flutter kick slightly. Fins can provide propulsion only when pushing against water, so you must shorten the upward portion of your kick stroke to keep your fins underwater. You also can swim on your back or side while using the flutter kick. This allows a wider stroke, helps keep the fins underwater, and is a good change of pace from face-down swimming (Figs. 9-15 and 9-16).

Fig. 9-15. On the surface, you also can swim on your side.

Fig. 9-16. Many divers prefer to swim on their backs while on the surface.

Whenever you are surface swimming, be sure that just enough air is in your buoyancy compensator (BC) to make you positively buoyant. If you find yourself tiring, stop and rest before swimming any further. As long as you have positive buoyancy, you can rest without effort for as long as you need.

Other strokes besides the flutter kick can be done with fins, and your instructor will teach you the most popular of these: the dolphin kick. This is an undulating motion performed with your entire body while your feet are together. Imagine a wave

passing through your entire length (Figs. 9-17 and 9-18). This kick usually is used only for scuba diving, not for skindiving.

You must learn more than one way to kick with fins so that you can change methods if your muscles tire from one type. You also must also learn how to swim with only one fin in case the other breaks or is lost.

Fig. 9-17. Use the dolphin kick for a change of pace underwater. In this kick, your whole body undulates.

Fig. 9-18. Completion of one cycle of the dolphin kick. Note that both legs are kept together throughout the kick.

SURFACE DIVES FOR FREE DIVING

Various types of dives are used to get underwater rapidly when free diving. These dives are commonly referred to as "surface dives," and they work best for skindiving. As you will learn in the discussion of scuba descents, the best way to leave the surface when you are on scuba is to simply sink feet first. This technique, however, does not work for skindiving.

The principles involved in performing a surface dive are simple. First, you must be weighted so that you are just barely positively buoyant at the surface. If you have too much positive buoyancy, it will be difficult or impossible to get below the surface. Your instructor will check your buoyancy and make sure that it is correct, and you will learn the technique as well so that you can apply it yourself.

To start a head-first dive, turn your body upside down so that your legs stick out of the water and your head points toward the bottom. The weight of your legs will help push you beneath the surface (Fig. 9-19). Kicking while your legs are still above water wastes energy and will not help you descend until your fins are underwater. With these steps in mind, now consider two versions of head-first dives.

Head-first surface dives can be executed from either a swimming or stationary position. If you want to descend while swimming at the surface, simply bend forward at the waist until the trunk of your body is vertical, then lift your legs above you to form a straight, vertical line in the water. Combined with your forward motion from swimming, the weight of your legs will carry you well below the surface, where you can begin kicking to continue your descent (Fig. 9-20).

If you begin your dive from a stationary position, first pull your knees to your chest in a tuck position, then roll forward using your hands to get into a head-down position. Extend your arms and

trunk downward, and extend your legs upward. At this point, you should be in the same position as you would be with the swimming dive (Fig. 9-21).

Both dives should be carried out in one smooth, continuous motion. It helps to imagine that you are trying to stand on your hands when beginning a surface dive. With some practice, however, these skills soon come quite naturally.

There also are feet-first dives that are used for free diving in areas with aquatic plants such as kelp. In these dives, you assume a head-up, vertical position in the water. By extending your arms and legs out and away from your body and then bringing them to your sides as quickly as possible, you will propel your body up through the water. Then, as your body sinks back below the surface of the water and the surface layer of plants, turn and begin swimming toward the bottom.

Fig. 9-21. To make a surface dive from an upright position, pull your knees to your chest and invert yourself while holding the tucked position.

Fig. 9-19. The weight of your legs will help you to get under the water in a surface dive.

Fig. 9-20. Surface dives that are combined with forward momentum usually are more efficient.

TEST THE DEPTH OF YOUR KNOWLEDGE

See if you can recall the following key concepts concerning the use of your mask, snorkel, and fins:

1 Briefly describe how to walk, if you must do so, out of the water when wearing fins.

2 List two ways to prevent losing your balance when you are donning your fins.

3 In what direction is the head tilted when clearing a purge-valve mask?

4 Name three methods of clearing a snorkel, including one that is not recommended.

5 Which method for clearing a snorkel requires the least amount of energy?

6 List three things that you should not do when swimming with fins.

USING SCUBA EQUIPMENT

This section teaches you how to prepare scuba equipment for use. You also will learn the correct techniques for donning gear, various breathing patterns, and disassembly procedures. These skills are essential for using scuba gear properly.

Setting up Your Weight Belt

How you set up your weight belt is important, because it affects your comfort and safety. You want to have the correct amount of weight, and you want those weights to be balanced on the belt. The length of the belt is important as well. The tail that hangs out the end of the belt must be long enough for you to grab with your entire hand but not so long that it gets in your way. If you use a conventional belt with molded lead weights, the belt must be equipped with some means to keep the weights from sliding.

With experience, you will be able to estimate the approximate amount of weight that will be required for different situations. Initially, however, your instructor will suggest an amount for you to try. Adjust or select a belt that, when 2 inches are allowed for each weight and 6 inches of excess strap is included, will be the correct length. String the weights onto the belt so that they will be balanced over each hip and your middle-back will be clear. The weights may be prevented from slipping by threading clips onto the belt, or you can put a twist into the belt as it is passed through the last weight. This will keep the weights from sliding off when the belt is handled in the water. Finally, try the belt on and check both the length and the position of the weights.

Donning Your Dive Suit

Depending on where you learn to dive, you may use anything from a Lycra® dive skin to a dry suit for skin and/or thermal protection underwater. There are different specific procedures for donning each type of suit. Your instructor will show you the techniques whichever suit you will be using.

No matter which type of suit you wear, sit down while donning the bottom portion. This is especially important if you are diving from a boat that is rocking as you dress. Normally, you will don the suit bottom first, followed by your booties or other foot protection, and then the jacket of your suit. The hood will follow the jacket or upper portion of the suit.

If the weather is warm, you probably will want to set up all of your scuba gear before you don your suit. If the weather is cold, you may be more comfortable if you don the suit before making any other preparations to dive.

If you grow too warm after you have donned your suit, take steps to cool yourself before you dive. Hose yourself down with cold water, or enter the water if possible.

Assembling Your Scuba System

Scuba gear consists of a tank, backpack, and regulator. The BC may be integrated with the backpack, or it may be a separate item. By learning and practicing a few simple rules, you will be able to assemble these items correctly and efficiently. An instructor or divemaster can easily tell whether someone is an experienced diver just by watching how they assemble their diving gear.

To begin assembling your scuba gear, first mount your BC on the tank (if it is not already in position). To accomplish this, look for the opening where the air comes out of the tank valve. When the BC is oriented correctly on the tank, the opening where the air comes out of the valve will face toward the backpack. Your first step is to properly orient the pack when positioning it on the tank (Fig. 9-22).

There are many different styles of BCs, but the following general rules apply when positioning yours. The openings for your arms always will be located near the top of the tank, closest to the valve. The waist belt or cummerbund will be located below the arm openings.

There also are several types of bands, with different locking mechanisms to secure the backpack to the tank. Your instructor will show how yours works. Remember that the band must grip the tank tightly so that the tank cannot slip out of the backpack while you are wearing it. If the

Fig. 9-22. Your scuba cylinder must be positioned at the correct height in relation to the backpack.

bands are made of cloth, they must be wet before you make any adjustments or they will slip.

After securing the backpack to the tank, grasp the top of the pack and try to move it up and down on the tank. You must not be able to move the pack. If movement occurs, you must tighten the band (Fig. 9-23).

In addition, the backpack must be mounted at the correct height on the tank. If the tank is too high, your head will bump the valve as you swim; if the tank is too low, it will be too low on your back and throw you off balance. Your instructor will point out the height adjustment for the type of backpack you will be using. Remember the position of the band for subsequent water-skill sessions.

The next step is to attach the regulator to the tank, and this procedure is illustrated here. Note particularly the following points:

1. The regulator must be oriented so that the second-stage hose comes over your right shoulder. It helps if you place the tank in front of you with the pack facing away from you. If you then imagine that you are standing behind the person who will be wearing the tank, you will be able to orient the regulator correctly (Fig. 9-24).

2. Briefly open the tank valve before attaching the regulator. This will blow out any water that might be in the valve opening and helps keep that water from being blown into your regulator first stage.

3. After the regulator seat has been positioned carefully over the "O-ring" (i.e., a black or white

Fig. 9-23. Grasp the top of the backpack, and try to move it up and down. It should be secure on the tank with no movement.

Fig. 9-24. Proper orientation for a yoke regulator connection.

rubber ring that is used for high-pressure seals) on the tank-valve outlet, the first stage of the regulator should be tightened onto the valve. The regulator first stage must be hand tightened only, because when the air is turned on, that high-pressure air will seal the regulator first stage tightly (Figs. 9-25 and 9-26).

4. The tank valve operates like a faucet. It is opened by turning it counter-clockwise and closed by rotating it in the opposite direction. If you stand behind the tank with the valve opening facing away from you, open the valve by turning the handle toward you; close it by turning the handle away from you.

When opening the valve, slowly open it all of the way while aiming the pressure gauge away from your face, then turn it back from its fully opened position by one quarter of a turn. When closing the valve, do so gently. Excessive force during closing will damage the valve. Close the valve just tightly enough to shut off the flow of air.

5. Always check the pressure gauge after turning on the air to make sure that the tank is filled (Fig. 9-27). Do not hold the pressure gauge toward your face or anyone else when you first open the valve. The regulator also must be tested to make sure that it is functioning properly. Typical problems include "free-flowing" (i.e., a constant flow of air from the mouthpiece) or a stuck exhaust valve. Your instructor will show you how to handle minor problems such as these.

Sometimes, the O-ring will not seal properly when the air is turned on. Do not be alarmed by

Fig. 9-25. Tighten the set screw on the regulator yoke by hand. Do not apply force.

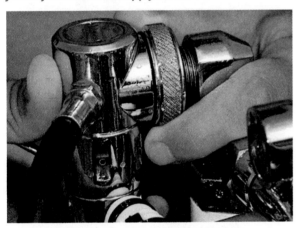

Fig. 9-26. DIN fittings also need only be screwed hand tight.

Fig. 9-27. Check the submersible pressure gauge to be sure that your tank is full.

Fig. 9-28. Connect the low-pressure inflator hose on your power inflator.

Fig. 9-29. Test breathe the regulator before you get in the water.

Fig. 9-30. Lay your equipment down if you will not be using it immediately.

loud, hissing air rushing from the tank. Simply turn the valve off and get assistance from your instructor to correct the problem.

Using a low-pressure inflation system on the BC is highly recommended. You must know how to connect and disconnect the low-pressure hose as well as how to operate the inflator mechanism (Fig. 9-28). You also must learn the various ways that the BC can be inflated and deflated and practice these techniques out of the water. Become thoroughly familiar with your BC before using it. If you buy or rent a different type, you must understand how to use it before you dive with it. Any time that you get a new piece of gear, you should try it out in a pool or other confined space before using it in open water (Fig. 9-29).

Once your scuba equipment is assembled, tested, and ready for use, lay it down with the backpack facing up while you prepare the rest of your gear (Fig. 9-30). If you leave the scuba unit standing, it may fall or be knocked over. If this happens, the valve or regulator could be damaged, or the unit could injure someone.

Donning Scuba Equipment

Develop the habit of having your buddy assist you with your scuba unit. You and your buddy should help each other don your tanks before each dive.

The main thing to remember when donning your equipment is that your weight belt must be clear for removal if you need to quickly establish positive buoyancy. With some buoyancy jackets, it is easier to put the weight belt on before the jacket. Just be sure that nothing is placed over the weight belt, such as a BC crotch strap, that might prevent the belt from falling clear if it is released.

The recommended method of donning your weight belt out of the water is to hold both ends and step through it (Fig. 9-31). You then can lift the weight belt into position on your back and hips and let gravity hold it there as you bend forward and fasten the buckle. The same principle applies in the water. Lie face down when positioning the belt so that its ends will have no tension on them and can be fastened easily. When donning the belt in water, your snorkel should be in your mouth so that you can breathe.

A right-handed release is standard for weight belts. This can be achieved by placing the buckle on the left side when you don it. Always handle a belt by the end without the buckle, because this will prevent the loss of weights. If you always hold the end of the belt without the buckle in your right hand, you will end up with a right-handed release whenever you don the belt.

The shoulder straps must be loosened so that they will slip on easily. Your buddy should hand you the ends of the waistband once the tank is in place on your back. The regulator hoses must be placed on your shoulders so that they are not trapped under the strap when the waistband is secured. Bend forward and balance the tank on your back while you pull the slack out of the straps before securing the waistband (Fig. 9-32).

The tank must feel balanced and secure. You can test its height adjustment by tilting your head back while standing. If your head hits the tank valve, the tank is mounted too high in the backpack.

After your BC has been donned, check its adjustment to make sure that it will not ride up on you when it is inflated in the water. To check this, lift up on the BC and then make adjustments as needed.

Once all of your equipment is in place, take a moment to familiarize yourself with the location of the controls and releases. You must be able to find all of them without looking. Note that their

Fig. 9-31. Hold both ends of your weight belt and step into it.

Fig. 9-32. It is easiest to don your tank if your buddy holds it for you.

positions will change in the water. Your instructor will show you some ways to locate them quickly.

Position your gauges and octopus rig so that they are properly restrained and will not cause any environmental damage. Your octopus rig or other alternate air source must be positioned within the "golden triangle" so that it is instantly accessible if needed (Fig. 9-33).

Fig. 9-33. Be sure that your octopus rig and gauges are fastened so that they will not cause any environmental damage. Your octopus rig must be fastened where it is easily accessible and visible to another diver facing you.

GETTING IN AND OUT OF THE WATER

Every time that you dive, you must get into and out of the water. The situations in which you will do this are numerous, so varied techniques are required. You will learn some general rules that apply to all entries. There also are some special techniques that do not apply to the majority of situations and some general procedures for exiting the water.

Become familiar with a variety of entries and exits so that you gain an overview of what is involved in getting into and out of the water. You will learn specific local techniques from your instructor and practice these, as well as the commonly used procedures, during your water-skill sessions and open-water training.

Preparing to Enter

Time the start of your entry procedures so that both you and your dive partner will be ready to enter the water at the same time. When you are both suited up, you will be eager to get into the water, but you must pause long enough to inspect each other's equipment. Familiarize yourself with how your buddy's gear is fastened and operates, and you will need to ensure that it is operating correctly. To inspect equipment, it helps to begin with the tank valve and work your way down, checking four major areas as you go. These are:

1. Be sure that the tank valve is turned all the way on and then backed slightly toward closing. Make sure that the regulator hose is oriented over the right shoulder and that the regulator functions correctly when the purge valve is depressed. Check the submersible pressure gauge to make sure the tank has sufficient air for the dive. Also, check that the tank is secure in the backpack.

2. Any alternate air source must be properly secured. Octopus rigs should be secured with their mouthpieces pointed "down" to avoid free-flow.

3. Check the BC. Make sure that the low-pressure inflator hose is connected and that the mechanism functions properly. Note how to operate the controls on the BC, and make sure that it is properly inflated or deflated for the type of entry that you will make.

4. Finally, check the weight belt. Be sure that it is clear for ditching, is secured with a right-hand release, and that no hoses are trapped beneath it.

These are the major items to inspect, but also take a few moments and check your partner from head to toe to make sure that all equipment is donned properly. It usually is easier to correct a problem before a dive than after you enter the water. No matter how experienced and skilled a diver you are, always have your buddy inspect your gear before a dive, and do the same for your buddy (Fig. 9-34).

Fig. 9-34. You must be familiar with your buddy's gear and your own. Do a good equipment inspection before you enter the water.

Entries

When you and your buddy are both prepared and ready to enter the water, remember some rules that almost always will apply. Generally, your BC should be partially inflated to provide buoyancy. Hold your mask firmly to avoid flooding or dislodging. Breathe from your regulator during the entry, especially if you are using the giant stride entry from a height. Also, make sure that the entry area is clear and sufficiently deep for the type of entry being used.

There is only one objective for an entry: to get into the water with minimal effort and effect on both you and your equipment. Any entry that accomplishes this is a good entry. Several commonly used entries are presented here, and your goal is to be able to determine when each is appropriate.

The "Seated" Entry

The seated entry is easy and quite controlled. Whenever you can sit at the water's edge, make final preparations, and then lower yourself into the water, this entry is a good choice. Appropriate situations for this entry include getting in the water from the side of a swimming pool, a ledge at water-level in a quarry, or a water-level boat dock. When seated, you are not as likely to lose your balance as you are when standing. You also are close to the water, so the impact of your entry is minimal.

To perform this entry, apply the general rules, place both hands on the same side on the entry edge, and then turn and lower yourself into the water. This should be done in one continuous movement. The entry is simple, easy, and effective (Fig. 9-35).

Using the "Giant Stride" Entry

When entering from a boat or dock where the distance to the water is no more than 6 or 7 feet, the giant stride entry is recommended (Fig. 9-36). This entry involves stepping off into the water, landing in the stepping position, and pulling your legs together to stop your downward momentum and remain at the surface. This entry is appropriate when the water is deeper than 7 feet and there are no objects underwater that a diver might strike while entering.

When carrying out this entry, look at the water first to check the entry area, but look at the horizon during the actual entry. Do not jump or leap from the platform; simply step out with one bold stride. Leave the trailing foot behind you. Both feet will enter the water simultaneously. It is especially important to apply the general rules during this type of entry.

Fig. 9-35. The seated entry is very controlled.

Fig. 9-36. Giant stride entries are commonly used for diving from large boats.

Once you are in the water, swim clear of the entry area, exchange your regulator for your snorkel, and watch as your buddy as he enters the water in case any of his or her gear comes off. When using the giant stride entry from heights of greater than 6 or 7 feet (2 m), bring your legs together before you reach the water.

If there is a current, be sure to immediately grab onto the anchor line, stern of the boat, or any trailing "current line" that has been set up for this purpose, no matter which entry you use. You must be in a position where you provide a clear space for the next diver to enter the water.

Using the "Back Roll" Entry

The back roll entry is used from a small boat where standing to enter could result in injury from loss of balance. The entry is performed by sitting with your back to the water and pulling your knees to your chest as you roll backward into the water. You also will want to tuck your chin to your chest (Fig. 9-37).

Several problems can occur with this type of entry if you are not careful. Keep your legs tucked to your chest until you are in the water. If you extend your legs as you roll backward, your heels can clip the edge of the entry area.

You may experience some dizziness as you roll into the water when using the back roll entry. This results from spinning the fluids of the equilibrium centers in your ears as you turn. Do not be overly concerned, however; you will reorient in a few seconds. Just wait until your body stops rolling before you begin swimming to avoid swimming into the bottom of the boat. Also, be sure to check your mask strap, because it will have a tendency to slip off your head during this type of entry.

With the back roll, or any other entry as well, emphasis on the general rules for entries is essential. Always remember to make certain that nothing is behind and below you before you roll into the water. Also, watch your buddy as he or she enters to make sure that no equipment is lost.

Wading Entries

In many areas, wading into the water is an easy method. Wading creates less impact than giant stride and back roll entries, which are used when you are going directly into water where the depth is over your head.

When you can walk into shallow water to begin a dive, it usually is an easy entry, but some precautions are necessary. Depending on the location, it may be acceptable to wade waist-deep into the

Fig. 9-37. Back roll entries are used for diving from small boats.

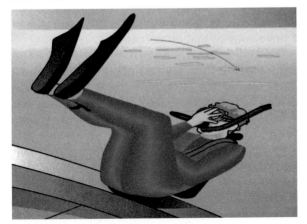

water and then don your fins. In other areas, particularly if there is surf, fins should be put on before entering the water (Fig. 9-38).

Fig. 9-38. Wading entries are easy when the conditions are calm.

Find out what is recommended for a particular site, and then adopt the accepted technique. Whether wearing fins or not, shuffle your feet along the bottom rather than stepping. This detects holes and rocks or obstructions, helps prevent loss of balance, and will chase bottom-dwelling animals from your path. Good practice in wading entries is to lie down and begin swimming as soon as possible; typically, this is when the water is approximately knee deep. Also, if you lose your balance during entry, do not try to stand. Crawl forward on your hands and knees and begin swimming rather than exerting yourself to stand again.

Entries through surf require special training. Generally, however, you must time your entry to coincide with a lull or low point in the wave action. Keep your knees bent, pause as the force of the wave is encountered, watch the approaching waves continuously, and avoid stopping in the surf zone. Duck under breaking waves while breathing from your regulator. If the surf is big, there must be no air in your BC during entry so that you can easily dive beneath it. When a float is used, it must be trailed behind you on a line.

This is only a brief introduction to surf entries; special instruction is definitely a prerequisite. If you are trained and have a NAUI Scuba Diver Certification in an area without surf conditions, you will need additional training in such entries and exits before attempting to dive in those areas.

Exits

Just as an airplane that goes up must come down, a diver who enters the water must exit from it. Procedures vary greatly depending on the situation, and this section provides some general rules and typical useful methods.

Conditions can change during a dive, so you must take a few minutes to evaluate the exit area before proceeding. During this time, make sure that all of your equipment is in place and secure. It helps to think out the steps of your exit in advance.

If you will be exiting onto a small boat or from water too deep for you to stand, it is a good idea to first remove your weight belt and then your scuba unit before trying to climb out of the water. Any items you may be carrying should be handed up first and then followed by the gear being removed (Fig. 9-39). If you are wearing a horsecollar BC, or a dry suit, and using a low-pressure inflator, remember to disconnect the low-pressure hose before removing the tank. If you will be exiting onto a large boat, you will in most cases continue to wear your tank and weight belt until you are back aboard.

Your fins must remain in place as long as possible. If you must lift yourself out of the water, use your fins to help. If you are exiting on a ladder, keep your fins on until you are ready to climb and then hold onto the ladder while removing them. Never get under another person on a ladder while you are waiting to exit the water or are making your own exit. If the other person falls, you could be seriously injured, especially if they are wearing their tank or weights.

Fig. 9-39. When exiting the water onto a small boat, it usually is easiest if you remove your scuba gear and hand it up to whoever is aboard.

When the exit area is a flat area or platform and wave action is present, your approach to that area must be coordinated with the wave action so that water movement will help lift you onto the exit area. Factors such as this show the need for orientations to local diving procedures.

When you will be wading out of the water, simply reverse your entry procedures. Swim in as far as possible before standing, and breathe from your regulator. Once you stand and begin moving, shuffle your feet along the bottom. Keep your knees bent and feet spread to maintain balance. Usually, it is a good idea to wear your fins and keep all other gear in place as well until you are clear of the water.

In surf, it often is practical to exit by crawling from the water (Fig. 9-40). Avoid allowing your enthusiasm for discussing the events of the dive to interfere with your concentrating on the exit procedures. Never stop in the surf zone. It is acceptable to have your BC partially inflated during a surf exit so that you can more easily ride the waves back in to shore.

Fig. 9-40. In surf, it may be more practical to crawl out of the water.

It is not uncommon to lose equipment during exits because of inattention. Be patient, and save your discussions until you and your buddy are out of the water. Also, if you exit onto a charter boat, do not stop in the exit area. Collect your gear and move away so that others can exit.

It would take an entire book to present all of the considerations for entries and exits and to describe and illustrate all of the accepted techniques. This chapter merely attempts to introduce the topics in this section and impress you with the need to learn the entry and exit techniques that are unique to each area. You will learn local methods from your instructor, but never assume that you know how to enter and exit the water everywhere. Always get an orientation to the diving procedures for every new site and region.

TEST THE DEPTH OF YOUR KNOWLEDGE

See how much you have learned about entries and exits by answering the following questions:

1   When preparing to enter the water, what are the major areas to be checked during the equipment inspection?

2   List three general rules that apply to entries.

3   What is the objective of an entry?

4   State an example of when it is appropriate to use each of the following entries:
   A. Giant stride
   B. Back roll
   C. Seated

5   List three general rules that apply to wading entries.

6   List two actions that should be avoided during exits.

EXCEPTIONAL BREATHING TECHNIQUES

For the most part, breathing from scuba is just a matter of breathing slightly deeper than normal. This becomes automatic with experience. Of course, you always must remember to keep breathing so that you will not trap expanding air in your lungs during an ascent. There are a few situations, however, where your breathing must be modified. These include breathing either with a flooded mask or no mask, removal of the regulator from your mouth, breathing from a free-flowing regulator, and sharing air with a single mouthpiece.

Breathing with a Flooded Mask or Without a Mask

At times, your mask may become partially or completely flooded or even be knocked off of your face. When this happens, you must concentrate on your breathing to avoid inhaling water (just as you would when clearing water from your mask).

During normal underwater conditions, all breathing must be done through the mouth. You must learn to both inhale and exhale through your mouth. Only when you are clearing or equalizing pressure in the mask will you need to inhale through your mouth and exhale through your nose.

If you lose your mask underwater or the faceplate breaks, you must make a conscious effort not to inhale through your nose as you return to the surface. The best way to help prevent this is to maintain a bubble of air in your nostrils but continue to inhale through your mouth and exhale through your nose. You must be able to function without needing to hold your nostrils closed, because in many situations, you will need to be able to use both of your hands.

Train Yourself to Exhale Whenever Your Regulator Is Out of Your Mouth Underwater

If for any reason the regulator must be removed from your mouth, remember that you still have compressed air in your lungs. You must overcome your natural tendency to hold your breath, because the air in your lungs will expand during ascent and damage lung tissues. To be sure that no air-expansion problems occur, develop the habit of exhaling a tiny stream of bubbles whenever you are breathing compressed air and the regulator is not in your mouth (Fig. 9-41). Whenever possible, the regulator must remain in your mouth, but you will discover a few situations where its removal is required.

Whenever a regulator is removed from your mouth while underwater, the mouthpiece will flood and must be cleared of water when it is reinserted into your mouth. The quickest and easiest way to do this is simply to exhale into the regulator (as you do for snorkel clearing). Depending on the regulator design, the air will force the water out of the bottom or side of the regulator, where a nonreturn exhaust valve is located. Note that most regulators must be in an upright position for

Fig. 9-41. You must exhale whenever the regulator is out of your mouth underwater.

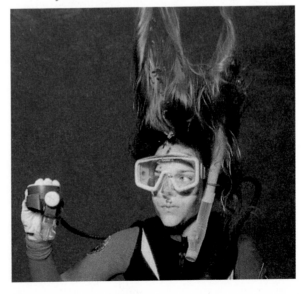

all of the water to be cleared from the chamber; regulators with a side-mounted exhaust can be cleared in any position.

If you do not have enough air in your lungs to clear the mouthpiece, you can clear the chamber by depressing a button on the regulator housing. This is called the "purge button," because it purges water from inside the regulator. You must block the mouthpiece opening with your tongue while depressing the button so that the water will be forced out through the exhaust valve and not back into your mouth and throat. This is a simple procedure.

Sharing Air with Another Diver

The preferred way of sharing air with another diver is to give the person needing air a second mouthpiece from which to breathe. This can be done with either an octopus rig or a completely independent scuba system. Carrying this extra item of equipment is highly recommended (Figs. 9-42 and 9-43).

Fig. 9-42. An octopus rig is one of the preferred methods for sharing air while underwater.

Fig. 9-43. Note how the donor and receiver are linked in this octopus-assisted ascent.

If you have a combined power inflator/regulator unit, the "air donor" uses the combined unit and passes his or her primary unit to the diver needing air. The short hose on most combined units usually makes it difficult or impossible for the diver needing air to breathe from them in a comfortable position (Figs. 9-44 and 9-45).

If for some reason an extra second stage is not available, it is possible to share air by exchanging a single regulator. This procedure will be further explained and demonstrated by your instructor. Basically, the procedure involves "passing" the regulator back and forth, with each diver taking two breaths at a time. The diver who is supplying air maintains control of the regulator at all times, and the person who is receiving the air guides the regulator into his or her own mouth.

Fig. 9-44. If you have a combined power inflator/regulator unit, the donor passes his or her primary unit to the diver needing air.

Fig. 9-45. Ascending with a combined power inflator/regulator unit in an out-of-air emergency.

For the first exchange only, the diver needing air may require additional breaths to re-establish controlled breathing. Thereafter, each diver must take two breaths only. The dive buddies must hold onto each another during the exercise, and the diver who is not breathing from the regulator always must be exhaling a continuous stream of bubbles.

How to Deal with a Regulator Free–Flow Underwater

When a regulator begins delivering air continuously, it is said to be "free-flowing" (Fig. 9-46) Fortunately, this is about the only problem that you might ever have with a regulator, and it usually is not serious.

You must not dive with a free-flowing regulator, but if one begins to flow continuously during a dive, there is a way to breathe from it while you ascend. If the regulator is sealed in your mouth, the free-flow of air from the tank can build up enough pressure to damage your lungs. To prevent this, simply remove the mouthpiece from inside your mouth and place it against your lips, breathe the air you need, and allow the excess to escape in the form of bubbles. When you reach the surface, have your buddy close your tank valve so that you do not drain all of the air from your tank.

Using the Oral Inflator on Your Buoyancy Compensator Underwater

There is another situation where your regulator occasionally is removed from your mouth. In the absence of a low-pressure inflation system for your BC or if your power inflator fails, the alternative is

Fig. 9-46. Most regulators will free-flow if they are turned upright when out of your mouth. To stop this, turn the regulator so that the mouthpiece faces the bottom.

oral inflation. In this situation, you must remove the scuba mouthpiece, depress the exhaust button on your inflator mechanism, and exhale into the mouthpiece or vent hole (Fig. 9-47). Then, reinsert the scuba mouthpiece, clear it, and repeat the process as needed to achieve the desired buoyancy. Remember to keep sufficient air in your lungs to be able to clear the regulator.

Switching from Regulator to Snorkel

There is a time during every dive when the regulator must be removed from your mouth, and this is after you surface. Also, when you prepare to descend for a dive, your snorkel is replaced in your mouth by your regulator mouthpiece; on surfacing, the regulator should be replaced with the snorkel. You will practice these snorkel/regulator exchanges at the surface until they are simple and easy for you to perform (Fig. 9-48).

Fig. 9-47. You must be able to use the oral inflator for your buoyancy compensator if your power inflator fails.

Fig. 9-48. Switching from regulator to snorkel should be smooth and easy.

How to Recover Your Regulator if It Is Knocked from Your Mouth Underwater

During this course, you will learn how to recover the regulator hose from behind your shoulder. You can reach back over your right shoulder with your right hand, grasp the hose where it emerges from the tank, and slide your hand along the hose to the end where the mouthpiece is located (Fig. 9-49).

If you are unable to reach the regulator hose where it attaches to the first stage, you generally will find it hanging either at your side or slightly toward your back. Simply reach down your side and feel to your side and behind you along your body. The regulator usually can be found this way.

Another way to find your regulator is to swim horizontally and then roll to your right and slightly downward. If the regulator is caught on your BC or tank, it normally will fall forward when you are in this position (Fig. 9-50).

In a "worst case" situation, you can always use your own octopus rig or redundant scuba system for breathing if you cannot find your regulator. Use these alternate air sources, however, only until you can get your dive buddy's attention and assistance to free your primary second stage. If you are separated from your dive buddy, you should surface.

Fig. 9-49. Not everyone has the flexibility to recover their regulator by reaching behind them like this.

Fig. 9-50. Even if you are unable to reach behind you to recover your regulator, you can roll to your right and the regulator will fall forward.

DISASSEMBLY OF YOUR SCUBA GEAR

After diving, you must disassemble your scuba equipment and rinse it with clean freshwater. Rinsing procedures are covered in the equipment section; for now, we will discuss how to disassemble the gear.

First, turn off the air. Stand behind your tank, with the backpack facing away from you, and turn the air off by twisting the valve handle away from you. The valve handle turns in a clockwise direction to shut off the air.

Before you can remove the regulator from the tank, you must relieve the air pressure inside the regulator. It is virtually impossible to unscrew the regulator first stage from the tank valve until you do. Push the purge button on the regulator second stage, and allow the air to escape (Fig. 9-51).

Next, unscrew the regulator handwheel from the tank valve. After removing the regulator from the tank valve, be sure to dry and replace the protective cap that covers the inlet on the first stage. It is best to use a dry towel or other cloth, but if none is available, hold the dust cap against the air opening on the valve and carefully open that valve until air hisses out to blow the water off. Be careful not to open the valve too far, because it is easy to lose the O-ring from your tank this way. Also, keep water from entering the regulator air inlet, because it can affect the efficiency of your regulator (Figs. 9-52 through 9-54). Water inside your first stage can lead to expensive repair bills as well.

With the regulator now removed from the tank, all that remains is to secure the straps on the backpack so that they will not drag and get in the way. If you must change tanks or you are finished diving for the day, you will want to remove the backpack or BC from the tank. To do this, simply release the bands holding the pack on the tank and slide it off.

Breathing underwater is not difficult. The hardest part is putting the gear on, and even that becomes easy with experience. Aside from developing proper breathing habits for various circumstances, there isn't much else that you must learn to use the scuba gear. Learning the other skills of diving, such as buoyancy control, entries, and emergency procedures, requires more training and practice. You will develop these skills through your Scuba Diver Certification and additional NAUI training courses.

Fig. 9-51. If you want to remove your regulator from the valve, you must purge the air from the regulator after you have turned off the air in your tank.

Fig. 9-52. Once the regulator has been purged, you can loosen the handwheel on the first stage.

Fig. 9-53. Dry the dust cap with a towel.

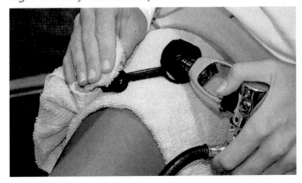

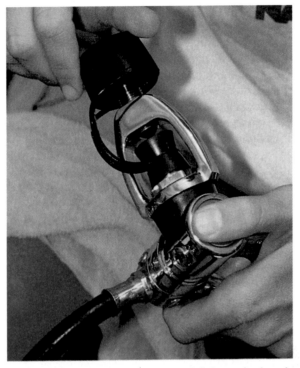

Fig. 9-54. Install the dust cap, and tighten the hand wheel.

TEST THE DEPTH OF YOUR KNOWLEDGE

See how much you have learned by answering the following questions:

1 There are three points to remember when attaching a backpack to a scuba tank. What are two of these?

2 How should a regulator be oriented when you mount it on a scuba tank?

3 A scuba tank valve is turned on when it is rotated in which direction?

4 What are two recommended steps that you should take as part of donning your scuba unit?

5 What action should you take whenever a scuba regulator is removed from your mouth underwater?

6 What are two methods of clearing water from a regulator?

7 How many breaths should each diver take when air is being shared with a single regulator?

8 What is the main thing to avoid when breathing from a free-flowing regulator?

TESTING YOUR BUOYANCY

Proper buoyancy is the key to enjoyable diving. To have good buoyancy control, you must begin your dive being properly weighted. In other words, you must be neither too light nor too heavy.

Buoyancy testing begins at the surface, with your BC completely deflated. Take a deep breath, hold it, assume an upright and motionless position in the water, and relax. Do not kick or use your arms to maintain position. If you are weighted correctly, you will float at eye level in the water. Adjustments in weight may be required to achieve this.

As a final test, exhale once you are floating at eye level. If you sink, you are weighted for neutral buoyancy. Look up as you perform this part of the exercise. As soon as you sink, swim back to the surface and establish positive buoyancy by adding air to your BC.

Once you are weighted for neutral buoyancy, add some extra weight, which will allow you to complete your precautionary decompression stop at the end of your dive. This extra weight enables you to hover motionless at a depth of 15 feet when you have 500 p.s.i. (34 bar) or less of air remaining in your tank. You must be able to complete your stop with no air in your BC or dry suit (if you are using one). The amount of weight that you will need to add depends on the type of tank that you are using, but it usually will not exceed 4 pounds (1.8 kg) (Fig. 9-55).

Your buoyancy will change underwater because of the compression of your suit, your BC, items that you collected during the dive, and air used from your tank. You frequently will be changing and testing your buoyancy underneath the surface by adding or removing air from your BC.

Fig. 9-55. Your buoyancy should be such that you can complete a hovering, precautionary decompression stop at the end of a dive at a depth of 15 feet with 500 p.s.i. or less of air in your tank.

To see if you are neutrally buoyant underwater, assume a facedown position in the water and breathe slowly and deeply. When your buoyancy is correct, you will begin to slowly rise in the water following your inhalations and start to sink following each exhalation. Your breaths must be very long and slow before this response can be noted. Air will need to be added or vented from your BC to achieve this state. Remember that with air in a BC and when wearing a wet or dry suit, your buoyancy will vary with depth. Initially, you will need to check your buoyancy whenever you change your depth, but with experience, you will learn how to make adjustments without even thinking about it.

Learn to dive being properly weighted. It is tempting to wear extra weight at first, especially while training in a swimming pool, because it seems easier to function underwater when overweighted. It will prove to be a disadvantage, however, and is even a hazard in the long run. Diving overweighted requires you to add more air to your BC, creating more drag when you swim and leading to fatigue, which in turn can lead to exhaustion or panic.

CONTROLLING YOUR DESCENTS AND ASCENTS

There are two categories of descents in diving and four categories of ascents, and you will become familiar with them in this section. You will be introduced to them in training, and you will be able to perform them in open water by the end of this course. Descending and ascending are among the most important skills that you will acquire during your training, so concentrate on the points that are presented here. Be sure to make an extra effort to master these skills during confined-water work.

Descents

Once you and your partner agree to leave the surface and descend, preparations need to be made. You must exchange your snorkel for your regulator and note the exact time so that you can keep track of your dive time for no-decompression diving. If you are using a dive computer and it is on, the computer automatically will begin tracking your bottom time when you descend.

With the regulator in place and cleared, you are ready to note the time before beginning your descent. Even if you are using a dive computer, you must still make a note of the time, both as a backup and to properly log your dive. During training, you may not have a timing device, but you may simulate checking the time by tapping on your wrist with one finger. This helps you remember to note the time when you do have a timer, and it helps remind your buddy to do the same.

The next step is to deflate your BC. When you are weighted correctly, you will sink only when all of the air has been vented from your BC and you have exhaled. First, you must get all of the air out of your BC; to do this, the exhaust must be the highest point in the BC. It also will help if you look at the deflator so that you can see if the air is escaping. Get all of the air out, but close the valve once the air is exhausted. You also may be able to hear the air venting from the BC and will notice your body sinking lower in the water.

After the BC is vented, exhale to begin your feet-first descent. It will take a few moments for anything to happen, so hold your exhalation until you begin sinking, then take a quick breath and exhale again. Keep your lung volume low during the first few feet of your descent. If you cannot get down by exhaling, you may need to add weight if it is available. Descending feet first provides better orientation, buddy contact, and makes it easier to equalize pressures than if you descend head first (Fig. 9-56).

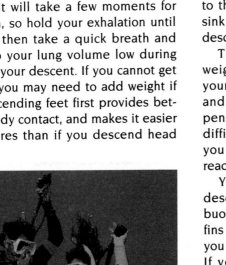

Fig. 9-56. It usually is easiest to descend feet first.

You must clear your ears and equalize pressure before you start down as well as continually throughout your descent. The techniques for what to do if your ears will not cooperate are covered in the section on ear equalization, but at no time should you continue a descent if you feel any discomfort. When a descent is performed correctly, no discomfort should be experienced.

On any dive, you and your buddy must descend together. Remain close enough to touch each

other and maintain eye contact throughout the descent. If one of you has a problem with equalizing pressure in an ear, the other must wait while this is corrected. Continuous buddy contact is important (Fig. 9-57).

Your rate of descent must not be rapid. The recommended maximum descent rate is 75 feet (22.9 m) per minute, which is a little over 1 foot (0.3 m) per second. Remember that you and your buddy must descend together.

When you wear a wetsuit and make descents in open water, there are other considerations as well. You will lose buoyancy as pressure compresses your suit, so from time to time, you will need to add some air to your BC to control your descent. If you are wearing a dry suit, you will need to add air to the suit itself and not the BC. You must never sink out of control; you must be able to stop your descent at any time by inhaling a full breath of air.

The compression of your suit will affect your weight belt if it is not a compensating type. As your suit "shrinks," your belt can become loose and shift around on your waist. When this happens, the buckle can change position, making it difficult to locate. The belt must be checked as you descend and then checked again once you reach the bottom.

You should not need to use your fins during a descent. Your control should be maintained by buoyancy, not by kicking. Any movement of your fins near the bottom may stir up clouds of silt as you approach the bottom and ruin your visibility. If you inhale maximally and still continue to descend, you are too heavy and air must be added to your BC to help control your descent.

Because so many things are happening at once during a descent, your first one in open water will be controlled. This means that you will descend

Fig. 9-57. Be sure to equalize frequently throughout your descent, and maintain good buddy contact.

on a line or along the contour of the bottom to help you control your progress while you learn to equalize pressure, maintain buddy contact, control your buoyancy, and perform the other parts of a proper descent. Once you can do these things, you will be introduced to free descents, which are vertical descents in water without a descent line. When you can execute free descents in a controlled manner, you will be well on your way to becoming a qualified diver.

Ascents

For every descent that you make, you also will make an ascent. To do this, you need to know the standard ascent procedures, those for assisted ascents, and those for ascending in an emergency situation. You should rarely, if ever, need to make anything except a standard ascent, but you must be familiar with the procedures for exceptional circumstances. Practice them so that you will feel confident and be prepared for any problems that might occur.

Normal Ascents

Before making any normal ascent, it is essential to stop for a minute and prepare. Locate your power inflator or other exhaust mechanism. Make sure that you are prepared for the ascent and that any accessories that you are using, such as a goody bag or camera, are properly prepared as well. For example, you would want the goody bag to be closed or the flash on a camera turned off. If you are using a dry suit that is equipped with an automatic exhaust valve, make sure that the valve is open before beginning your ascent.

A normal ascent consists of swimming slowly to the surface with your buddy while looking up and around, controlling your buoyancy, and breathing regularly (Fig. 9-58). Several steps must taken to accomplish this. You and your buddy must agree to ascend by responding to the "up" hand signal. If you have introduced air into your BC to compensate for suit compression, several kicks should lift you enough to allow you to gain additional buoyancy. The deflator for your BC should be held in your hand throughout the ascent, and air should be expelled from time to time to maintain a slight degree of buoyancy.

If you are wearing a dry suit with an automatic exhaust valve, you must raise the exhaust valve until it is at least equal in height to or above the level of your shoulder. On most dry suits, the exhaust valve is located on the left upper arm, and to vent the suit, you will need to lift your elbow (Fig. 9-59).

Fig. 9-58. A normal ascent should be slow and controlled.

Fig. 9-59. If you are wearing a dry suit, you must vent air from the suit as you ascend.

Your rate of ascent must not exceed 30 feet (10 m) per minute if you are using the Dive Tables. This is only 6 inches per second, and it is much slower than the rate at which you are naturally inclined to proceed. Do not pass the smallest bubbles from your exhaust as you rise with them through the water.

If you are using a dive computer, your ascent rate almost always will be slower than 60 feet per minute. Your instructor will explain the rate of ascent for your particular computer. Remember that many computers use varying ascent rates over different ranges. Most computers usually require slower rates the closer you get to the surface. Monitor your dive computer continuously throughout your ascent, and follow any instructions that it gives you.

At first, it will help to time your ascents and compare them with the depth so that you can gauge your rate. You must develop a feel for the correct rate, and your instructor will help you do this. The ascent rate is important, because it allows gas that is dissolved in your tissues under pressure to come out and be expelled without causing you any problems. If you ascend quickly, however, that gas can cause the bends (i.e., decompression sickness).

Keep looking up and around as you ascend. Extend one hand upward during the ascent, especially if visibility is low, to help avoid running into any objects overhead. Remember to maintain contact with your buddy throughout the ascent.

As you reach a depth of 30 feet (10 m), your ascent must begin to slow. When you reach a depth of 15 feet (5 m), stop your ascent and hover for 3 minutes to complete a precautionary decompression stop. It is much easier to complete a precautionary stop on a line or by following the bottom contour than it is in midwater.

On surfacing, note the elapsed time of the dive. At this point, you also must establish positive buoyancy by partially inflating your BC. Remember to exchange your regulator for your snorkel as well.

Assisted Ascents

If you forget to check your pressure gauge and run out of air at depth, you have several ascent techniques to choose from depending on the situation. Two of these are performed with assistance from your dive buddy, and these are introduced first. Two independent methods are presented as well.

Dependent Emergency Ascents. The preferred dependent method of ascending when your own air supply is unexpectedly depleted is by breathing from a secondary regulator that is provided by your buddy. This means that your buddy has an extra regulator or independent air supply, and also that you are close to your buddy underwater and experienced in using the secondary regulator.

Your buddy may elect to "give" or have you take the extra regulator, or he or she may want you to use the primary one. In an actual out-of-air situation, you may get no warning that your partner needs assistance. Most divers who are out of air will grab the first regulator they see—usually the one that is in your mouth!

The exact procedure for sharing an alternate air source varies with equipment configurations and personal preference, but the important point is that it be worked out in advance and agreed to by both divers. You must know which regulator to use, where to find it, and if you are to use the secondary regulator, how it is attached.

Breathing from an extra regulator is just as easy as breathing from your own, but ascending is more difficult. This is because you must coordinate your ascent with the person who is supplying you air. When two people ascend from depth together, changes in buoyancy can be large.

Proper contact between buddies during an assisted ascent is critical. This includes both physical and eye contact. Extra-regulator configurations vary considerably, so position yourself comfortably in front and to one side of your buddy after you have located and secured the mouthpiece. Then, when you both are ready, carry out the ascent, incorporating the various parts of a standard ascent. Once you have the extra regulator and are positioned properly, this type of assisted ascent is quite easy.

The other type of dependent ascent also involves sharing your buddy's second stage and air supply. If your buddy does not have a secondary regulator, you may need to share air by exchanging the single regulator. This procedure is somewhat complex, but it is useful in certain circumstances.

"Buddy breathing" can be used while ascending, but you must be skilled at simultaneously sharing air and making a proper ascent. This can be done successfully with training and practice, but frequent review is required to make buddy breathing a successful option for shared-air ascents. Buddy-breathing ascents are complex, requiring a high level of proficiency on the part of both divers.

If your buddy is not equipped with a secondary regulator, you should rehearse buddy-breathing techniques before entering the water. Practice again just beneath the surface, at the beginning of every dive, to renew the skill and coordinate procedures.

Several points must be remembered during any buddy-breathing ascent. First, as the regulator is passed back and forth, the diver without the regulator must exhale to prevent air from expanding in his or her lungs and causing injury. Next, buoyancy must be controlled by both divers. Continuous physical contact also is essential.

Whenever a buddy-breathing ascent is initiated, it should be continued all the way to the surface. Attempting to change techniques during an ascent results in confusion and could lead to an accident.

Unless you practice buddy breathing on a regular basis, it is unrealistic to expect that you can do this in an emergency situation. There have been numerous accidents involving divers who were not proficient in buddy breathing but who attempted to do so anyway during an emergency.

Independent Emergency Ascents. If you find yourself without air and unable to obtain it from your buddy, you must make an unassisted ascent. In shallow water, this is not difficult and is in fact preferred to a dependent ascent. A "controlled emergency swimming ascent" simply is a matter of swimming to the surface while preventing the air in your lungs from overexpanding.

Lung volume during a controlled emergency swimming ascent is maintained at midvolume. To control your lung volume, keep the airway to your lungs open by exhaling continuously. You must control your rate of exhalation, however, or you will have either too little or too much air in your lungs.

Unlike emergency ascent practice in confined waters, where you left the bottom after inhaling, you begin an actual emergency ascent following an exhalation and an ineffective attempt to inhale. Keep the regulator in your mouth, and exhale through it to control your exhalation rate and maintain your lung volume so that it is neither too low nor too high (Fig. 9-60).

Attempt to inhale briefly from time to time during an emergency swimming ascent. As the water pressure decreases during your ascent, some air may become available from your tank. It

Fig. 9-60. Keep the regulator in your mouth during an emergency ascent.

is hard to imagine exhaling air as you ascend through water and then surfacing with plenty of air in your lungs, but this is exactly what happens in this type of ascent.

An emergency swimming ascent from shallow water is not particularly difficult. If you find yourself in a situation where you do not feel that you can exhale all the way to the surface, however, a greater-than-normal buoyancy must be established to aid your ascent. This extra buoyancy can be achieved by discarding your weight belt or not venting your BC if it contains air. You also can use a carbon-dioxide cartridge to inflate your BC if it is equipped with a CO_2 mechanism. Generally, buoyant emergency ascents are only used to ascend from deeper depths when no extra source of air is available.

If you find yourself without air, you undoubtedly will wonder which method of ascent that has been discussed here should be used and when. This depends on the situation, but the following general guidelines should help you decide which technique is most appropriate:

1. Emergency procedures for a dive must be discussed and agreed on before the dive. You must know what signals will be used, what equipment is available, and how to use whatever method you have agreed on.
2. The best independent procedure is use of a backup scuba. Carry a pony bottle and second regulator. This is the easiest and safest method for reaching the surface if you find that your primary scuba has no air. Simply place the backup mouthpiece in your mouth, and continue breathing while you ascend.
3. An independent emergency swimming ascent is a good choice if your depth is less than 40 feet (12 m) or your buddy with an alternate air supply is not close to you.
4. A buoyant ascent is appropriate if an alternate air source is not available and your depth is greater than 40 feet (12 m).
5. The most highly recommended dependent ascent is breathing from your buddy's air supply with an octopus rig.
6. The least desirable option for a dependent ascent is buddy breathing. This can be used if you are deeper than 50 feet (15 m), your buddy is nearby, both of you are proficient in buddy breathing, and no alternate air source is available.

It should be obvious that not running out of air in the first place is the best course of action. Frequently monitor your submersible pressure gauge—more frequently the deeper you dive—to avoid running out of air. In this way, all of your ascents can be normal ascents, and you will not need to worry about decisions regarding emergency ascents.

TEST THE DEPTH OF YOUR KNOWLEDGE

See if you can recall some of the key points concerning ascents and descents by answering the following questions:

1 What are three steps that you should take to prepare for a descent?

2 What are three actions to be performed during every descent?

3 What are three actions to be performed as part of a normal ascent?

4 How do you know which of your buddy's two regulators to use during an assisted ascent?

5 What is the primary prerequisite to ensure that a buddy-breathing ascent will be executed properly by trained divers?

6 When is it appropriate to choose a buoyant emergency ascent?

CONTROLLING YOUR BUOYANCY UNDERWATER

If you had to select a single skill for determining a person's diving ability, buoyancy control would certainly have to be considered the most important. It consists of numerous subskills that can be learned quickly by understanding and applying basic principles. Proper buoyancy control makes diving easier, adds to your enjoyment, and helps protect the underwater environment (Figs. 9-61 and 9-62).

Fig. 9-61. You can help control your buoyancy by controlling your breathing pattern.

Dealing with Changes in Buoyancy

Many factors affect your buoyancy in water. You must be aware of all of them, and you must know the various means that are available to you for remaining in control of your buoyancy at all times.

The principal means of controlling buoyancy are the amount of weight that you wear, the amount of air in your BC (or dry suit), and the amount of air in your lungs. You also can help control your buoyancy simply by varying the average amount of air in your lungs. You must always keep breathing, but you can take shallower breaths to be less buoyant or deeper breaths to be more buoyant.

If you are learning to dive using a dry suit, you will control your buoyancy by using the suit itself, even though you will be wearing a BC as well. The BC is used for surface flotation and backup.

Frequently, your breathing pattern can be used to control buoyancy until adjustments can be made with your BC. For example, if you feel yourself beginning to drift upward, you can exhale completely to stop the upward progress and then vent some air from your BC (or dry suit) to rid yourself of the excess buoyancy.

As you pick up objects underwater and carry them with you, it probably will be necessary to increase your buoyancy to offset their weight. Add air only in short bursts. In addition, heavy objects must not be carried in this way. Excessive buoyancy will result if a heavy object is dropped and a runaway ascent will probably occur. Even with fairly light items, remember that you will become buoyant if you set down those items on the bottom.

When you have compensated for buoyancy at depth, note that the air in your BC or dry suit will expand as you ascend. Thus, your buoyancy increases as the depth decreases. When you move upward in water, especially shallow water, it will

Fig. 9-62. Maintaining neutral buoyancy while underwater is a key to enjoyable diving.

be necessary to dump air from your BC (or dry suit) to keep from being carried out of control to the surface. How much air must be dumped and how often depend on the situation and the depth. You can gauge your buoyancy during an ascent by your progress through the water coupled with your swimming efforts.

If you find yourself rising through the water, you should exhale, turn to an upright position, and vent air from your BC (or dry suit). The upright position is required, because the exhaust valves in BCs are located at the top and you cannot get the air out of the device if it is upside down. On a dry suit, the exhaust valve usually is located on the left upper arm of the suit.

Slow your fin kicks from time to time as you ascend to test your buoyancy. If you float up without kicking, you are too buoyant. If you begin sinking, you have released too much air. You will learn to gauge this with practice and should strive to control your buoyancy so well that you can stop at any depth any time and remain suspended there without using your fins or hands. This is an evaluation of your buoyancy control and will be part of your open-water training. When you are able to hover at any depth any time during your dive, you are demonstrating the ability to control your buoyancy correctly.

TEST THE DEPTH OF YOUR KNOWLEDGE

See how much you have learned by answering the following questions:

1. What are four major factors that affect your buoyancy?

2. What must you do as the air in your BC or dry suit expands during ascent?

HANDLING YOUR SCUBA EQUIPMENT IN WATER

Typically, you will don your scuba equipment out of the water, go diving, and remove your equipment after exiting the water. There will be instances, however, where you may need or want to don or remove and replace your equipment in the water. For example, you may discover that it is easier and cooler to don your tank in the water, or the boat that you are using may be too small to permit much equipment handling while on board.

An item of gear also may require adjustment in the water, and that usually necessitates its removal before the adjustment can be made. If your scuba unit gets caught in something, you may be able to free it by removing the unit so that you can see the problem and correct it. It is fairly common to remove some of your equipment in the water before exiting into a small boat. As you can see, there are many reasons why you must become proficient at working with your equipment while in the water.

Removing Scuba Gear on the Surface and Underwater

Removal of the scuba unit in water is as simple as removing a jacket. The waistband is released, the shoulder strap is released, and the tank is slipped from the left shoulder and then from the right. Good control and balance can be maintained if the tank is brought forward under the right arm. If the BC is attached to the tank, it must be only slightly inflated. If the BC is not attached to the tank or you are using an older-style BC, be sure to disconnect the low-pressure inflation hose from the BC before you remove the tank.

To don your tank at the surface, put just enough air in the BC on the tank so that it will just float. Position the tank in the water so that the tank rests on the backpack. Ideally, you should be slightly buoyant. Duck under the tank as you slip your arms through the shoulder straps, make sure that your snorkel is clear, and lie back on the unit while securing the waistband. Pay particular attention to the following points:

1. You must be slightly buoyant when donning scuba at the surface. If the BC is attached to the tank, vent most of the air so that you can work easily with the unit. It is difficult to don a very buoyant scuba unit. Retain some buoyancy, however, so that you will not sink while putting on the tank (Fig. 9-63).

Fig. 9-63. Donning your tank on the surface is easier if you have positive buoyancy.

2. Do not forget to refasten the shoulder strap before donning the tank.

3. Work with the tank in front of you.

4. It usually is a good idea to breathe from your regulator while donning the tank, even when doing so at the surface. You can don your tank in two ways. First, you can put it on like a coat; second, you can raise it up and duck beneath it. If you duck beneath the tank, the regulator must be in your mouth while you don the tank. If the tank is being put on over your head, the entire hose (from the first stage on the tank to the second stage in your mouth) must be between your arms. If a loop of the hose is on the outside of your arm, the hose will be trapped beneath your shoulder strap when you lower the tank into place.

5. When the tank is in place on your back, locate the waist straps and pull on them to position the unit. Before securing the straps, check that the shoulder straps are not twisted and that all of your hoses are clear. Learn to buckle the waist strap by feel, because it is not easy to see your waist while wearing a mask (Fig. 9-64).

The technique for removing and replacing the scuba unit while underwater is similar to that used at the surface. Buoyancy is the difference. You do not want the scuba unit to be buoyant when working with it on the bottom, and your overall buoyancy must be slightly negative. Just as you prepare to don the scuba, it helps to exhale fully and breathe shallowly as you position the unit. It is best to work at a slow, steady pace (Figs. 9-65 to 9-67).

It is desirable for you to be able to handle your equipment independently, but nothing is wrong with obtaining assistance from your dive buddy when a problem arises. An extra set of hands and eyes can be quite useful and save time.

Fig. 9-64. Before securing the waist straps, make sure that the shoulder straps are not twisted.

Fig. 9-65. Donning your tank underwater requires both negative buoyancy for you and your buoyancy compensator.

Fig. 9-66. Slide into your buoyancy compensator as you would a jacket.

Fig. 9-67. Fasten the waist belt or cummerbund.

Weight Belt Handling

Handling a weight belt in the water can be very awkward, but if you remember a few key points, you will find that with practice, working with this item is not as difficult as it seems. When you remove the belt and hold it, the belt will swing to a vertical position and tend to pull you over in water as it tries to sink. The weights will hang in a direct line toward the bottom (Fig. 9-68). This problem can be offset, however, by holding the belt close to your stomach.

Gravity also pulls on the belt when you try to buckle it after putting it in place. You can use this to your advantage by assuming a facedown position so that gravity keeps the belt in place across your back. In this way, there will be no tension on the buckle while you tighten and secure it. These two ideas will make working with your belt easier in water.

Removing a weight belt in water sometimes is more difficult than it might seem. Belts tend to catch on the most unexpected things. Therefore, if a belt is being discarded to gain buoyancy during an emergency, it is essential not only that you release it but that you also pull it clear of yourself and your equipment before releasing it.

If you are not discarding but only removing the belt to hand it out of the water or make an adjustment on it, hold it by the end without the buckle. This helps prevent any weights from sliding off it (Fig. 9-69).

When donning the belt, keep the end without the buckle against your midsection while holding it in your right hand. Then, tip your body to the right and roll to the left as you maneuver the belt across your back. Turn your body to a horizontal position. Using this technique, you can position

Fig. 9-68. When you remove a weight belt underwater, the weights will hang in a direct line toward the bottom.

Fig. 9-69. If you are removing but not discarding the belt, hold it by the end without the buckle.

the belt across your back. Of course, make sure that the weight belt is between the tank and your back and not over the tank. It then is simply a matter of making sure that the belt is free of twists, checking that the weights are correctly positioned, and securing the buckle.

Some divers prefer to don the belt while holding both ends in one hand. For this method, place the belt behind your back, grasp each end of the belt in separate hands, and pull the belt into place. If this is done, immediately turn to a facedown position as the belt is pulled against your back.

The same procedures for donning a weight belt apply at the surface as well as underwater. Be careful not to release the belt underwater, because in shallow water, you will instantly attain positive buoyancy and float to the surface.

Mask Removal and Replacement

You may wonder why you would want to remove your mask while underwater. Generally, you would not, but someone else may inadvertently do it for you. Your mask can be bumped and dislodged, or it may catch on something and be pulled free. In such instances, you must be able to calmly relocate and easily replace the mask.

Your vision without a mask will not be good, but you will be able to see. Make use of your eyes. Learn to open them while working without a mask, because they will be more useful than you might think.

When you are wearing contact lenses, you run the risk of losing the lenses if your mask floods or comes off your face underwater. In this situation, keep your eyes closed unless you need to see to locate your mask. If your mask is lost, you will need to open your eyes to surface, even if it means possibly losing your lenses (Fig. 9-70).

To replace your mask underwater, orient it into the correct position and then grasp it by the strap on either side. Place the seat of the mask on your forehead, and hook the strap over the back of your head. Move the mask down into position on your face, then clear the area under the skirt all of the way around the mask. Items to be cleared include hair and the hood if one is worn. Then, clear the water from the mask before positioning the strap (or you can reposition the strap first). This method of working the mask into position in stages is recommended, because it works well both with and without a hood.

Handling Fins in Water

If a strap on your fin works loose or pulls free, you must be able to remove the fin, correct the problem, replace the fin, and continue. With a little thought and practice, you will be able to do this easily.

It usually is easier to correct a fin problem on the bottom than it is to fix it at the surface, so you may choose to work with your fin while underwater. Unless the water is extremely cold, you also may find it easier if you remove at least one glove so that you will have more dexterity working with the strap and the buckles. When working with a fin at the surface, establish positive buoyancy so that the need to kick will be reduced or eliminated. Your instructor probably will have you do exercises with one fin removed to get you accustomed to functioning with a single fin.

Fig. 9-70. Keep your eyes closed if your mask comes off your face and you are wearing contact lenses underwater. If you lose your mask, however, you will need to open your eyes to surface, even if it means losing your lenses.

You will quickly feel confident with your ability to handle your equipment in water. The more practice and experience that you have, the easier it will become. Your goal is to make working with your equipment as easy as your instructor makes it look.

If you find yourself fighting with your gear, this indicates that you do not understand something about how it works. Learn to work slowly and deliberately. Think of the steps involved in handling a given item of gear, and then execute them one at a time. Working this way, you will do well. It is simply a matter of time, practice, and developing a feel for handling scuba equipment

TEST THE DEPTH OF YOUR KNOWLEDGE

See how much you have learned by answering the following questions:

1. What is the primary difference between donning your tank at the surface and donning it underwater?

2. How can you keep the regulator hose from becoming trapped when you don your tank over your head?

3. What two points that you should recall will make handling your weight belt easier in water?

4. What are the five recommended steps for replacing a mask underwater?

OPEN WATER DIVING SKILLS

You have learned many skills in this NAUI course so far, but they have been learned under controlled conditions to prepare you for open-water diving in your area. Whether you will eventually be diving in the ocean, a lake, river, or some other body of water, the diving conditions likely will be quite different than those in which you learned the needed skills.

Open water contains greater changes in pressure and buoyancy, because you dive to greater depths. The visibility may be less, and there will be currents and waves. You can only learn to cope with these conditions by diving in them. This section gives you an additional preview of the skills that you will need for open water.

Buddy-system Techniques

It is easy to keep track of a diving partner in controlled conditions, where visibility is good and the area limited. Unless a few proven techniques are employed, however, maintaining buddy contact will not be as simple in open water. Diving is supposed to be fun, but there is no fun in spending most of your time looking for your buddy. By applying the following procedures, however, both you and your buddy can remain together without detracting from your enjoyment.

Begin by discussing the dive beforehand and agreeing on the location, purpose, activity, and general course that you will follow. This preplanning will prove to be beneficial.

As much as possible, you and your buddy should maintain the same position relative to each other once you reach the bottom. If you are supposed to be on the right, stay on your buddy's right throughout the dive. Diving abreast is preferred to a leader-and-follower configuration.

When a direction of underwater travel has been established, the dive team must maintain that heading until a change of direction is suggested by a signal and then acknowledged. When you know the direction of travel, you will have a general idea of where to locate your buddy if you become separated.

If separation does occur, search briefly for your buddy at the bottom, then ascend a few feet and look for bubbles. Total search time must not exceed 1 minute (Fig. 9-71). If you are unsuccessful in reuniting with you buddy during that minute, surface and wait for your buddy to do the same. Then, you can get back together, descend again, and continue the dive. This is the fastest and best method for locating a lost teammate in most situations.

Fig. 9-71. If you become separated from your buddy, ascend a few feet and look for bubbles. Your search time should not exceed 1 minute, however, before you surface to regroup.

As you and your buddy gain experience together and get to know one another, it becomes easier to remain together. You will become familiar with each other's diving styles, and you will be able to function as a true team with minimal effort. Developing this harmony should be your goal, because diving with a good buddy is diving at its best.

Your buddy also can make things easier by helping you with your equipment. For example, if your tank unexpectedly slips from the backpack, it is much easier for your buddy to assist you in refastening it than it is to remove your BC and fix it yourself (Fig. 9-72).

Fig. 9-72. It is much easier for your buddy to help you solve problems underwater, such as a tank that has slipped from the backpack.

Underwater Navigation

Out of the water, you constantly employ simple navigational procedures. Maps, street signs, and landmarks help you locate a destination and aid you in returning to your point of origin. There are no street signs underwater, but there are navigational aids that can be used to help keep track of where you are during a dive. This section introduces you to some of the fundamentals of underwater navigation; you can learn more about this very useful skill in a NAUI Underwater Navigation Specialty Program.

Learn to use natural aids in navigation. These quickly can become as useful to you as street signs. If you know that ripple marks on the bottom form parallel to shore and are closer together the closer that you are to shore, you will have one reference. If you note the relative position of the sun and shadows at the start of the dive, you will have another.

The back-and-forth movement of water caused by wave action near shore is called "surge." Its movement is toward and away from shore, and it provides yet another clue to your location. Depth is another useful indicator.

Underwater "landmarks," such as an unusual formation, large and unique plant, unusual crevice, or wreck become reference points on a dive as well. By paying attention to such natural aids while diving, you and your buddy can keep track of your position underwater and be able to return to the starting area without surfacing (Fig. 9-73).

You can avoid long surface swims by ending your dive at predetermined locations. To know where you are and be able to get where you want to go is the objective of underwater navigation. By recognizing and using natural aids to navigation, you should be able to do this. This is called "piloting."

When natural aids are not available or cannot be used, such as when diving at night or in limited visibility, a compass and depth gauge are used as references. Not only do these help you find your way by dead reckoning, they allow you to navigate very accurately. The depth gauge is equivalent to an airplane's altimeter; it tells your vertical position in the water. The compass serves as your relative direction indicator (Fig. 9-74).

An underwater compass is filled with liquid, has a reference line (called a "lubber line"), and must have some means of setting a reference course with a movable index point. Because a compass is magnetic, it will be affected by any metal objects in close proximity.

Fig. 9-73. A reef formation such as this arch is an excellent natural aid to navigation underwater.

When using a compass, the lubber line must be kept aligned with the center line of your body. Compasses may be worn on the wrist, held in your hand, or mounted on an instrument console along with other gauges. Where the compass is carried is not critical, but aligning it properly for reference is essential. When referencing a compass, always check that you are lined up with the lubber line and that the compass is level (Fig. 9-75).

A compass provides relative directional information and can serve as a reference for maintaining a selected course. Both are accomplished by referring to the direction of the needle, which will always point to magnetic north as long as no magnetic influences, such as a steel scuba tank, are brought near it.

If you point the lubber line toward shore and the compass needle points to the left, you will know that whenever the needle is pointing left you are swimming toward shore. Conversely, if the needle points to the right, you are heading in the opposite direction, away from shore.

You should be able to see why setting the reference marker on your compass at the beginning of a dive is helpful. If you decide to begin a dive in a

Fig. 9-74. The underwater compass helps make navigation more accurate during a dive.

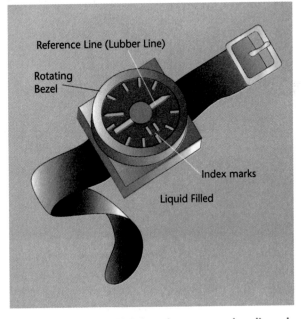

Reference Line (Lubber Line)

Rotating Bezel

Index marks

Liquid Filled

Fig. 9-75. It is essential that the compass be aligned with the center line of your body.

Fig. 9-76. The lubber line must be aligned with the direction you want to swim.

certain direction, you can set the movable reference marker so that it aligns with the needle when the lubber line is pointed in the desired direction. By keeping yourself aligned with the lubber line and the compass needle with the reference marker, you can maintain your desired course very accurately (Fig. 9-76).

When using a compass, you must look across the top rather than down on it. Usually, you only need to occasionally reference the compass to make sure that you are on course. If you want to

navigate precisely, however, such as when returning to the boat at the end of a dive, you must reference the compass frequently.

As the dive progresses and you follow your chosen course, there will be a point where you must start back so that you will have enough air to reach your final destination. Your return heading (called a "reciprocal course") is easily found if your outbound course was a straight line. In this case, all you need to do is turn yourself until the compass needle is directly opposite the original reference marker, then you will be heading in the proper direction. In essence, what you are doing is making a 180° turn, and the compass enables you to do this very precisely.

What if you do not travel in a straight line during the dive? If you follow a course such as a square or rectangle and keep track of the turns that you made, you can still navigate quite well with practice. This is another reason why constant reference to the compass is so useful.

Even if you follow no particular pattern during a dive, the compass will still be helpful. You and your buddy can surface near the end of the dive, point the compass in the direction of the exit point, set your heading with the movable reference marker, submerge, and follow that heading to your destination. Return underwater if possible, because swimming underwater almost always is much easier than swimming on the surface.

Simple navigational techniques such as those presented here make diving more enjoyable. By knowing where you are underwater, not only will you be able to avoid long surface swims at the end of a dive, you also will be able to relocate interesting areas. You will save time and air and can devote it to enjoying the objective of your dive.

You must be able to perform the basics of navigation that are taught in this course. To learn more about underwater navigation, enroll in a NAUI continuing education course, such as the NAUI Advanced Course.

Monitoring Your Air Consumption

As discussed in Chapter Two, monitoring your air consumption by frequently checking your submersible pressure gauge is essential. At a minimum, you must check your gauge once every 5 minutes in shallow water (i.e., less than 30 feet [10 m]) and more frequently the deeper you dive. You also must check your pressure gauge more frequently when your tank pressure drops below 800 p.s.i. (54 bar) (Fig. 9-77).

Initially, your air consumption will be quite high, and you will be surprised by how short your dives will be. As you gain experience and your comfort level in the water increases, however, your air will last longer and longer. Of course, when you are cold, diving deep, or working hard on a dive, your air consumption will increase. Under these conditions, it is essential to monitor your air supply more frequently.

On dives to 60 feet (18 m) or less, begin ascending when your tank reaches a minimum air pres-

Fig. 9-77. Monitor your air consumption frequently while diving.

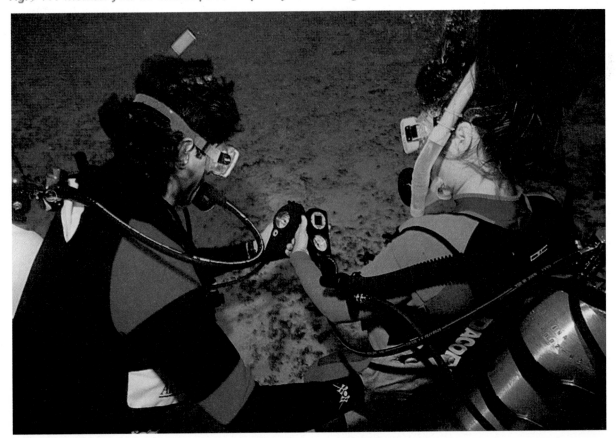

sure of 500 p.s.i. (35 bar) or more. On deeper dives, begin your ascent with even more air, even as much as 800 p.s.i. (54 bar) or more, depending on the depth and conditions.

Enjoying Open-Water Diving

Open-water training involves application of all skills learned under more controlled conditions plus the introduction of new skills that are needed for diving, skills that can only be learned in the actual environment. When you can perform the basic skills of diving as well as the skills presented in this section comfortably in open water, you will be qualified for certification as a scuba diver and be able to learn even more about diving in other courses. You will find that your open-water dives will be fun as well as provide an evaluation of your skills, and you will realize even more why divers are so enthusiastic about their sport (Fig. 9-78).

TEST THE DEPTH OF YOUR KNOWLEDGE

(S)ee how much you have learned by answering the following questions:

1 What are three recommended techniques that help maintain buddy contact while diving?

2 Briefly describe the steps to reunite if you become separated from your buddy while diving.

3 What are three natural aids to navigation?

4 What are two principles to be applied when using a compass for underwater navigation?

5 Define a "reciprocal course."

Fig. 9-78. Diving in open water requires that you use all of the skills you will learn during this course.

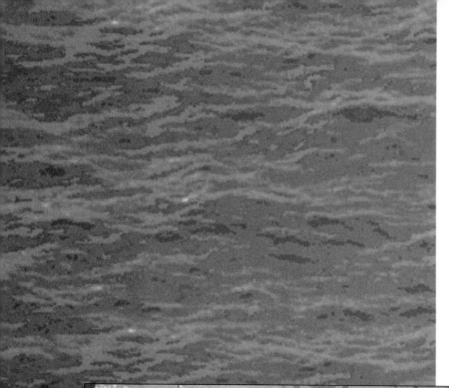

CHAPTER TEN

To get the most enjoyment out of diving, it is essential to plan and prepare your dives in advance. Part of this preparation is considering how you will deal with any problems that may occur during the dive.

Diving always entails some degree of risk. Even if you do everything right, there is still a slight but real possibility that you may be injured, or even killed, while underwater. Fortunately, however, diving accidents are rare, but even so, you must be prepared to accept responsibility for your participation in diving.

LEARNING OBJECTIVES

By the end of this chapter, you must be able to:

1. State two reasons why you must plan your dives.
2. List the three phases of dive planning.
3. Explain the reason for not combining multiple activities, such as photography and hunting, during a single dive.
4. List three factors that must be considered in advance planning for diving.
5. State the order in which your dive gear should be packed.
6. List and explain the four points to be discussed with your buddy just before entering the water for a dive.
7. List the emergency information that you must have before making a dive.
8. Demonstrate the NAUI standard hand signals for the following messages:
   - Go up
   - Go down
   - Low on air
   - Out of air
   - I need to share air
   - Okay (when given underwater)
   - Okay (when given on the surface)
   - Danger
   - Help (when given on the surface)
   - Stop
9. List two additional methods of communication underwater, not including standard hand signals.
10. Explain the recommended action to be taken if a diver develops leg cramps.
11. State the most likely point of entanglement for a diver underwater.
12. List three equipment problems that can occur while diving, and explain the techniques for dealing with them.
13. State the procedure for dealing with a power inflator that is frozen in the "on" position while underwater.
14. State the procedure for dealing with coughing and choking underwater while on scuba.
15. Define "vertigo" as it applies to diving, and state one possible cause.
16. List and explain the three steps for assisting a conscious diver who is in distress at the surface.
17. Describe two variations of the tired-swimmer's carry that may be used for scuba divers.
18. List and describe the steps for dealing with an unconscious diver who is at the surface.
19. List and describe the steps for dealing with an unconscious diver who is underwater.
20. State the ventilation rate to be used for artificial respiration.
21. List three diving emergencies where using oxygen to treat the victim is highly desirable.
22. State the purpose of the Divers Alert Network.
23. List the five major categories of injuries that you must be prepared to render aid for while diving.
24. List the three major categories of injuries from aquatic life to which a diver may be subjected.
25. State the correct first-aid procedure for a jellyfish sting.
26. State the correct first-aid procedure for a sea-urchin wound.

The best way for you to help minimize any problems while diving is to plan your dives. To do this, we need to define "planning" as it applies to diving. For our purposes, planning is all of the arrangements that you make for a dive, from the time that you decide to go diving until any planned dives are complete.

The task is broken into three parts: 1) planning to dive, 2) preparing to dive, and 3) making the planned dive. You will want to know what to do and how to do it so that you can enjoy all the pleasures of a well-planned dive. This includes having all of the needed equipment in good working order, knowing what to expect at the dive site, and avoiding any last-minute rushing. In some instances, just being able to go diving is possible only because you have made reservations ahead of time for this popular activity. When you, your equipment, and your buddy are well prepared for a dive, you have the best possible chance of having a pleasurable experience, which is the goal of recreational diving.

There are many things to do while diving, but you must select one activity—and only one—as the purpose of your planned dive (Fig. 10-1). It is unwise, and can be unsafe, to combine activities on a dive. If you try to spear fish and take pictures, you are not likely to do either one very well. Therefore, your first step is to decide the purpose of your dive and who your buddy will be. It also helps greatly if you and your buddy have similar interests.

Fig. 10-1. Whenever you dive, concentrate on only one activity. Underwater photography, for example, takes great concentration to do well.

PLANNING YOUR DIVES

D ive planning begins several days before you actually "hit the water" to dive. If you wait until the night before the dive to begin, it usually is too late to pull everything together effectively to have a successful dive.

Your first decision will be when you want to dive. This will be influenced by a variety of factors, including your work schedule, weather, tides, boat availability and schedules, regulations that affect game collection, and so forth.

Be aware of any conflicting activities that may affect the date that you want to dive, including plans you have made for the night before the dive. It is unwise and unsafe to dive the morning after attending a party that you had forgotten was planned when you scheduled your dive. You must not use alcohol within 24 hours of a planned dive, and you must be well rested.

The time of day for your dive also is a consideration. Local winds may be light in the morning and strong in the afternoon, or vice versa. Try to schedule your dive during high tide, because visibility usually is the best at this time.

Once you and your buddy have decided on the date and objective of the dive, you must agree on the location. An alternate location also must be discussed in case conditions are unacceptable at the primary site. Remember points such as marine-life preserve areas, boat traffic, and courtesy to fishermen when deciding where to pursue your underwater goals (see Diver Etiquette in the Appendix).

If the dive site is unfamiliar to you, research it. Books are available that provide information on popular locations, but you also should find a con-

tact person in that area to obtain knowledge about the proposed site. Sources include dive resorts, dive stores, dive clubs, and diving instructors. The more that you can learn in advance, the better prepared you will be.

Whenever possible, look at the dive site in advance. This will tell you a great deal about its accessibility, parking, fees, conditions, facilities, as well as entry and exit points. You also may find divers who can point things out and explain the best procedures for that location (Fig. 10-2).

Your next step is to make some phone calls. These include reservations for a plane, boat, hotel, and so forth. You may want to get information on the dive site at the same time if you are speaking to someone who knows the area. Take some time to obtain emergency contact information as well; the specific information that you must have is presented later in this chapter.

When you have acquired knowledge about the planned dive, you can determine the equipment you will need. For example, if the water temperature is different from that in which you usually dive, you may need to obtain a different type of protective suit. Different dive suits will change the amount of weight that you wear to ensure good buoyancy control throughout the dive. Estimated water temperature is particularly useful information that you must make sure to obtain.

It is vital to prepare a list of things to do for arranging your dive. Keep it handy so that you can add to it as thoughts occur. Develop a checklist that will be useful to help in planning future dives as well. Do not rely on your memory (see the Appendix for a sample checklist).

You need to inspect your equipment several days before the dive to make sure that it is in

Fig. 10-2. Picking a dive site is something that you and your buddy should do together. It helps to visit the site before diving in any new location for the first time.

good condition and ready for use. Make any minor repairs that you are qualified to make, such as replacing dried and cracked straps on your fins, at this time. Have any complex equipment with problems, such as those involving a regulator or power inflator, serviced at your dive store well in advance of your trip.

Avoid waiting until the last minute to buy items that you will need for the trip. Typical items include tickets, air fills for your scuba tanks, film, sunscreen, seasick pills, and a fishing license. Determine what you need, write it down, and get it in advance. Your list also should include spare parts for your diving equipment. Having an extra mask strap or O-ring for your tank can save both time and frustration if they are needed at the dive site.

As the day of the dive draws near, check weather trends, water conditions, tides, and the long-range weather forecast. Your NAUI Instructor will advise you about available sources for such information. If you know in advance that the weather may be bad on the day that you plan to dive, you may be able to avoid wasting a trip.

Finally, remember to get yourself as well as your equipment ready to go diving. Be fit for diving. Exercise to develop stamina, and practice skills to keep them sharp (Fig. 10-3).

Planning a dive may seem like a lot of trouble, but it becomes easy and fun to do after a few times. You will enjoy "talking diving" with your buddy and others from whom you seek information. A good feeling comes from being well pre-

Fig. 10-3. Stay fit for diving through regular, related exercise, such as swimming with a mask, fins, and snorkel.

pared to do something. To be comfortable with your diving, you must arrive at your selected dive site feeling that you have done everything possible to ensure your success.

Preparing to Dive

Once all of your plans and long-range preparations have been completed, it should be fairly easy to complete the last-minute details of preparing for a dive. This section identifies those details.

The day or evening before your scheduled dive, gather all of your equipment and personal articles together in one place. The use of a checklist is recommended. Your gear should be packed into two bags: one for your diving equipment, and one for your personal items, such as towel, jacket, snacks, camera, and clothes (i.e., things that you want to keep dry).

Your weight belt must not be packed with your dive gear. The weights will make your bag too heavy and could even damage it. The easiest way to carry your belt usually is to wear it.

Your backpack should be mounted on your tank. The tank also can be carried by wearing it.

Packing your diving equipment in reverse order of its use is helpful. Put the fins, which are donned last, on the bottom and your exposure suit, which is donned first, on top.

A last-minute check of the weather and water conditions is recommended as well. Leave a copy of your plans, along with information on your destination and estimated time of return, with someone who is not going on the dive. This way, assistance can be summoned to look for you if you are unusually late in returning. Do not forget, however, to notify the person holding your plans if you are going to be intentionally late.

Be sure to get a good night's rest and avoid alcohol before diving. You must be well rested, in good health, and have a good feeling about the dive.

Making a Planned Dive

When you and your buddy arrive at the selected site, agree on how you will conduct your dive before entering the water (Fig. 10-4). First, evaluate the conditions to determine if they are acceptable for your planned activity. If the conditions are bad, travel to an alternate location or abort the dive entirely. Never be afraid to say that you do not feel good about diving in poor conditions. The purpose of a dive is enjoyment, and there is no fun if the conditions are bad.

Once you decide to go ahead with the dive, you must plan the dive itself. This includes discussion and agreement on the following points:

Fig. 10-4. You and your buddy must agree on how you will conduct the dive before entering the water.

1. One member of the dive team must be in charge of decision-making for the dive. This person will decide when to change course, to begin the return leg, and to surface. Partners always can make suggestions, but it must be agreed that most decisions be left to the dive leader. The person in charge does not necessarily need to be the most experienced or most qualified member of the team. The person who is most familiar with an area should lead on the first dive, and then the buddies or other team members can take turns leading subsequent dives.
2. You must agree on the activity and objective of the dive. Discuss what you want to do, how you want to do it, and any special signals that you may need to use. Standard hand signals (which are presented later in this chapter) also must be reviewed. Communicate as much as possible before the dive, because it is much more difficult after you descend beneath the surface.
3. Next, outline the course to be followed on the dive. Where will you enter? What pattern will you follow and for what distance? What will be your limits for depth, time, and air supply? Where do you intend to surface? Where is your exit point? Both divers must understand the course to be followed and agree on it.
4. Finally, discuss contingency plans, emergency procedures, and accident management. Agree on what to do if air is needed underwater. Agree on what to do if a buddy pair is separated underwater. In this case, a good rule is to stop, listen, and retrace your previous course for up to 1 minute; if contact is not made, both members must surface and get together. Every effort should be made to prevent diver separation. If it should happen, however, and quick contact is not made at the surface, another

course of action is necessary. Agree on how help can be summoned if it is needed. Discuss the steps to be taken if an accident or injury should occur. Have the local emergency contact information, and make sure that you know the location of the nearest phone. (It is essential to make sure that the phone is working as well.) Take some time to be prepared for emergencies, because little time will be available if one occurs. Accidents can happen any time that you are diving; be ready for them.

Dive Your Plan

It is essential that you carry out the plans you have made for your dive. The dive plan must not be abandoned midway through a dive. If something occurs that alters your plan, terminate the dive long enough to make new plans rather than trying to change them underwater. You and your dive buddy must be coordinated while diving. This is difficult even when you agree on what you intend to do, so if one team member varies from the plan, confusion will result (Fig. 10-5).

Plan ahead while diving. Remind one another of the limits that you have agreed on for depth and time, and carry out your plans throughout the dive.

Fig. 10-5. Plan your dive, and then dive your plan.

Accomplishing what you set out to do and ending a dive exactly where you planned is very rewarding. Consider dive planning and the ability to execute your plan as a challenge. This will add to your enjoyment of the dive while making that dive much more effective and safer.

Many benefits result when you are prepared for a dive, and these are worth the time that it takes to properly plan and prepare. As you work with others to coordinate your dive, that work will become easy. You will find yourself enjoying the preparations involved for the dive as well as the dive itself.

Always make plans for your dives. All good divers do this.

TEST THE DEPTH OF YOUR KNOWLEDGE

Ｓee how much you have learned by answering the following questions:

1   What are three reasons why dives should be planned?

2   What are 10 steps involved in long-range preparations for diving?

3   What are four steps involved in last-minute preparations for diving?

4   What is the first step that you should take after arriving at the selected dive site?

5   What are five items that you and your buddy should agree on before diving together?

COMMUNICATIONS

Ｙou probably have already realized that communication is not easy underwater. The need to communicate as much as possible before making a dive was emphasized earlier; however, there are some standard signals used for communicating underwater that you must know. This section introduces you to certain methods that work well for diving.

Standard Hand Signals

The NAUI Diving Hand Signals are standard among the US diving community, and they are recognized in many other countries as well. As a certified diver, you must be able to correctly identify and use each one. These signals will be easy to remember once you begin using them (Fig. 10-6).

When hand signals are given, they must be displayed distinctly and then acknowledged by either repeating the signal or responding with the "OK" sign (Fig. 10-7). Along with the standard hand signals, local and personal hand signals also are popular. Some divers even learn American Sign Lanauge to expand their vocabulary for underwater communication. Remember that hand signals must be reviewed before each dive.

Other Means of Communicating

There are several ways to communicate while diving, both at the surface and underwater. What are the available means for each of these situations?

At the surface, various forms of visual and audible communication can be used. Some of the standard hand signals are in fact surface signals. For example, a diver must not wave to anyone while in the water, because this is a distress signal.

While diving, divers occasionally are recalled with a special flag to a dive boat (Fig. 10-8). When the flag is hoisted and flown, it means that all divers who surface are to return to the exit point.

Audible communications are possible at the surface, but yelling is not effective at long distances over water. A whistle, however, produces a loud sound that can be heard at considerable distance. The other big advantage to using a whistle is that little energy is required to produce the sound. A repeated series of four short blasts on a whistle is the standard distress signal.

Aside from hand signals, underwater communication also includes written messages on underwater slates (Fig. 10-9). This is a handy way to prevent a trip to the surface, because detailed messages can be given. In addition, communication is achieved by touching your buddy to gain his or her attention, or to let another diver know that you are nearby. Try to avoid touching other divers when you are behind them, especially if they are not aware of your presence. It is easy to frighten someone in this situation.

Audible signals may be used underwater as well. Sound signals include rapping on a tank to gain attention, special electronic communication devices, or some noise-producing device to serve as a prearranged recall signal. Most charter dive boats use some type of underwater recall device, which sounds similar to a siren, if they need to get all of the divers to surface or return to the boat. If the recall signal is heard while you are underwater, you must surface and look to the exit point for instructions. Broadcasting of the recall signal does not necessarily mean that you

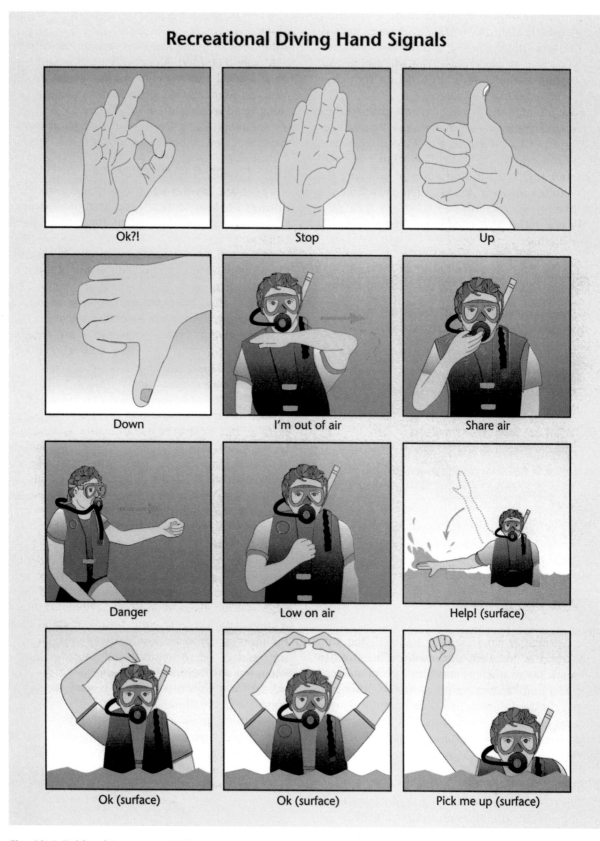

Fig. 10-6. Table of Recreational Diving Hand Signals.

Fig. 10-7. When a hand signal is given, it must be acknowledged by either repeating the signal or responding with the "OK" sign.

Fig. 10-8. The diver recall flag is flown from charter dive boats when the divemaster wants everyone to return.

Fig. 10-9. Writing on a slate is an extremely effective means of underwater communication.

should exit the water, but you must surface and look for instructions from the boat.

The key point to remember is that to be effective, any signals you plan to use must be discussed and agreed on before diving. Proper use of signals is crucial to all dives.

TEST THE DEPTH OF YOUR KNOWLEDGE

See how much you have learned by answering the following questions:

1 What are four means of communicating while underwater?

2 What are three means of communicating at the surface while diving?

3 What action should you take when you are given a hand signal underwater?

4 What is the most important point to remember regarding diving communications?

DIVING NUISANCES

A "nuisance" is defined as an annoyance, and that is just what the following diving nuisances are. Most underwater problems can be overcome if you stop to analyze and cope with them calmly. As long as you have air to breathe, you can deal with almost anything. Keep this thought in mind, and you will soon view perplexing underwater situations as what they are: mere annoyances.

Leg Cramps

Cold, exertion, restricted circulation, or some combination of these factors can lead to cramps, which usually occur in the legs. The best way to deal with this problem is preventing cramps before they occur. Avoid becoming chilled or exhausted, and avoid wearing protective clothing that is too tight.

If you experience a cramp, stretch the cramped muscle and massage it (Fig. 10-10). For cramps in the calf or foot, pulling on the tip of the fin while straightening the leg usually is effective. This stretches the muscles that are responsible for the cramp.

Once a cramp has been removed, rest and recover, then continue at a slower pace. Employing a different type of kick may help keep the cramp from returning.

Fig. 10-10. A cramp can be relieved by quickly stretching the affected muscle.

Entanglements

Entanglements typically occur in underwater plants, fishing line, or fishing nets. It is imperative that a knife be available so that you can cut yourself free, but that should not be your first reaction to an entanglement. First, determine where you are caught and, if possible, what is causing the entanglement.

You may be able to free yourself by pulling the plant, line, or net clear, or by getting your dive buddy to free you. Frequently, you can reverse direction and achieve freedom. Remember that you have buoyancy control, which allows you to move up and down and thus provides another dimension of movement. Also remember that you must remain calm while working to free yourself (Fig. 10-11).

One of the most likely points of entanglement is the tank-valve area on your scuba unit. Unfortunately, you cannot see this area. Your dive buddy can, however, so try to use his or her eyes and hands to help you. If for some reason your buddy is not near, you usually can free yourself. Avoid turning in the water while you are entangled, however, because this will only make matters worse. If you cannot cut yourself free, the next option is to remove your scuba unit, free it, and then don the unit again and proceed.

If none of these actions clears you of an entanglement, consider using a knife to cut yourself free; however, use caution and work both slowly and deliberately. Panic is your worst enemy, not the temporary entanglement.

Fig. 10-11. Remain calm if you become entangled. There usually is no rush to free yourself, and hurrying only compounds the problem.

Equipment Problems

Equipment problems include gear that is or becomes improperly adjusted, undone, or lost while diving. It also includes gear that malfunctions. Any good diver can handle these nuisances, so you will want to learn how to handle them as well. Your instructor will help you develop this skill by giving you typical equipment problems to solve as your training progresses.

Nearly every piece of equipment can be adjusted while in the water. If you must make an adjustment, think first about what needs to be done, then work slowly to accomplish the adjustment. If you become excited and find yourself working hard, stop the activity, recover, think, and start again slowly. Working with your gear in the water is good practice to keep many of your diving skills sharp.

Lost equipment could include your mask, snorkel, fins, or weight belt. While each is valuable and needed for diving, you must be able to either recover a lost item and continue or reach the surface and exit the water without the missing item. Practice swimming with missing items of equipment to develop the needed techniques for handling this type of nuisance.

Occasionally, the power-inflator mechanism on your buoyancy compensator (BC) or dry suit may "stick" or "freeze" in the open position, causing these pieces of equipment to inflate rapidly. If this happens, you must immediately disconnect the inflator hose and vent air from whatever gear has inflated. If this is not done, you will experience a rapid ascent that could lead to a lung overpressure injury or decompression sickness (Fig. 10-12).

Fig. 10-12. If the power-inflator mechanism on your dry suit sticks in the open position, disconnect the inflator hose.

Fig. 10-13. If you feel starved for air underwater, stop what you are doing and relax.

One way that you can slow your ascent is through "flaring." To flare, try to get your body faceup and parallel to the surface of the water, similar to the position of skydivers as they "fall." Get your arms and legs out and away from your body, and hold the blades of your fins parallel to the surface of the water. The purpose of this technique is to try to create as much drag as possible to slow your ascent.

Regulators rarely fail in the "off" position, where they will not deliver air. If this does happen, however, or if your regulator floods because of a worn exhaust valve or other malfunction, it must be treated as an out-of-air emergency. Follow the procedures for out-of-air emergencies that are outlined in Chapter 9 of this book.

Air Starvation

This problem has been presented before, but because of its importance, it deserves to be emphasized again. Any time that you find yourself feeling starved for air, either underwater or on the surface, or if you feel that your regulator is not delivering enough air, stop what you are doing and relax. Concentrate on breathing slowly

and deeply until you regain control of your breathing, and the feeling of air starvation will pass (Fig. 10-13).

If your tank valve is not fully opened, it is possible that the valve could be restricting your flow of air. Check this yourself if you can reach behind you, or have your buddy check it if you cannot.

Coughing and Choking Underwater

Breathing through a regulator while underwater occasionally can result in some water being accidentally inhaled, so you must know how to handle a situation where you begin to cough or choke. If you can prevent this from ever happening, it will be more pleasant than dealing with it once the situation has occurred.

The first breath that you take after clearing a snorkel or regulator must be shallow and cautious. You also can raise your tongue to the roof of your mouth to form a barrier, keeping drops of water from going through your mouth and into your throat.

If you must cough, you can do so into a snorkel or regulator. Keeping the mouthpiece in place while you recover can help you avoid drawing in more water, which would increase the problem. In addition, if you swallow several times in rapid succession, your recovery will be quicker. The main idea is to trust your regulator. You can cough or sneeze into it and through it, so instead of spitting out the mouthpiece, hold it in place. You will quickly learn how to avoid inhaling water and how to recover if you do.

Temporary choking may occur if water enters the windpipe leading to your lungs. If this happens, it may be difficult or impossible to breathe without considerable effort for a few moments. Training without a facemask while underwater usually conditions divers so that this phenomenon is unlikely to occur. If it should, however, deliberately relax your body and wait for your airway to relax before resuming proper breathing.

Seasickness

Suffering from seasickness is an unpleasant situation that no one enjoys. If you can avoid it by using medication, do so. When the situation is serious, however, do not try to cure the problem by diving, which frequently is recommended by well-meaning divers. Vomiting underwater is hazardous and must be avoided if possible.

Several recommendations to reduce that problems caused by motion sickness are included in the section on Boat Diving, and these actions may help control the problem. One comforting note is that with time and experience, most people adapt and overcome motion sickness.

Disorientation

Disorientation, or not knowing where you are, can occur in several ways while diving (Fig. 10-14). Sensory deprivation, where you cannot see anything in the water around you, can occur during poor visibility or night diving. It can produce dizziness or "vertigo," which is described as a whirling feeling. Ear problems and the inability to equalize easily while ascending also are common contributors to vertigo.

Novices should postpone diving at night or in poor visibility until they have acquired confidence through dives with good visibility. All divers must exercise reasonable caution if they are aware of ear problems that might preclude the ability to equalize middle-ear pressure. Vertigo most commonly occurs during ascent, when one ear equalizes more rapidly than the other. Understanding this phenomenon is important. Sensations of verti-

Fig. 10-14. Problems of disorientation rarely are serious. The typical problem is not knowing your relative position when submerged.

go will pass in a few moments, but the diver must not become excited if vertigo does occur.

The two most important actions to take if you experience disorientation are to overcome dizziness and discern which way is up. To overcome vertigo, hold onto a solid object or hug yourself until the dizziness passes. To know which way is up, watch your bubbles.

Problems of disorientation rarely are severe. The most likely problem is not knowing your position underwater relative to your exit point. This can force a long surface swim at the end of the dive. This type of disorientation can be avoided, however, by using both natural and compass navigation, which are presented in Chapter 9 and developed further in your advanced training. Develop the ability to know where you are, and you are not likely to experience the nuisance of disorientation.

Being able to handle annoyances without stress signifies you as a good, skilled diver. By the time that you complete your training, you should feel capable of handling any problem described here. This feeling of confidence will make you much more relaxed so that you can fully enjoy diving.

TEST THE DEPTH OF YOUR KNOWLEDGE

For each of the following nuisances, list at least one correct action that you can take to overcome the problem:

1 Cramp in the leg.

2 Entanglement.

3 Air starvation.

4 Choking.

5 Lost item or gear.

6 Extreme dizziness.

7 A power inflator that is stuck "on" and inflating your BC or dry suit.

8 What is the primary advantage of being able to cope with the nuisances described?

HELPING OTHER DIVERS

As a diver, you have two responsibilities to your buddy. First, you must help keep problems from occurring. Second, you must help your partner overcome any problems that do occur.

Diving problems may be classified as either minor or an emergency. This section describes how to assist a dive buddy in overcoming minor problems; later, you will learn how to perform rescues in emergency situations. While the situations described here are rare and should be prevented before they ever occur, you need to know what to do just in case.

The Three Primary Steps in Assisting Your Buddy

It may seem strange, but most diving problems occur at the surface rather than underwater (Fig. 10-15). If your buddy is in distress at the surface, you must take three actions to assist. These are helping the buddy to establish positive buoyancy, getting him or her to rest, and providing assistance where needed.

You can help your buddy establish positive buoyancy in several ways. If you can instruct your buddy to get buoyant and obtain a correct response, this is the best. If your partner does not respond to instructions, however, extending a surface float is an excellent alternative method for providing buoyancy quickly. When neither of these options is workable, you must drop the other diver's weight belt or inflate his or her BC to accomplish your task (Fig. 10-16).

First, approach your buddy from the left side or the back, and try to inflate the BC with the low-pressure inflator. If this is unsuccessful,

Fig. 10-15. Divers who are in distress at the surface usually remove their masks and either wave their arms or flail the water.

Fig. 10-16. To assist another diver, first make the person buoyant or provide buoyancy.

Fig. 10-17. If you want to inflate another diver's BC, do so from a position behind that diver's back.

reach around your buddy, release his or her weight belt, pull it clear, and discard it (Fig. 10-17). Work from a position where your companion cannot easily grasp you. Once your buddy is buoyant, move out of touching distance and begin step two.

The second step is to get your buddy to rest and breathe deeply. Have your buddy discard any hand-carried items or give them to you so that you can discard them if necessary. Give your buddy assurance and encouragement, and if possible, help your buddy recover and overcome the difficulty without your direct interference. Establish positive buoyancy for yourself, and remember to control your own level of exertion. Your main task is to remain close to your buddy and give optimistic encouragement and advice.

The third step is to provide assistance as needed. You must try to get your buddy to solve his or her own problem. If this is not possible or your directions are not followed, you will need to provide assistance. Your help may consist of working out a cramp, solving an equipment problem, or assisting the other diver to the exit point.

If you must help your buddy through the water, various swimming assists and tows can be used. Two variations of the tired-swimmer's carry are possible. If your partner does not feel comfortable with this arrangement, he or she can be moved by grasping the upper arm and pushing the person along. This assist provides control and allows good eye and voice communication between you. A diver must not be allowed to swim to shore or a boat alone. You and your buddy should practice swimming assists from time to time, because you must learn how to function as both the diver needing assistance and as the one providing it.

A tired diver also can be pushed through the water by having them hold their legs straight and placing their feet against your shoulders. Place your hands under their legs, and grasp their legs behind the knee or on the calf. With this position, you can push them easily through the water.

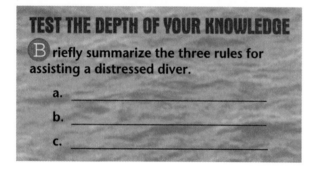

TEST THE DEPTH OF YOUR KNOWLEDGE

Briefly summarize the three rules for assisting a distressed diver.

a. _____

b. _____

c. _____

DIVING RESCUES

Divers usually can avoid trouble underwater. If not, however, they frequently can overcome their problems either independently or with help from their buddies. Most emergencies in the water are preventable, and many occur because divers violate safety rules.

As a diver, you must know the fundamentals of rescuing an incapacitated diver, even though it is unlikely that you will need to apply what you learn. This way, if you need to rescue someone, you will at least have some idea of how to proceed. Further training in diver rescue techniques is included in NAUI continuing education courses, and this is recommended (Fig. 10-18).

You should have some training in first aid and artificial respiration. Everyone (diver or not) should be prepared to administer first aid, especially cardiopulmonary resuscitation (CPR). If you have not taken courses to acquire these skills or refreshed your knowledge for several years, you should complete one of the programs that are readily available through the American National

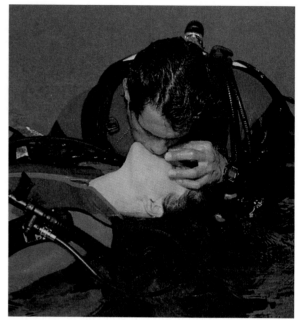

Fig. 10-18. Administering mouth-to-mouth artificial respiration requires additional training beyond what you receive in this course.

Red Cross and American Heart Association. As a diver, you also should complete training in oxygen administration either through NAUI or the Divers Alert Network (DAN).

One category of diving emergency occurs when a diver is unconscious and, perhaps, not breathing. Possible causes include drowning, a lung expansion injury, head injury, or drugs in the diver's system. Such injuries are rare, but you must to be able to help if another diver is unable to care for himself or herself.

Dealing with an Unconscious Diver at the Surface

If a diver is unconscious at the surface, make contact and establish positive buoyancy for yourself. Pull the victim to a face-up position, and establish positive buoyancy for the other diver. This can be accomplished by ditching the victim's weight belt; if more buoyancy is required, inflate their BC.

Remove the victim's mask, and ensure that he or she is breathing. If the victim is not breathing, call for assistance and administer artificial respiration as taught by your NAUI Instructor. These ventilations must be continued as you transport the victim to the exit point.

If you are far away from assistance, consider ditching the victim's tank. This procedure can be time-consuming, so tank ditching is done only if necessary. It is best to wait for assistance before removing someone from the water; the exception to this rule is if the person requires CPR (see the

Appendix), which cannot be administered effectively in water. Whether your exit point is a boat or the beach, you must remove both the victim's tank and your own to get the victim out of the water.

You need both training and practice to become proficient at in-water artificial respiration. Only the basics are learned in this course.

Dealing with an Unconscious Diver Underwater

If you find a diver who is unconscious underwater, your primary concern must be transporting the victim to the surface (Fig. 10-19). If this diver is breathing, simply hold his or her regulator in place while you swim that person to the surface. If the regulator has fallen out of the victim's mouth, leave it out. You probably will need to make the person buoyant to swim him or her up without overexerting yourself. This can be accomplished by inflating his or her BC or ditching the weight belt.

During the ascent, hold onto the victim. Do not waste time worrying about expanding air trapped inside the victim's lungs; it will escape naturally from an unconscious person. Your major concern is bringing the victim to the surface, where you can administer first aid. After reaching the surface, turn the victim to a face-up position, open his or her airway by tilting the head back,

Fig. 10-19. When you locate an unconscious diver underwater, getting that diver to the surface is your primary concern.

and check for breathing. If the diver is not breathing, begin artificial respiration immediately. If you have a pocket mask for administering artificial respiration, this device will work satisfactorily in the water.

In-Water Artificial Respiration

With the victim at the surface and buoyant, hold the victim with one hand while using your other to push his or her head back and open the airway. Quickly check the victim's mouth to be sure that it is clear of obstructions. The head can be turned slightly toward you to make it easier to seal your mouth over the victim's for mouth-to-mouth resuscitation.

After the customary two full breaths, ventilations are continued at a rate of 12 breaths per minute (i.e., one every 5 seconds). Again, training in first aid, CPR, life-saving, oxygen administration, and diver rescue are helpful and recommended. Also, take care to prevent water from entering the victim's mouth and being blown into the lungs.

Unless the distance to the shore or boat is short, keeping water out of the diver's lungs and maintaining mouth-to-mouth resuscitation must be emphasized. This usually is more important than rapidly transporting the victim without attempting to ventilate. Learn to pace yourself so that you will not become too exhausted to be of assistance. By the end of your entry-level course, you will be able to perform the fundamentals of in-water artificial respiration, but additional training and practice are required for you to become proficient. Even your NAUI Instructor must practice this activity regularly to maintain his or her proficiency in this skill.

TEST THE DEPTH OF YOUR KNOWLEDGE

See if you can answering the following points emphasizing the important aspects of handling diving emergencies:

1 By definition, what is a diving emergency?

2 List four types of emergency training that are recommended in this chapter.

3 What is the first action that you should take when providing assistance to an unconscious diver at the surface?

4 How do you prevent a lung-expansion injury in unconscious divers when bringing them to the surface?

5 What are the two most important points regarding in-water artificial respiration?

EMERGENCIES AND FIRST AID

To be a qualified dive buddy, you must be able to assist or rescue your partner, render proper first aid, and manage an emergency situation. While few diving accidents are life-threatening, injuries and fatalities do occur, just as in most physical activities. You must be prepared to cope with injuries ranging from cuts and bruises to wounds from aquatic animals to respiratory and cardiac arrest. You may be the only person available to offer immediate assistance.

Being Prepared

To prepare yourself to handle emergencies, you need training, emergency equipment, emergency contact information and plans, and the determination to take action. An overview of emergency training was presented earlier in this chapter. Periodically, you must strive to update your training in first aid, CPR, and diving-rescue techniques. Practicing with your dive buddy several times a year is a good way to keep emergency skills sharp. It is surprising how quickly an ability is lost if it is not applied regularly.

Emergency equipment can be extensive, but at a minimum, you should have a first-aid kit available. Recommendations for the contents of this kit are listed in the Appendix. Several first-aid kits that are designed especially for diving are available. Other useful equipment includes a continuous-flow oxygen unit (oxygen is extremely valuable for treating serious diving injuries), a cloth or space blanket, and a supply of clean freshwater. Emergency equipment must be ready at the dive site and replaced promptly after use.

Oxygen is extremely valuable in first-aid treatment for serious diving injuries such as air embolism, bends, and near-drowning (Fig. 10-20). Some states prohibit the use of oxygen resuscitators by nonmedically trained personnel. Continuous flow units are readily available, however, and may be used without restriction. Dive boats usually are equipped with emergency oxygen systems. Check with your instructor about the laws in your area. NAUI believes that oxygen is vital in effecting first aid on site, as recommended by diving medical advisers.

You also must know how to call for help. In some areas, a special number is available for reporting diving emergencies. In most regions, however, you will need to know who to call for medical attention, recompression treatment in a chamber, or other emergency needs. There is a nationwide emergency network of hyperbaric chambers and diving physicians—DAN—that can

Fig. 10-20. Oxygen is vital in treating diving emergencies such as air embolism and decompression sickness.

help provide consultation, transportation, and treatment through a single, 24-hour emergency telephone number: (919) 684-8111. You also must have a phone number for the local emergency medical service. Write these local numbers as well as the DAN number on a card, tape coins for calls to that card, and include it in your first-aid kit.

The last requirement for preparation is being determined to act in an emergency. Rather than become involved, most people tend to stand by and watch as an accident occurs. You must decide in advance that you will take action if you are present at the scene of a diving accident.

Basic First-Aid Procedures

First aid must include the following:
1. A quick examination of the victim to determine the nature and extent of injury.
2. Treatment for life-threatening emergencies such as cessation of breathing.
3. Treatment for less serious injuries and shock.
4. Arrangement for medical care and transport.

There are five major categories of injury for which you must be prepared to administer first aid. You must be able to stop severe bleeding, maintain respiration if a person has stopped breathing, and maintain circulation if a person's heart has stopped beating. Also be sure to treat for shock, which is a factor in all serious injuries. In addition, you need to be able to render the proper first aid for serious diving accidents such as lung expansion injuries and decompression sickness. Emergency training in first aid will teach you to properly respond in the first four areas.

First aid for air embolism and decompression sickness includes laying the victim down and maintaining his or her respiration and circulation. You also must treat for shock, administer oxygen (if available), constantly monitor the patient, and transport the victim to the nearest recompression chamber (Fig. 10-21).

NAUI recommends that you participate in the NAUI Rescue Techniques course, where you can learn and practice how to handle accident management. See your instructor for more information about this important course.

Aquatic Life Injuries

General first-aid training does not cover treatment of injuries from aquatic life, although most of the general procedures apply to this specialty area as well. Additional general guidelines are presented here as basic information. These are

Fig. 10-21. In addition to administering oxygen for a diving emergency, you must treat for shock, monitor the patient, and transport them to the nearest recompression chamber.

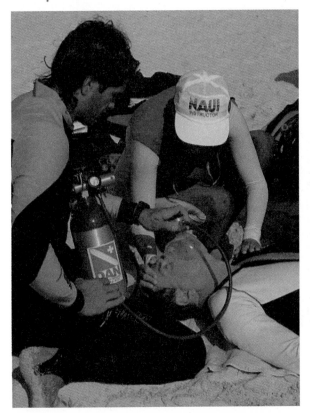

intended only to make you aware that you must find out from local diving instructors how to treat any injuries that you could receive from aquatic animals where you dive.

Injuries from aquatic life are classified in one of three major categories: 1) punctures, 2) stings, and 3) bites. Puncture wounds can be caused by sea urchins, spiny fish, or sting rays. If possible, any material in the wound must be removed. Toxin may have been injected and must be treated by soaking the wounded area in water as hot as the victim can tolerate for 20 minutes. Just as some individuals are allergic to bee stings, some divers may be hypersensitive to wounds from marine animals. Medical attention usually is required.

First aid for stings, such as those from jellyfish or coral, includes removal of the stinging materials and application of a neutralizing agent. Your instructor will advise you on the correct procedures for neutralizing stings that are caused by creatures in your local area. Medical attention is required if the injury is serious or the victim shows signs or symptoms of an allergic reaction.

If a diver is bitten by an aquatic animal, first aid can range from simple, antiseptic cleaning of the wound to control of serious bleeding. Medical attention is required if the injury is serious, significant blood loss occurs, or the patient shows signs or symptoms of an allergic reaction.

Injuries from aquatic life are as varied as the diving environment. You must know what wounds are likely to occur in a given area as well as the first aid for them. Even more important, learn how to avoid being wounded.

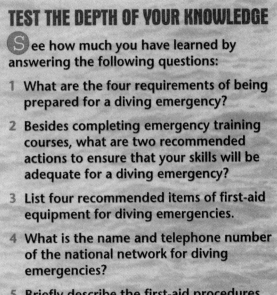

TEST THE DEPTH OF YOUR KNOWLEDGE

Ⓢee how much you have learned by answering the following questions:

1 What are the four requirements of being prepared for a diving emergency?

2 Besides completing emergency training courses, what are two recommended actions to ensure that your skills will be adequate for a diving emergency?

3 List four recommended items of first-aid equipment for diving emergencies.

4 What is the name and telephone number of the national network for diving emergencies?

5 Briefly describe the first-aid procedures for an unconscious diver.

SAFETY IN SUMMARY

What is the overall impression that you now have of diving safety? Do you feel that it primarily is a matter of knowing the rules, following them, and of being prepared? If so, your perception is correct. Being aware of safe diving practices, both generally and locally, and desiring to follow them will do more than anything else to ensure your safety. If something unexpected does occur, being prepared to deal with the situation can make it simply inconvenient rather than insurmountable.

Diving safety primarily involves attitude. "Safety" occurs when a diver respects the environment and wants to be properly prepared for diving. For divers who are prepared for emergencies and follow the buddy system as well as other good diving practices, safety is simply a byproduct of that attitude.

You must develop a desire to abide by the NAUI Recommended Diving Practices, which are presented in the following paragraphs and summarized in the Appendix. By applying these principles, you will see for yourself that the saying "Diving safety is no accident" is not merely a play on words.

RESPONSIBLE SCUBA DIVING PRACTICES

You must be trained for what you do in diving, and you must resist the temptation to teach others unless you become certified as a NAUI Instructor. Your training should continue with advanced, specialty, and refresher courses to keep your knowledge and skills current.

Only dive when you are feeling well, both mentally and physically. Annual physical examinations by a diving doctor are important. Do not dive under the influence of drugs, including alcohol. Keep yourself in good physical condition, know your limits, dive within them, and maintain a reserve of energy and air as a margin of safety. If you grow cold, tired, ill, or low on air while diving, exit the water immediately.

Your equipment must be maintained properly and checked before each dive. Have it serviced professionally as the manufacturer recommends, and use all recommended equipment when diving. Be properly weighted, and avoid diving over-weighted. Also, never loan your equipment to friends who are not certified to dive.

Know the location where you will dive. Respect the environment, and avoid dangerous sites and poor diving conditions. Fly the dive flag to warn boaters of your presence, and then dive near that flag. Exercise moderation concerning depth and time limits.

Take the time to properly plan your dive, and follow your plan. Know the rules of the buddy system, and abide by them for your own enjoyment as well as security. Dive regularly, or renew your skills after a period of inactivity before diving again. Your dives should be logged to help you remember the details and experiences.

If you follow the Recommended Diving Practices that are presented by your NAUI Instructor from the outset of your training, they will soon become part of your routine and be accomplished with little effort. Make this your goal, and you will set yourself on a good course to avoid the hazards of diving. Safety is an attitude, and this is reflected in the NAUI motto "Safety Through Education."

CHAPTER ELEVEN

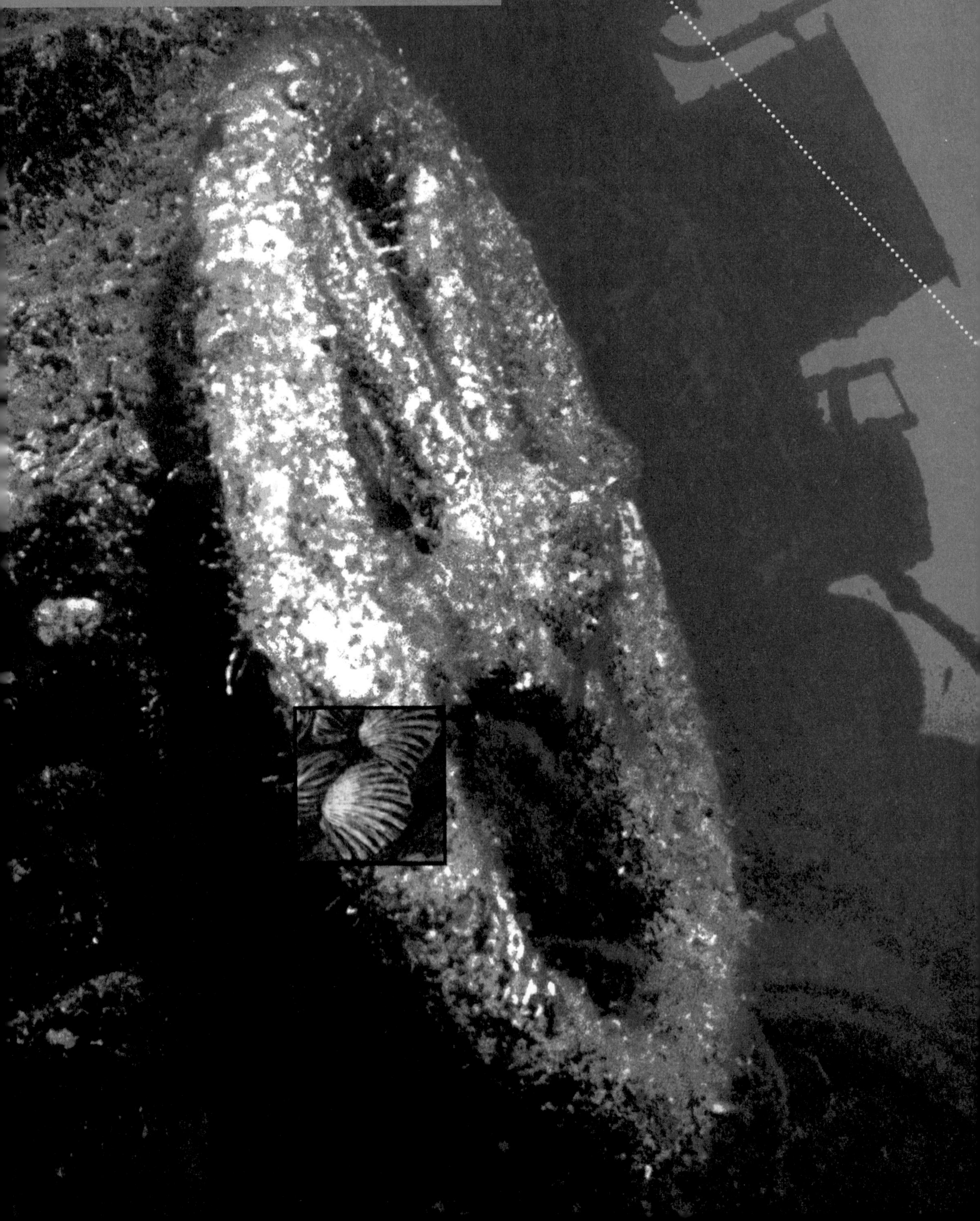

DIVING ACTIVITIES

By now, you have acquired (or nearly acquired) the knowledge, skills, and experience that allow you to enjoy scuba diving, and soon, you will earn NAUI credentials that will be your passport to the underwater world. It has taken study and physical effort to develop the needed ability. You can be proud of all that you have accomplished, and it now is time to look ahead. What should you do after you have obtained certification? What can you do to keep learning and stay informed? To what activities will you apply your diving ability? This chapter explains the available options.

LEARNING OBJECTIVES

By the end of this chapter, you must be able to:

1. Define "IUF," and list the services that it offers.
2. List two additional diving courses beyond Scuba Diver Certification, and give a brief description of each.
3. State your nine responsibilities as a NAUI Certified Scuba Diver.

HOW TO GET INVOLVED

We recommend that you become involved with other divers right away. Local dive clubs are an excellent way to find diving companions, learn about the local area, and be introduced to many diving activities. Be sure to inquire about joining a dive club in your area (Fig. 11-1).

For a larger perspective and to get involved as part of a national organization, we recommend that you join the NAUI International Underwater Foundation (IUF). This group provides you with an excellent news magazine, offers educational programs and an international conference, saves you money, and identifies you as part of the large, collective voice of recreational divers. You will receive an application to join IUF, and we suggest that you join right away. The NAUI IUF offers many opportunities for you to become actively involved in diving programs and projects.

DEVELOPING A SPECIAL INTEREST

Donning scuba equipment and exploring the world beneath the surface of the water are exciting. You will quickly find, however, that diving is simply a means that allows you to do something in the underwater world rather than being an end in itself. Soon, you will want to inspect old wrecks, take pictures, take game, collect things, or dive in unusual places. Such challenges make diving both exciting and rewarding. Remember that specialty areas can be learned much more quickly and easily through training than by trial and error (Fig. 11-2).

One reason that you should get involved with local divers and the IUF is to learn what the special diving interests are in your area and how to be introduced to them. When you have an underwater objective, your enthusiasm for diving multiplies

Fig. 11-1. Get involved with a dive club or other divers in your area as soon as you complete this course.

Fig. 11-2. It is important to develop a special-interest area in diving, such as developing your knowledge about marine life.

many times over, and you will have some of the best times of your life developing and refining your interest area.

Little compares with the feeling of accomplishing a goal in the underwater world, whether it be taking a perfect photograph of a rare fish, finding an ancient wreck, or exploring a site where no diver has ventured previously. Imagine the excitement and satisfaction that you can experience. Realize that relatively few people learn how to dive and will ever feel the exhilaration that you experience because of your success in "inner space." Diving can provide some of the most cherished moments in your life, and these moments usually relate to a special interest. Learn about the "special" activities of diving, and get involved (Fig. 11-3).

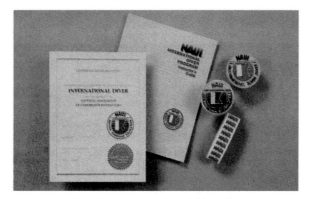

Fig. 11-3. The NAUI International Diver Program recognizes you for diving in new and exciting places.

ADDITIONAL TRAINING

The best way to remain involved in diving after this course is to continue your diving education. By completing this Scuba Diver Certification course, you will be prepared to dive unsupervised by an instructor under conditions similar to those encountered during your entry-level course. There are many other aspects of diving, however, that you will need to learn or develop further. You must consider your initial certification as a "License to Learn" how to dive. Experience and additional training are needed for you to dive under other conditions.

To further enhance your diving, you can learn diving specialties by taking a NAUI-sanctioned specialty course, such as those dealing with night diving, rescue diving, cavern diving, or photography (Fig. 11-4). While experience is said to be a good teacher, it frequently gives you the test before the lesson. This results in frustration and wasted time. It also can be unsafe. To get the most from a diving specialty, and to get it quickly in today's fast-paced world, complete a NAUI specialty course. This way, you will quickly achieve success in your endeavor and be able to take advantage of your NAUI Instructor's years of experience in your area of interest.

After you have completed several specialty courses, we suggest that you take the NAUI Master Scuba Diver course. You need not be an "expert

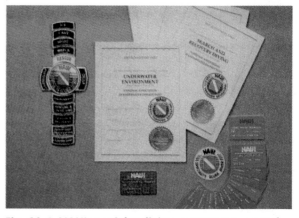

Fig. 11-4. NAUI specialty diving courses are a good way to learn new activities that will expand your diving experiences.

diver" to take this course, but you should have the desire to learn more advanced skills. This course provides you with an additional eight supervised dives, acquisition of other useful skills, amplification of your current knowledge, and further introductions to various specialty areas. Underwater navigation, limited-visibility or night diving, search and recovery, light salvage techniques, and deep-diving procedures are included (Fig. 11-5).

Every diver should graduate from a Master Diver course. At this level, you will have the knowledge, skills, and ability to enjoy diving in a variety of conditions and locations.

Once you have completed Master and Specialty ratings, you probably will want to seek the NAUI

Fig. 11-5. You need not be an expert diver to take the NAUI Master Diver course. This course will teach you those advanced skills.

Divemaster rating. For this, you will need I year of experience and a minimum of 25 logged dives, but you can set this as your goal right now.

Perhaps you will want to get involved in a leadership role in diving. This is the special interest area that we just suggested above, and it is one of the best. It is personally rewarding to help others realize the dream of becoming a diver or having an underwater adventure. NAUI has the finest leadership programs and training that are available. If you find that diving becomes more than a hobby to you, remember that through NAUI, there are many opportunities to work as a professional. By becoming qualified as a NAUI Divemaster or Instructor, you can profit from your diving ability, training, and experience. Your instructor is an example of this, and he or she will be glad to provide you with information on leadership training programs (Fig. 11-6).

Fig. 11-6. NAUI leaders teach diving in locations all over the world.

The field of diving is always changing. Equipment is constantly being improved and new types developed. Physiologic discoveries continually change our understanding of the effects of pressure on divers. Therefore, continuing education is important. You should belong to IUF, subscribe to diving magazines, attend diving seminars and conferences, take refresher courses every year or two, and obtain the highest level of certification that is possible.

RESPONSIBILITIES

When you are certified as a NAUI diver, you will continue to learn through your diving experiences. During these experiences, however, you should remember that you have certain responsibilities to yourself, your buddy, and others. The following is a partial list of what is expected of you as a NAUI diver:

1. Keep yourself mentally and physically fit for diving.
2. Continue your diving education.
3. Use complete, correct, well-maintained equipment.
4. Know your dive site, and avoid or abort diving in hazardous conditions.
5. Be prepared to handle emergencies.
6. Always dive with a buddy, and remain together while diving.
7. Avoid running low on air, control your buoyancy at all times, and ascend properly.
8. Keep conservation in mind regarding the environment.
9. Demonstrate the proper etiquette toward boaters, fishermen, and the general public.

It now is time to look ahead to fun, adventure, and all of the excitement that you envisioned when you began this course. That strange, wonderful world of "inner space" is finally accessible and waiting for you to enter. Enjoy yourself, and fulfill your responsibilities as a NAUI diver. Your instructor looks forward to working with you again soon in your next NAUI course.

TESTING THE DEPTH OF YOUR KNOWLEDGE

Page 19

1 Fit, comfort.
2 Purge valve.
3 Small inside diameter, sharp bends, excessive length.

Page 25

1 A "J" valve has a reserve; a "K" valve is an on/off valve.
2 Ease of breathing.
3 Install the dust cap.
4 Convenience, low price, integrated system. Completely independent air supply.
5 Aluminum and steel.
6

Page 28

1 Back flotation systems, buoyancy jackets, integrated weight systems.
2 Overinflation valve, oral inflator.
3 To prevent damage to the buoyancy compensator.

Page 29

1 Quick release.
2 To prevent the belt from sliding around on the waist.
3 Comfort, less likely to cause damage or injury if dropped.

Page 32

1 Dive skin.
2 Wet suit.
3 Dry suit.
4 False.

Page 36

1 Capillary depth gauge.
2 Submersible pressure gauge.
3 Dive computer.
4 Pressure proof.

Page 38

1 To cut rope or line underwater.
2 To display the flag only when diving, and to dive near the flag.
3 May be required for proof of recent diving experience to obtain diving services; documentation of diving experience for leadership training.

Page 46

1 20.9% oxygen; nitrogen.
2 False.
3 False.
4 6.4 pounds (2.9 kg).
5 By streamlining to reduce cross-sectional area.
6 Because air increases in density as the depth increases, there is more resistance to the movement of air for breathing.
7 Water conducts heat rapidly; water has a greater capacity to absorb heat.

Page 48

1 34 (10.3 m); 33 (10 m).
2 Five.
3 3 atm.

Page 49

Pressure	Volume	Density
Doubles	Halves	Doubles
Triples	One third	Triples
Halves	Doubles	Halves
Quadruples	One fourth	Quadruples

Page 51

1 Volume of the object; density of the object; density of the water.
2 Change amount of weight that is worn; change amount of air in the buoyancy compensator; change amount of air in the lungs; change equipment that is worn.
3 Decrease.
4 Remove weight.

Page 53

1 Conduction; respiration.
2 Lowering the temperature of the air.
3 The saliva reduces the surface tension of water so that it does not allow beads of moisture to form on the mask lens.
4 To prevent dehydration that can be caused by breathing dry scuba air.
5 As the temperature increases, the pressure inside a scuba tank will increase.

Page 54

1 Larger; closer.
2 The diver would not be able to determine the direction from which the sound was coming.
3 Cold numbs your sense of touch; you will be wearing gloves.

Page 55

1 Cold; mental state; physical activity; depth; body size
2 By using their submersible pressure gauge.

Page 61

1 Ears; sinuses; lungs.
2 It would be difficult or impossible to equalize pressure in your sinuses.
3 Exhale into your mask to equalize pressure in it and eliminate the mask squeeze.

Page 64

1 Squeeze.
2 Sudden, extreme vertigo; ear infection; permanent hearing loss.
3 Swollen or congested sinuses, as when you have a cold.
4 Mask squeeze.
5 The most common ear-clearing technique, which is known as the "Valsalva maneuver," is attempted exhalation against your closed nose and mouth.
6 Failing to equalize pressure in the ears during descent; by means of a very forceful Valsalva maneuver

Page 66

1 Reverse block.
2 Holding your breath; not breathing properly.
3 Neutral.

Page 68

1 Carbon dioxide.
2 Slow and deep.
3 Stop all activity, rest, and breathe deeply.
4 Keep the regulator in place.

Page 70

1 Conduction; respiration.
2 Muscle numbness; loss of strength; loss of memory; affects ability to think clearly; unconsciousness; death.
3 Stay out of sun; get wet.
4 Get dry, put on warm clothes, and drink warm liquids. Avoid alcohol.

Page 73

1 Have tanks filled with compressed air only.
2 Have tanks filled at a reputable air station.
3 Dive within time and depth limits for various depths.
4 Limit diving to depths shallower than 100 feet.
5 Ascend to shallower water.
6 Cold; shorter duration; narcosis; decompression sickness.

Page 74

1 You must be able to perform at full capacity while diving.
2 A woman should not dive when pregnant or the effects of menstruation are bothersome.
3 False.
4 Dive regularly.
5 Medications only mask the symptoms of your illness, but the illness still exists, affects your physiology, and can be hazardous.

Page 81

1 Temperature; visibility; currents; plants; water movement; animals; seasons; weather; bottom formations; shoreline configuration; bottom composition.
2 Slope; drop off; holes.
3 Cavern diving; ice diving; wreck diving.
4 NAUI Instructor; NAUI Divemaster.

Page 83

1 An abrupt transition from a layer of water at one water temperature to another at a distinctly different temperature.
2 Locality; season; weather; water movement; bottom composition.
3 Disorientation.

Page 87

1 Tides; gravity; winds; Earth's rotation.
2 Swim parallel to shore and downcurrent of the primary current flow.
3 Against the current.

Page 88

1 Sand; mud; silt; clay; rock.
2 Visibility; entries and exits; activity of the dive; marine life; swimming activity.
3 Low visibility; difficulty with entries and exits.

Page 90

1 False.
2 Learn to identify hazardous life forms in the area where you will be diving; move slowly and look carefully while diving; stay clear of things that can hurt you; if you don't know what something is, don't touch it.
3 Helps you know what to look for; helps you know where to look for it.

Page 92

1 Go with an experienced diver or group to learn the correct techniques; study boat-diving procedures, and get training if possible.

2 Take suitable medication; get fresh air; watch the horizon; stay near the center of the boat; lie down with your eyes closed.

Page 92

1 Use sunscreen; keep out of the sun as much as possible; wear protective clothing.
2 Learn of possible entanglements; be on the lookout for possible entanglements; advance planning.
3 Display the dive flag; dive in the vicinity of the dive flag; pause during ascent to listen for approaching boats.

Page 99

1 Breakage; silt.
2 Shells that are already dead.
3 Sea turtles.
4 Snip the rings open.

Page 105

1 "Ingassing" is the process of accumulating increased nitrogen in the body under greater-than-normal pressures.
2 Bubble formation occurs during "outgassing," when the pressure is reduced faster than the excess gas can be eliminated from the body.
3 20 feet (6 m).
4 55 minutes.
5 Nitrogen in excess of normal levels remaining in your body after diving.

Page 108

1 60 ft/30 min (18 m/30 min).
2 1:25; 2:20.
3 55 minutes.
4 With a letter group designation.
5 15 feet (5 m); 3

Page 109

1 30 feet (9 m); 10.
2 60 ft/30 min (18 m/30 min); 50 ft/20 min (15 m/20 min); 30 ft/40 min (9 m/40 min).
3 40 ft/40 min (12 m/40 min).

Page 113

1 31 minutes.
2 2:29.
3 60 feet (18 m).

Page 119

1 A precautionary decompression stop is recommended for every dive.
2 10 minutes.
3 80 ft/30 min (24 m/30 min)
4 24 hours.
5 1000 feet.

Page 126

1 Ascend.
2 20 feet (6 m).
3 100 feet (30 m).
4 False.

Page 131

1 Initializing.
2 Scrolling.
3 Decompression sickness.
4 Beeping; flashing lights; warning display.

Page 142

1 Shuffle fins while walking backward.
2 Sit down; steady yourself by holding onto someone or something with one hand.
3 The head is tilted forward when clearing a purge valve mask so that the purge will be the lowest point in the mask and the water will flow out at that point.
4 Blast method; displacement method; removing the mouthpiece to pour out the water (not recommended).
5 Displacement method.
6 You should not swim with rapid, short kick strokes; bend the knees sharply; swim rapidly; swim with your arms; kick your feet above the surface of the water.

Page 151

1 **Air supply:** valve, regulator hose orientation, regulator function, submersible pressure gauge, tank security in pack; **Buoyancy compensator:** low-pressure inflator hose connected, function, operation of controls, partially inflated; **Weight belt:** clear for ditching, right-hand release, no hoses trappedbeneath.
2 Buoyancy compensator should be partially inflated; mask should be held firmly; breathe from regulator during entry; be sure entry area is clear and sufficiently deep.
3 The objective of an entry is to get yourself into the water with minimal effort and effect on both you and your equipment.
4 Use giant stride when the distance to the water is several feet; use a back roll entry from a low, unstable platform or small boat; use a seated entry whenever you can sit at the edge of the water and lower yourself into the water.
5 Determine when it is best to don fins for the location; shuffle feet along bottom rather than stepping; lie down and swim as soon as possible; time the entry to coincide with a lull in wave action; trail float behind with a line.
6 Don't take tank off without disconnecting the low-pressure hose to a horse collar–type buoyancy compensator or dry suit; don't remove fins until absolutely necessary; don't exit with items in your hands; don't talk about the dive until you are out of the water; don't linger at the exit point after exiting water.

Page 155

1 The opening in the valve should be oriented toward the pack; the band must hold the tank securely so that the tank cannot slip; the pack must be mounted at the correct height on the tank.
2 The regulator should be mounted so that the regulator hose will come over the user's right shoulder.
3 Counterclockwise.
4 Have your buddy assist you; place the hoses on your shoulders so that they are not trapped under the strap when the waistband is secured; bend forward and balance the tank on your back when working with the straps; test the height adjustment.
5 Blow a continuous stream of small bubbles so that you will not be holding your breath with compressed air in your lungs.

6 Exhalation; use of purge valve.
7 Two, except the receiver may take up to four during the initial exchange.
8 Do not seal your mouth around the regulator when breathing from a free-flowing regulator.

Page 161

1 Exchange snorkel for regulator; note the time; deflate the buoyancy compensator.
2 Maintain eye-to-eye contact with buddy; equalize pressure in air spaces often; control buoyancy; control rate of descent.
3 Signal buddy; agree to ascend; note time; look up; reach up; swim up; control buoyancy; ascend at 30 feet (9 m) per minute.
4 You and your buddy should agree before the dive which regulator will be used.
5 Recent practice with the person with whom you may need to buddy breathe.
6 When no source of air is available and the depth is greater than 40 feet.

Page 162

1 Amount of weight you wear; the amount of air in your BC (or dry suit), the amount of air in your lungs, objects you pick up underwater; distribution of weights on belt for balance; amount of excess strap; means to prevent slipping of weights.
2 Vent air through the exhaust.

Page 165

1 You want to be positively buoyant at the surface and negatively buoyant at the bottom.
2 Have the hose entirely inside your arms.
3 Hold the belt close to your midsection; assume a facedown position so that gravity will keep the belt in position across your back.
4 Orient into the correct position and then grasp the strap on both sides; place seat of the mask on your forehead and hook the strap over back of head; position mask on your face and then clear area under skirt; clear water from the mask; reposition the strap.

Page 169

1 Discuss the dive beforehand and coordinate; maintain a general heading until you both agree on new direction; maintain the same position relative to one another.
2 Search briefly; ascend a few feet and look for bubbles; total search time should not exceed 1 minute; surface and wait for your buddy.
3 Sunlight; ripples; natural formations.
4 The lubber line of the compass must be aligned with the center line of your body; have a reference setting on the compass; look over a compass rather than down on it.
5 A reciprocal course is a heading 180° from an original heading (e.g., in the opposite direction from which you started).

Page 179

1 Have the best possible time; have a safe experience; have all equipment in good working order; avoid last minute rushing.
2 Determine the purpose of the dive; select your dive buddy; determine primary and alternate locations; research dive site if it is unfamiliar; select date and time for the dive and schedule on calendar; make any necessary reservations; obtain emergency contact information; determine needed equipment; inspect equipment to ensure readiness; purchase advance items (e.g., tickets, air, film, license); inventory spare parts kit; check long-range weather forecast.
3 Check weather and water conditions; ensure that you are physically and mentally ready to go diving; collect all equipment, and use a checklist to prevent omissions; pack equipment in the reverse order that it will be used; pack personal items in separate bag from dive gear; leave information on destination and estimated time of return with someone.
4 Evaluation of conditions to determine suitability for diving.
5 Decide who will be in charge of the dive; review hand signals; agree on the general course to be followed during the dive; agree on entry and exit locations and techniques; agree on emergency procedures.

Page 181

1 Hand signals; sign language; underwater slate and pencil; tank rapping; noise-producing device; touch.
2 Hand signals; flags; whistle; voice.
3 Acknowledge the signal by repeating it or responding with the "OK" signal.
4 Signals must be reviewed and agreed on before diving.

Page 184

1 Stretch and massage cramped muscle, and proceed slowly with a different swimming stroke after recovery.
2 Determine where you are caught and try to get clear by reversing direction or sinking, removing scuba unit, or cutting yourself free with a knife as the last resort.
3 Stop all activity, rest, and breathe deeply.
4 Keep mouthpiece in place, and swallow several times in rapid succession.
5 Recover lost item if possible, or surface and exit water.
6 Hold onto a solid object or hug yourself until the dizziness passes.
7 Disconnect inflator hose, and vent buoyancy compensator or suit.
8 A feeling of confidence helps you relax so that you can enjoy diving.

Page 186

1 Establish buoyancy.
2 Help the diver overcome his or her difficulty if possible.
3 Provide assistance as needed.

Page 187

1 When a diver is unconscious and perhaps not breathing.
2 First aid, cardiopulmonary resuscitation, diving rescue, life saving.
3 Establish buoyancy for yourself.
4 Don't worry about it, because the air will escape naturally; keep water out, and maintain the breathing cycle.

Page 189

1 Training; equipment; contact information; determination to take action.
2 Update training periodically; practice frequently with dive buddy.
3 First-aid kit; oxygen; blanket; supply of

DIVER ETIQUETTE

As a responsible diver, you must follow certain "etiquette" guidelines:

* Manage your equipment and vehicles as compactly as possible so that you do not block sidewalks, driveways, or public accesses. Maintain a tidy equipment area to avoid a "cluttered" look to the dive site.
* Take care with spear guns. Loaded spear guns are forbidden on land, and any spear should be restricted from crowded beach areas.
* Ask before using or crossing private property, whether to gain access to a dive site or for recreation after a dive.
* Do not change clothes in public. Be discreet, and use vehicles, changing robes, or tents. Think of others who are passing the site or using the beaches.
* Try to create a "good guy" impression about divers. Talk pleasantly to interested nondivers who are curious about your sport. Be careful of your language and behavior, particularly regarding the use of alcohol or drugs before a dive.
* Do not violate the rights of others to enjoy the environment, run businesses, or have a pleasant town to live in.
* Obey all laws, whether they are fish and game regulations or designated parking and access areas. Cooperate with local police.

* Do not litter beaches or otherwise destroy property. Beach environments often are fragile ecologic systems that require your careful use if they are to survive.
* Patronize local merchants. Divers can have a greatly positive economic impact on an area, from restaurants to dive stores to motels. Good economic rapport with a community means continuing good communication and access for divers.
* Begin your dives early in the day for optimum diving conditions, less crowded beaches, more parking, and more freedom of choice regarding dive sites. Do not exceed your diving capabilities in selecting your site. Ask local residents or divers about possible sites, and rely on their knowledge of water and bottom conditions.
* Make sure that your fishing license is current, and obey local fishing regulations. Only take as much game as you can use. Collect as little as possible, clean fish only in designated areas, and dispose of any waste properly.
* Be helpful to other users of our aquatic environment. It makes you, as a diver, better than the faceless crowd, and it gains respect for your sport. Also, it removes many "hassles" of diving and makes you a happier, and thus calmer and safer, diver.

NAUI RESPONSIBLE BOAT DIVING PRACTICES

The NAUI Responsible Boat Diving Practices include the following:

1 Select a Coast Guard–licensed boat that is fully equipped with all required safety equipment as well as diver support and safety equipment.

2 Ask to receive Boat Diving Techniques training as part of your Advanced or Master Diving courses.

3 Rely on the skipper's knowledge of the most suitable dive sites. Plan your dive using the specific site information that the crew or divemaster provide.

4 Only sign up for trip destinations that are consistent with your ability and dive plan.

5 Arrive at the boat at least one-half hour before departure. Stow your well-marked gear in the assigned locations, and respect the boat facilities, which means no wet suits in the bunk room or dropping tanks or weight belts on the deck.

6 Between dives, keep your gear in your bag to avoid lost or broken equipment, and always sssist your buddy with his or her tank. Do not sit on the deck to put your tank on, or you may get hit on the head by another diver's tank.

7 Use your equipment to dive both easily and safely. Do not overweight yourself. Only use your buoyancy compensator to fine-tune your buoyancy during the dive or compensate for a heavy game bag at the end.

8 Loaded spear guns are *never* allowed on the boat or boarding ramp. Bring a container for your game. Help keep the deck clean and clear.

9 Use the boat exit points that are recommended by the crew. Move away from the boat exit once you are in the water, and either snorkel clearly on the surface or begin your descent down the anchor line. Do not use scuba to "skim" just beneath the surface; by doing so, you cannot be seen by passing boats and other divers.

10 Fins should be put on last, while you are waiting near the exit. Do not walk around the deck while wearing fins.

11 Be sure to use a compass and submersible pressure gauge. Plan your dive so that you end with a reserve of air and are able to return to the boat while still underwater.

12 Be aware of changes in current conditions during the dive. Use natural clues such as seaweed. Look for current lines trailed behind the boat on the surface, and do not hesitate to pull yourself hand-over-hand back to the boat using this line.

13 Use common sense, training, and experience; ask questions if you are unsure. Allow for a "margin of reserve," and do not push your endurance limits. Watch for other divers who are waving one arm while on the surface; this signals a diver who is in distress. Divers who maintain personal control and are comfortable in the water have safe, enjoyable experiences underwater.

Explore the far away places. Boat dive often.

DIVE PLANNING

Advance Planning

Advance dive planning includes the following:

1 Determine the purpose of the dive.
2 Select your dive buddy.
3 Determine both a primary and alternate location for the dive.
4 Research the dive site if it is unfamiliar.
5 Select both a date and time for the dive, and schedule this on your calendar.
6 Make any necessary reservations.
7 Obtain emergency contact information.
8 Determine what equipment is needed.
9 Inspect your equipment to ensure its readiness.
10 Purchase advance items (e.g., tickets, air, film, fishing license).
11 Inventory your spare-parts kit.
12 Check the long-range weather forecast.

Final Preparations

Final preparations for your dive include the following:

1 Check the weather and water conditions.
2 Ensure that you are physically and mentally ready to dive.
3 Collect all equipment, and use a checklist to prevent omissions.
4 Pack equipment in reverse order of its use.
5 Pack personal items in a separate bag from your dive gear.
6 Leave information on your destination and estimated time of return with someone who is remaining behind.

On-Site Planning

On-site planning includes the following:

1 Determine that the conditions are acceptable for diving, move to the alternate location, or don't dive.
2 Decide who will be in charge of the dive.
3 Review hand signals.
4 Agree on the general course to be followed during the dive.
5 Agree on entry and exit locations and techniques.
6 Agree on emergency procedures, and know the location of a telephone.

Diving Your Plan

Diving your plan includes the following:

1 Abide by your predive plans.
2 Think ahead while diving.

Remember, plan your dive, and then dive your plan!

DIVING EQUIPMENT CHECKLIST

Primary Dive Gear

Gear bag
Fins, mask, snorkel, and keeper
Exposure suit
Hood
Booties
Gloves
Weight belt
Dive knife
Scuba tank (filled)
Backpack and/or buoyancy compensator
Regulator with gauge
Depth gauge, timing device (or computer), and compass
Float, flag, and float anchor
Dive tables

Additional Dive Gear

Dive light
Slate and pencil
Thermometer
Marker buoy
Game bag

Spare Equipment

Tanks
Weights
Mask and fin straps
O-rings
Snorkel keeper
Tools

Emergency Items

First-aid kit
Phone numbers
Coins for phone
Oxygen

Personal Items

Certification card
NAUI log book
Swimsuit
Towel
Hat or visor
Sunscreen lotion
Sunglasses
Lunch, snacks, and drinks
Jacket and extra clothes
Tickets and money
Seasickness medication
Toilet articles
Sleeping bag

SAMPLE DIVERS FIRST-AID KIT

A first-aid kit should be present at all dives. The contents may be simple or complex as your distance from medical assistance increases. The following items are basic and may be supplemented according to the personal needs and capabilities of the user as well as the local conditions.

General

General items for a first-aid kit include:
Sterile compress pads for severe bleeding
Roll of 2-inch gauze bandage
Assorted Band-Aids
Adhesive tape, 1-inch wide
Assorted gauze pads (sterile)
Cotton swabs
Assorted safety pins/needles
Triangular bandage
Antiseptic soap
Germicide spray
Seasick pills
Decongestant tablets
Scissors
Tweezers and/or splinter remover
Medicated stick
Isopropyl alcohol (approximately 70% solution or commercial product)
Sunscreen cream
Aspirin
Loose change and emergency phone numbers
White vinegar

Optional

Optional items for a first-aid kit include:
Cleaning agent (e.g., hydrogen peroxide)
Gauze scrub pads
Baking soda
First-aid book
Salt tablets
Waterproof matches
Drinking water and paper cups
Blanket

NAUI SPORT DIVING TABLES

The Sport Diving Tables were developed at the **Defence and Civil Institute of Environmental Medicine (DCIEM)** in Toronto. DCIEM is a world leader in the field of decompression research. The Sport Diving Tables are comprised of the following tables: (A) air decompression, (B) surface intervals, (C) repetitive diving, and (D) depth corrections for altitude dives. In addition to repetitive diving procedures, guidelines are also provided for multi-level diving.

TABLE A—FIRST DIVE NO-D LIMITS

1. A No-Decompression Limit **(No-D Limit)** is the maximum time that you can spend at a given depth without having to conduct a Decompression Stop before surfacing.
   Table A provides the No-D Limits for First Dives as well as the Decompression Stop(s) for dives which exceed the No-D Limits. Repetitive Group letters appear beside the listed Bottom Times.
2. To find a First Dive No-D Limit, select the depth and follow the row of numbers across to the bold vertical lines. The section to the left of the bold lines is used for No-D Dives. The largest number to the left of the bold lines is the No-D Limit (in minutes) for that depth.
3. The Rate of Descent is 60 feet (18 metres) per minute or slower. The **Ascent Rate** is 50' plus or minus 10' per minute. Divers are advised to spend two minutes between 10' (3m) and 20' (6m) while ascending from a No-D Dive.
4. **Bottom Time** includes both your descent time and the actual time spent at depth. Group letters appear beside the Bottom Times. If your exact Bottom Time is not listed, use the **Repetitive Group (RG)** for the next greater Bottom Time. (Where no RG appears beside your Bottom Time, cease diving for at least 18 hours. Example: 30'/9m for 360 minutes)
5. The section to the right of the bold vertical lines is used for **Decompression Dives**, dives which exceed the No-D Limits. Decompression Stops must be conducted before surfacing from these dives. Decompression Stop times are given in minutes.

Example: 1st Dive to 70' (21m) for 40 minutes
Group letter is 'F'
No-D Limit = 35 minutes
Stop time = 5 minutes at 10' (3m)

A: AIR DECOMPRESSION

Depth		No-Decompression Bottom Times (minutes)				Decompression Required Bottom Times			
20'	6m	30 A / 60 B / 90 C / 120 D	150 E / 180 F / 240 G / 300 H	360 I / 420 J / 480 K / 600 L	720 M / ∞				
30'	9m	30 A / 45 B / 60 C / 90 D	100 E / 120 F / 150 G / 180 H	190 I / 210 J / 240 K / 270 L	300 M	360	400		
40'	12m	22 A / 30 B / 40 C	60 D / 70 E / 80 F	90 G / 120 H / 130 I	150 J	160 K / 170 L	180 M / 190	200	215
50'	15m	18 A / 25 B	30 C / 40 D	50 E / 60 F	75 G	85 H / 95 I	105 J / 115 K	124 L	132 M
60'	18m	14 A / 20 B	25 C / 30 D	40 E	50 F	60 G	70 H / 80 I	85 J	92 K
Decompression Stops in minutes				at 10' 3m		**5**	**10**	**15**	**20**
70'	21m	12 A / 15 B	20 C	25 D	35 E	40 F	50 G	60 H / 63 I	66 J
80'	24m	10 A / 13 B	15 C	20 D	25 E	29 F	35 G	48 H	52 I
90'	27m	9 A	12 B	15 C	20 D	23 E	27 F	35 G	40 H / 43 I
100'	30m	7 A	10 B	12 C	15 D	18 D	21 E	25 F / 29 G	36 H
110'	33m		6 A	10 B	12 C	15 D	18 E	22 F	26 G / 30 H
120'	36m		6 A	8 B	10 C	12 D	15 E	19 F	25 G
130'	39m			5 A	8 B	10 C	13 D	16 F	21 G
140'	42m			5 A	7 B	9 C	11 D	14 F	18 G
150'	45m			4 A	6 B	8 C	10 D	12 E	15 F
Decompression Stops in minutes			at 20' 6m			-	-	5	10
			at 10' 3m			5	10	10	10

TABLE B—SURFACE INTERVALS

1. The time elapsed between surfacing from a dive and beginning descent on the following dive is called a **Surface Interval**. Surface Intervals are expressed in hours and/or minutes. The maximum Surface Interval in Table B is 18 hours.
2. By matching your Group letter with your Surface Interval, you can determine your Repetitive Factor (RF) - a residual nitrogen indicator. The highest Repetitive Factor is 2.0.

B: SURFACE INTERVALS

Rep. Group	0:15 ↗ 0:29	0:30 ↗ 0:59	1:00 ↗ 1:29	1:30 ↗ 1:59	2:00 ↗ 2:59	3:00 ↗ 3:59	4:00 ↗ 5:59	6:00 ↗ 8:59	9:00 ↗ 11:59	12:00 ↗ 14:59	15:00 ↗ 18:00
A	1.4	1.2	1.1	1.1	1.1	1.1	1.1	1.1	1.0	1.0	1.0
B	1.5	1.3	1.2	1.2	1.2	1.1	1.1	1.1	1.1	1.0	1.0
C	1.6	1.4	1.3	1.2	1.2	1.2	1.1	1.1	1.1	1.0	1.0
D	1.8	1.5	1.4	1.3	1.3	1.2	1.2	1.1	1.1	1.0	1.0
E	1.9	1.6	1.5	1.4	1.3	1.3	1.2	1.2	1.1	1.1	1.0
F	2.0	1.7	1.6	1.5	1.4	1.3	1.3	1.2	1.1	1.1	1.0
G	-	1.9	1.7	1.6	1.5	1.4	1.3	1.2	1.1	1.1	1.0
H	-	-	1.9	1.7	1.6	1.5	1.4	1.3	1.1	1.1	1.1
I	-	-	2.0	1.8	1.7	1.5	1.4	1.3	1.1	1.1	1.1
J	-	-	-	1.9	1.8	1.6	1.5	1.3	1.2	1.1	1.1
K	-	-	-	2.0	1.9	1.7	1.5	1.3	1.2	1.1	1.1
L	-	-	-	-	2.0	1.7	1.6	1.4	1.2	1.1	1.1
M	-	-	-	-	-	1.8	1.6	1.4	1.2	1.1	1.1

Repetitive Factors (RF) given for Surface Intervals (hr:min)

3. As the Surface Interval increases, the Repetitive Factor decreases. Any dive conducted while the Factor is greater than 1.0 is a **Repetitive Dive**. If the Factor is 1.0, use the No-D Limits in Table A. When the Factor is higher than 1.0, use the No-D Limits for Repetitive Dives in Table C.

4. Before conducting a Repetitive Dive, allow enough Surface Interval time to elapse for a Factor to appear in Table B. If an emergency situation forces you to dive before a Factor appears, take no Surface Interval credit. Apply the following guidelines:

a. For dives to the SAME DEPTH: add the Bottom Times together and use the total Bottom Time to determine your Group letter and decompression requirements;

b. For dives to DIFFERENT DEPTHS: Take the Group letter from your 1st Dive and find the same letter at the second depth. Begin the 2nd dive as if you had already spent the Bottom Time listed beside that Group letter.

Example: 1st Dive RG = F and 2nd depth is 50'/15m
Bottom Time for RG 'F' at 50'/15m = 60 minutes. Assume that you have already been at 50' for 60 minutes.

Flying After Diving

1. Allow **at least 24 hours** to elapse before flying after any dive other than a No-Decompression First Dive.

2. Although **12 hours** is the minimum time before flying after a No-Decompression First Dive, your Repetitive Factor must drop to **1.0** before you fly.

Example: RG 'E' requires 15 hrs

TABLE C—NO-D LIMITS FOR REPETITIVE DIVES

C: REPETITIVE DIVING											
Depth		1.1	1.2	1.3	1.4	1.5	1.6	1.7	1.8	1.9	2.0
30'	9m	272	250	230	214	200	187	176	166	157	150
40'	12m	136	125	115	107	100	93	88	83	78	75
50'	15m	60	55	50	45	41	38	36	34	32	31
60'	18m	40	35	31	29	27	26	24	23	22	21
70'	21m	30	25	21	19	18	17	16	15	14	13
80'	24m	20	18	16	15	14	13	12	12	11	11
90'	27m	16	14	12	11	11	10	9	9	8	8
100'	30m	13	11	10	9	9	8	8	7	7	7
110'	33m	10	9	8	8	7	7	6	6	6	6
120'	36m	8	7	7	6	6	6	5	5	5	5
130'	39m	7	6	6	5	5	5	4	4	4	4
140'	42m	6	5	5	5	4	4	4	3	3	3
150'	45m	5	5	4	4	4	3	3	3	3	3
Repetitive Dive No-D Limits given in minutes according to Depth and RF											

1. The No-D Limits for Repetitive Dives appear in Table C. Match the Depth with your Repetitive Factor to find the No-D Limit for your Repetitive Dive.

Example: Depth of 40' (12m) with a RF of 1.5
No-D Limit = 100 minutes

2. If you dive within the No-D Limits and conduct only two dives (one Repetitive Dive), no calculation is necessary. After 18 hours, go back to Table A.

3. If you plan to conduct a 3rd dive, you need to establish the **Effective Bottom Time (EBT)** for dive #2. The **EBT** combines your actual Bottom Time with additional time to compensate for residual nitrogen.

4. To establish your EBT, multiply your Bottom Time by your RF, or refer to the following chart. This chart is available on an underwater slate. Match Bottom Time (left hand column) with Repetitive Factor.

QWIK EBT TABLE

Minutes	1.1	1.2	1.3	1.4	1.5	1.6	1.7	1.8	1.9	2.0
10	11 1	12 2	13 2	14 2	15 2	16 2	17 2	18 2	19 2	20 2
20	22 2	24 3	26 3	28 3	30 3	32 4	34 4	36 4	38 4	40 4
30	33 3	36 4	39 4	42 4	45 5	48 5	51 5	54 6	57 6	60 6
40	44 4	48 5	52 5	56 6	60 6	64 6	68 7	72 7	76 8	80 8
50	55 5	60 6	65 6	70 7	75 7	80 8	85 8	90 9	95 9	100 10
60	66 6	72 7	78 8	84 8	90 9	96 9	102 10	108 11	114 11	120 12
70	77 7	84 8	91 9	98 10	105 10	112 11	119 12	126 12	133 13	140 14
80	88 8	96 9	104 10	112 11	119 12	128 12	136 13	144 14	152 15	160 16
90	99 9	108 10	117 11	126 12	135 13	144 14	153 15	162 16	171 17	180 18

Example: Bottom Time is 32 minutes
Repetitive Factor is 1.5
Effective Bottom Time (EBT) for 32 minutes is 30 minutes = 45 minutes; plus 2 minutes = 3 minutes
EBT = 48 minutes

5. Repetitive Group letters are found in Table A according to the depth and Effective Bottom Time.

Example: Repetitive Dive to 40' (12m) with a RF of 1.5 Bottom Time is 60 minutes.
EBT = 60 minutes X 1.5 = 90 minutes
Repetitive Group is 'G'

6. When the actual Bottom Time on a Repetitive Dive exceeds the No-D Limit given in Table C, a Decompression Stop is required. Decompression Stops are found in Table A according to the depth and EBT.*

*If your actual Bottom Time exceeds the Repetitive Dive No-D Limit but results in an EBT that is less than the First Dive No-D Limit, conduct a 5 minute Decompression Stop at a depth of 10 feet (3 metres).

Minimum Surface Intervals

Use Table B and Table C to find the Minimum Surface Intervals needed to conduct No-D Repetitive Dives.

1. In Table C, select the depth of the Repetitive Dive and find a No-D Limit that is equal to (or slightly over) the actual Bottom Time planned for the dive. The RF required to conduct the No-D Dive appears at the top of the column.
2. In Table B, match this RF with the Repetitive Group letter from the preceding dive. The Minimum Surface Interval is given at the top of the column.

Example: First Dive is 90' (27m) for 20 minutes
Repetitive Group = D
Repetitive Dive will be 50' (15m) for 40 minutes

In Table C, a RF of 1.5 provides a No-D Limit of 41 minutes for a Repetitive Dive to 50 feet. In Table B, a Group D diver acquires a RF of 1.5 after a Surface Interval of 30 minutes.

3. If multiple dives (3 or more) are conducted on 3 consecutive days, take a 24 hour Surface Interval after the 3rd day.

Repetitive Groups and Multiple Dives

When you plan to conduct more than 2 dives, The Repetitive Group for each dive must be higher than the Group letter from the preceding dive. Otherwise, add one letter to that of the preceding dive and use the higher Repetitive Group.

Example: 1st dive RG = C
2nd dive RG = D
3rd dive RG = C
The 3rd dive RG becomes 'E'

TABLE D—DEPTH CORRECTIONS FOR ALTITUDE DIVES

1. Any dive conducted at an altitude greater than 999 feet above sea level is an **Altitude Dive**. **Depth Corrections** are necessary when

D: DEPTH CORRECTIONS

Actual Depth	1000' ↳1999 / 300m ↳599		2000' ↳2999 / 600m ↳899		3000' ↳3999 / 900m ↳1199		4000' ↳4999 / 1200m ↳1499		5000' ↳5999 / 1500m ↳1799		6000' ↳6999 / 1800m ↳2099		7000' ↳7999 / 2100m ↳2399		8000' ↳10000 / 2400m ↳3000	
30' 9m	10	3	10	3	10	3	10	3	10	3	10	3	20	6	20	6
40' 12m	10	3	10	3	10	3	10	3	10	3	20	6	20	6	20	6
50' 15m	10	3	10	3	10	3	10	3	20	6	20	6	20	6	20	6
60' 18m	10	3	10	3	10	3	20	6	20	6	20	6	20	6	30	9
70' 21m	10	3	10	3	10	3	20	6	20	6	20	6	30	9	30	9
80' 24m	10	3	10	3	20	6	20	6	20	6	30	9	30	9	40	12
90' 27m	10	3	10	3	20	6	20	6	20	6	30	9	30	9	40	12
100' 30m	10	3	10	3	20	6	20	6	20	6	30	9	30	9	40	12
110' 33m	10	3	20	6	20	6	20	6	30	9	30	9	40	12		
120' 36m	10	3	20	6	20	6	30	9	30	9	30	9				
130' 39m	10	3	20	6	20	6										
140' 42m	10	3														
Add Depth Correction to Actual Depth of Altitude Dive																
10' 3m	10	3.0	10	3.0	9	3.0	9	3.0	9	3.0	8	2.5	8	2.5	8	2.5
20' 6m	20	6.0	19	6.0	18	5.5	18	5.5	17	5.0	16	5.0	16	5.0	15	4.5
Actual Decompression Stop Depths (feet/metres) at Altitude																

Published under government license by Universal Dive Techtronics, Inc.

diving at altitude because the reduced atmospheric pressure at the dive site makes the Altitude Dive equivalent to a much deeper dive at sea level.

2. Table D is used to convert the actual depth at high altitude to an Effective Depth which corresponds with the depth figures intended for use at sea level. Table D provides the Depth Corrections and Actual Decompression Stop Depths needed to conduct dives at altitudes between 1,000 feet (300 metres) and 10,000 feet (3,000 metres) above sea level.

3. Apply the following procedures after you have acclimatized at the altitude of the dive site for at least 12 hours:

a. Establish the actual depth and the altitude;
b. Find the required Depth Correction by matching the actual depth with the altitude;
c. Add the Depth Correction to the actual depth in order to determine the EFFECTIVE DEPTH - the equivalent sea level depth for an Altitude Dive. Apply the Effective Depth to Table A (or to Table C for Repetitive Dives);
d. If the dive exceeds the No-D Limit, decompress at the Actual Decompression Stop Depth given in Table D.

Example: Altitude = 6,000' (1,800m)
Bottom Time = 35 minutes
Actual Depth = 60' (18m)
Depth Correction = +20' (6m)
EFFECTIVE DEPTH = 80' (24m)
Dec. Stop Time = 10 minutes at 10' from Table A)
Actual Decompression Stop Depth is 8' (2.5m)*

*The imperial and metric figures given for Actual Stop Depths are not direct conversions. Due to the effect of rounding the numbers on the imperial table, the imperial equivalents may differ from the metric figures.

4. If you must dive before 12 hours have elapsed, start with the NEXT GREATER Depth instead of the actual depth. In the example above, begin the procedure as if the actual depth was 70'. The Effective Depth would be 90' (27m).
5. At altitudes below 5,000', the Ascent Rate is 50 to 60 feet per minute. Between 5,000' and 10,000', the Ascent rate is reduced to 40 to 50 feet (12 to 15 metres) per minute.

Omitted Decompression Procedures

1. A diver who omits a Decompression Stop may resort to one of the following emergency procedures. After using either of these procedures, do not dive again for at least **24 hours**.
2. If no signs or symptoms of Decompression Sickness (DCS) are present, divers may begin the following In-water Procedure:

Within seven (7) minutes of surfacing, secure an adequate air supply and immediately return to the Stop 10 feet (3m) deeper than the first omitted Stop. Decompress at this depth for the time of the first omitted Stop, then continue the decompression in accordance with the Table A schedule.

Example: First Dive is at 100' (30m) for 25 minutes (No-D Limit is 15 minutes). Decompression Stops required are 5 minutes at 20' (6m) and 10 minutes at 10' (3m).

Situation: On ascent, a diver omits decompression, but has no symptoms of DCS.

Reaction: Secure an adequate air supply and recompress for 5 minutes at 30' (9m), 5 minutes at 20' (6m), and 10 minutes at 10' (3m).

3. If a RECOMPRESSION CHAMBER (RCC) is available within seven minutes of surfacing, place the diver(s) in the RCC and recompress on Oxygen to a pressure equivalent to a 40 foot (12 metre) depth. The diver(s) must remain on Oxygen at this pressure for twice the total omitted decompression time. The RCC ascent time on Oxygen is 2 minutes.

MULTI-LEVEL DIVES

Many diving educators consider the following procedures for multi-level diving to be unsuitable for entry-level divers. The DCIEM multi-level procedures are intended for advanced and experienced divers.

1. A **Multi-level Dive** is a dive during which Bottom Time is spent at two or more depths.
2. Plan each Multi-level Dive to be a NO-DECOMPRESSION Dive. If a No-D limit is exceeded,

terminate the dive and proceed to the Decompression Stop(s) specified in Table A.
3. Conduct the DEEPEST PART of the dive FIRST. Ascend at least 20' (6m) between each of the 'Steps' in the dive profile. At depths greater than 100' (30m), ascend at least 30' (9m).
4. Immediately before surfacing, spend five minutes between 10' and 20'. After each Multi-level Dive, allow for a Surface Interval of at least one hour.

First Dive Multi-Level Procedures

1. Find your Repetitive Group for Step 1 according to the depth and Bottom Time.

Example: Step 1 - 90' (27m) for 15 minutes
No-D Limit = 20 minutes
Step 1 RG is 'C'

2. Find the equivalent time (in Table A) for RG 'C' at Step 2. Add your next Bottom Time to the equivalent time. The total time becomes your Effective Bottom Time (EBT) for Step 2. Your EBT must not exceed the No-D Limit given for Step 2.

Example cont'd: Step 2 - 50' (15m) for 20 minutes
No-D Limit = 75 minutes
Equivalent time for 'C' is = 30 minutes
Actual Bottom Time = 20 minutes
Effective Bottom Time = 50 minutes
Step 2 RG is 'E'

3. Find the equivalent time for RG 'E' at Step 3. Add your actual Bottom Time to the equivalent time. Your Effective Bottom Time must not exceed the No-D Limit for Step 3.

Example cont'd: Step 3 - 20' (6m) for 20 minutes (No-D Limit at 20'/6m is 'infinity')
Equivalent time for 'E' is 150 minutes
Actual Bottom Time = 20 minutes
Effective Bottom Time = 170 minutes
Final RG is 'F'.
(Step 3 meets the requirement to spend at least 5 minutes at a depth between 10' (3m) and 20' (6m) before surfacing.)

Surface Interval is 1 hour

REPETITIVE DIVE MULTI-LEVEL PROCEDURES

1. On a Repetitive Dive, the *actual* Bottom Time at Step 1 must not exceed the No-D Limit given in **Table C**.

Example: Repetitive Factor is 1.6 (based on RG 'F' following a 1 hour Surface Interval)

Step 1 - 60' (18m) for 25 minutes
(No-D Limit in Table C is 26 minutes)
Actual Bottom Time = 25 minutes
EBT = 25 min x 1.6 = 40 minutes
Repetitive Group for Step 1 is 'E' (60'
for 40 minutes)

2. **The RG for Step 1 must be equal to or greater than the Group letter from the preceding dive.**

Example: Since the RG from the preceding dive was 'F', and 'E' is lower than 'F', apply Group 'F' to Step 1.

3. The EBT for Step 2 (and for each subsequent Step) must not exceed the No-D Limit given in **Table A.**

Example: Step 2 - 40' (12m) for 15 minutes
(No-D Limit is 150 minutes)
Equivalent time for RG 'F' = 80 minutes
Actual Bottom Time = 15 minutes
Effective Bottom Time = 95 minutes
RG for Step 2 is 'H'
Step 3 - 15' (4.5m) for 10 minutes
(No-D Limit is 'infinity')
Equivalent time for RG 'H' = 300 minutes
Actual Bottom Time = 10 minutes
Effective Bottom Time = 310 minutes
Final RG is 'I'.

COPYRIGHT

The DCIEM Sport Diving Tables and Procedures are copyrighted, and published under government license by Universal Dive Techtronics, (UDT). The Procedures were prepared by Ron Y. Nishi of DCIEM and Gain Wong of UDT. The Sport Diving Tables and Procedures may not be reproduced in any form without the written authorization of Universal Dive Techtronics, Inc. All Rights Reserved.

The Defence and Civil Institute of Environmental Medicine, the Department of National Defence, Universal Dive Techtronics and the National Association of Underwater Instructors (NAUI) disclaim any and all responsibilities for the use of the Sport Diving Tables and Procedures.

Copyright Her Majesty The Queen in Right of Canada 1994.

Glossary

Absolute pressure: the result when atmospheric pressure is added to gauge pressures.

Actual Dive Time: the total time spent underwater from the beginning of descent until breaking the surface at the end of the dive. Does not include precautionary decompression time.

Adjusted Maximum Dive Time: the Maximum Dive Time for a specific depth minus the Residual Nitrogen Time for a specific letter group and depth.

Alternate air source: an additional second-stage regulator that provides air to a diver's buddy (body?) in an emergency. A true alternate air source would be a completely independent unit consisting of an air cylinder and regulator. See also *Octopus*.

ADT: Actual Dive Time.

Air embolism: the blockage of blood flow in the body by air bubbles escaping into the blood.

Ambient pressure: the surrounding pressure.

AMDT: Adjusted Maximum Dive Time.

Alveoli: the air sacs in the lungs where gas exchange occurs.

Atmospheric pressure: the pressure that is exerted by the atmosphere.

Back flotation system: a buoyancy control device that is attached to the scuba tank and does not wrap around the diver in any way.

Backpack: a piece of equipment that is designed to hold the scuba tank on the diver's back.

Backup scuba: a redundant second-stage or total scuba unit for use in out-of-air situations.

BC: Buoyancy Compensator.

Bends: another name for decompression sickness.

Bezel: a movable ring on a compass or watch that is inscribed with index marks. The ring may be rotated in one direction only and is used to measure elapsed time.

Buoyancy: an upward force on an object placed in water that is equal to the weight of the water displaced.

Buoyancy compensator: a piece of equipment that provides increased volume with little increase in weight, thus providing lift.

Buoyancy jacket: a buoyancy control device that is worn like a sleeveless jacket.

Boyle's Law: the inverse relationship between pressure and volume.

Buddy system: a system in which you never dive alone and always have someone to assist you (if necessary) and share experiences with.

C-card: Certification Card.

Carbon monoxide toxicity: a condition that results from breathing air that is contaminated with carbon monoxide.

Cardiopulmonary resuscitation: the first-aid procedure that sustains ventilation and pulse until a person's heart and breathing resume on their own or other medical procedures can be initiated.

Ceiling: a minimum depth to which a diver may ascend without risk of decompression sickness that is displayed by a computer.

Certification card: a card that NAUI awards as evidence of completing required training.

Clearing: the moving of air from the lungs to the other air spaces, such as the ear and sinuses.

CO_2 detonator: a mechanical device that allows the buoyancy compensator to be filled quickly with carbon dioxide to provide rapid flotation. This is an option and is not standard on all BCs.

Compass: a piece of equipment that aids in underwater navigation by indicating the direction of true north with respect to your position.

Condensation: water that forms on a surface because of the cooling of air containing water vapor.

Consoles: devices that are designed to hold assorted gauges and instruments around or in line with the submersible pressure gauge.

Coral: a marine animal without a backbone that usually lives together with other animals of the same species and forms a colony. Many corals produce a hard external skeleton.

CPR: Cardiopulmonary Resuscitation.

Currents: the movement of water in the ocean-like movement of a river. Currents flow in specific directions for a given period of time. Currents are caused by wind, temperature, the Earth's rotation, and other factors.

Decompression stop: the time that a diver stops and waits at a specified depth during ascent to allow nitrogen elimination before surfacing.

Decompression sickness: the formation of bubbles of inert gas within the body of a diver. When these bubbles act on various parts of the body, such as the nerves, they have a negative impact and cause a variety of signs and symptoms that signal the diver is suffering from decompression sickness.

Defog solution: a substance that is rubbed on the lens of the mask to keep it free of condensation. Saliva often is used as a defog solution.

Dehydration: lack of adequate body fluids.

Density: mass per unit of volume.

Depth gauge: an instrument or device that indicates the depth.

Dive computer: an electronic device that senses water pressure, measures time, continuously calculates the amount of nitrogen in several "compartments," and displays information to assist divers in avoiding decompression sickness.

Dive schedule: an abbreviated statement of the depth and duration of a dive expressed as depth/time, e.g., 70 feet |21 m| for 40 minutes, or 70 ft/40 min.

Dive time calculator: a rotary calculator containing the NAUI Dive Tables in a format that eliminates the mathematic calculations associated with the dive tables.

Drag: resistance that is encountered when moving through the water because of the water's density.

Drift diving: a dive that is made using a current as the primary means of propulsion.

Dry suits: protective suits that prevent water from coming into contact with covered portions of the body.

Eardrum: the membrane that separates the middle and outer ears.

Equalization: the methods of preventing and correcting "squeezes."

ESE Program: Entry Scuba Experience Program— a NAUI program to introduce nondivers to scuba diving. This program does not lead to certification.

Eustachian tube: the tube that connects the middle ear with the throat, though which divers can "clear" their ears.

Fins: a piece of equipment that increases the surface area of the foot to make propulsion easier.

Foam neoprene: a rubber-based material that is saturated with tiny gas bubbles to provide insulation. This material is used to manufacture environmental suits.

Gauge pressure: pressure that is indicated by a gauge but not including atmospheric pressure.

Goggles: a piece of equipment that covers only the eyes to prevent water from irritating them. Goggles are not an acceptable substitute for the mask.

Heat exhaustion: a condition resulting from overheating that is characterized by a pale, clammy appearance and a feeling of weakness.

Heat stroke: a condition resulting from overheating that is characterized by hot, dry, and flushed skin. This is a life-threatening emergency.

Hose protector: a piece of heavy plastic or rubber that fits over the end of a hose to relieve the stress that is caused by the weight of equipment.

Hydrostatic test: a test that is required to ensure the safety of scuba tanks. This test is done using water as the medium to provide pressure to check the expansion of scuba cylinder.

Hyperventilation: breathing much more deeply and rapidly than required. This lowers the carbon dioxide level of the blood, which decreases the desire to breathe.

Index marks: the points on a compass bezel that provide a place to aim the needle to stay on a desired course.

Integrated weight systems: systems in which weight is combined with the backpack and BC.

Letter group designation: a letter that is used to designate the amount of residual nitrogen in the diver's system after a dive.

Longshore currents: currents that run parallel to the coastline.

Low-pressure inflation device: a device that allows the flow of air from the scuba cylinder to the BC.

Lubber line: the "reference line" on a compass. The stationary line that will show the direction of travel.

Lungs: the part of the body that allows oxygen to transfer from inhaled air to the blood. One of the body's air spaces.

Mask: a piece of equipment that holds a pocket of air around the eyes to improve underwater vision. The nose is always included in any mask to allow the pressure inside it to be equalized.

Maximum Dive Time: the length of time that may be spent at a given depth without being required to stop during ascent to reduce the likelihood of decompression sickness.

MDT: Maximum Dive Time.

Mediastinal emphysema: the condition that exists when air from an overexpansion injury escapes into the chest area near the heart.

Middle ear: the space in the ear containing the auditory bones that is connected to the throat by the eustachian tube.

Multilevel dive: a dive with progressively shallower depths.

NAUI: National Association of Underwater Instructors.

Neutral buoyancy: the state that exists when an object neither floats nor sinks.

Nitrogen narcosis: the name that is given to the narcotic effect nitrogen has at increased pressure.

Octopus: an extra second stage that is attached to the regulator for use in out-of-air situations. An extra regulator.

One atmosphere: the force of the atmosphere on the Earth taken as a constant 14.7 psi or 1 bar.

Open Water I Diver course: the first course in NAUI's complete diver education program. This course leads to certification.

Overexpansion injury: injuries that are caused by the expansion of air in closed body spaces.

Overpressure valve: an important device that is built into BCs and allows the escape of expanding gas without loss of buoyancy or damage to the BC.

Oxygen: the gas that is necessary to sustain life. This gas makes up approximately 20.9% of the air.

Pneumothorax: the condition that exists when air from an overexpansion injury escapes into the chest area.

Positive buoyancy: the state that exists when an object floats on the surface of the water.

Precautionary decompression stop: three minutes spent at a depth of 15 feet (5 m) as a safety precaution even though the Maximum Dive Time has not been exceeded.

Pressure: the force of the weight of the air and water above a diver measured in pounds per square inch.

Pressure gauge: a piece of equipment that allows a diver to monitor the amount of air remaining in the scuba cylinder.

Pressure relief disk: a safety device that is built into tank valves and prevents pressure from reaching dangerous levels. This is a one time-use device and must be replaced if the disk bursts.

PSI: pounds per square inch.

Quick-release buckles: buckles that are designed to be operated with one hand so that they can be opened quickly in an emergency.

"Rapture of the Deep": an older, more romantic name for nitrogen narcosis.

Reference line: the "lubber line" on a compass. The stationary line that will show the direction of travel.

Regulator: the piece of equipment that reduces high-pressure air in the scuba cylinder to ambient pressure.

Relative humidity: the amount of water vapor in the air.

Repetitive dive: any dive that is made within 24 hours of a previous dive.

Required decompression stop: an amount of time that is specified by dive tables, a calculator; or a computer to be spent at a specified depth whenever the Maximum Dive Time is exceeded.

Residual nitrogen: dissolved nitrogen remaining in the body as a result of an earlier dive within 24 hours.

Reverse block: the opposite of "squeeze." The situation that exists when the internal pressure of an air space is greater than the external pressure.

Rip current: a transitory current that results when water pushed up on the beach by waves rushes back to the sea.

RNT: Residual Nitrogen Time.

SAC-Rate: Surface Air Consumption Rate.

Safety stop: see precautionary decompression stop.

Scrolling: a continuously flashed display on a computer between dives to provide the Maximum Dive Times for various depths in sequence.

Scuba: Self-Contained Underwater Breathing Apparatus.

Scuba Tank: the piece of equipment containing the high-pressure air to be breathed while under water.

Service pressure: the working pressure of the scuba tank. It is stamped on the shoulder of the tank; for example, with "CTC/DOT-3ALxxxx-S80." The "xxxx" would actually be a number indicating the working pressure.

Sinuses: air cavities within the head that are lined with mucus membrane. May cause problems equalizing if they are blocked because of a cold.

SIT: Surface Interval Time.

Skip breathing: the hazardous practice of taking a breath and holding it for a moment before exhaling while scuba diving. This dangerous practice is done to extend bottom time.

Snorkel: a tubular piece of equipment that allows a person to breathe while keeping his or her face in the water.

SPG: Submersible Pressure Gauge.

Squeeze: the condition that results when the pressure outside an airspace is greater than the internal pressure.

Standing currents: currents that are regular and steady.

Submersible pressure gauge: a piece of equipment that provides a display of tank pressure during the dive.

Surface Air Consumption Rate: the rate of air consumption converted to a surface rate.

Surface Interval Time: time that is spent on the surface between dives.

Skin diving: diving that is done by holding your breath. Also known as free diving or breath-hold diving.

Tank valve: a mechanism that controls the flow of air in and out of a scuba tank. The tank valve provides the attachment for the scuba regulator.

Test date: a date that is stamped on the scuba tank indicating the date of the last hydrostatic test.

Thermocline: the dividing line between water of different temperatures.

Tide: the change in water level of the ocean caused by the gravitational attraction amongst the Earth, Sun, and Moon.

Tidal currents: currents that accompany changes in the tide. They ar a direct result of water flowing into or away from an area, such as an inlet or bay.

Timing device: a device that is used to record the length of a dive. For example, a watch or bottom timer.

Total Nitrogen Time: the sum of Residual Nitrogen Time and Actual Dive Time following a repetitive dive.

Trail line: a line that is used while boat diving. It is let out from the back of the boat with a float attached to aid divers returning to the boat.

Transitory currents: currents that last only for a short time and, unlike a tidal current, do not occur with any predictability.

Valsalva maneuver: the attempted exhalation against a closed nose and mouth that ordinarily opens the eustachian tubes, allowing equalization.

Vertigo: a loss of the sense of balance. Severe dizziness.

Visual inspection: a periodic inspection of the scuba tank that checks for corrosion to ensure the integrity of the tank. Sometimes referred to as VCI (Visual Cylinder Inspection) or VIP (Visual Inspection Program).

Wet suit: environmental suit that allows a small amount of water to enter the covered area. This water is trapped inside the suit and warmed by the body, thus providing a certain amount of protection from the cold.

Index